THE WELL WROUGHT URN

STUDIES IN THE STRUCTURE OF POETRY

BY CLEANTH BROOKS

A HARVEST BOOK

HARCOURT, BRACE & WORLD, INC. · NEW YORK

ISBN 0-15-695705-1

V W X Y Z

To the members of English 300–K
(Summer Session of 1942, University of Michigan)
who discussed the problems with me
and helped me work out some of the analyses.

Certain chapters of this book originally appeared in *American Prefaces, The American Scholar, The Kenyon Review, The Sewanee Review, The Yale Review,* and in *The Language of Poetry,* which was published by the Princeton University Press in 1942. I wish to thank the editors of the magazines mentioned and the directors of the Princeton University Press for their courtesy in extending permission for the publication of these materials here.

PREFACE

Most of the chapters of this book have been published as separate essays; but I offer it to the reader, not as a miscellaneous collection, but as a book, a book with a defined objective and a deliberate plan. I have attempted to examine, in terms of a common approach, a number of celebrated English poems, taken in chronological order, from the Elizabethan period to the present. Whether or not the approach is really a common approach, and whether or not the examination reveals that the poems possess some common structural properties, are matters for the reader to determine. The last chapter attempts some generalizations upon these properties, and upon the characteristic structure of poetry.

There is something to be said, I think, for thus exhibiting the concrete examples on which the generalizations are to be based. If this procedure is frankly part of a strategy for securing conviction, it also constitutes, I may point out, something of a check on the generalizations made in the final chapter—a means of testing them. I could even hope that, if the worst came to the worst and the account of poetic structure itself had to be rejected, some of the examples might survive the rejection as independent readings of the poems concerned. At all events, the readings represent an honest attempt to work close to specific texts.

Yet, even when relieved by the concrete instances that

precede it, the final chapter may seem to some readers irritatingly abstract. I am sorry that this must be so. I quite agree that poetry is a "natural" activity, one of the fundamental human activities, and not an esoteric one. But I would point out that it is precisely our basic concerns which—like the indispensable terms of language—are hardest to define. The common-sense view of poetry works very well on some levels; but when we come to inquire into the essential nature of poetry, it does not work at all—it raises far more problems than it solves. Nevertheless, I have decided to relegate the more technical parts of this discussion to an appendix where they will be available for those readers who are interested, but will intrude as little as possible on the book proper.

A more formidable objection to the plan of the book might be that I have taken too little into account the historical backgrounds of the poems I have discussed. An adequate answer to this charge will have to be furnished by the book itself, but I should like to forestall some misapprehensions, here and now. If literary history has not been emphasized in the pages that follow, it is not because I discount its importance, or because I have failed to take it into account. It is rather that I have been anxious to see what residuum, if any, is left after we have referred the poem to its cultural matrix.

The temper of our times is strongly relativistic. We have had impressed upon us the necessity for reading a poem in terms of its historical context, and that kind of reading has been carried on so successfully that some of us have been tempted to feel that it is the only kind of reading possible. We tend to say that every poem is an expression of its age; that we must be careful to ask of it only what its own age asked; that we must judge it only by the canons of its age. Any attempt to view it *sub specie aeternitatis,* we feel, must result in illusion.

Perhaps it must. Yet, if poetry exists as poetry in any

meaningful sense, the attempt must be made. Otherwise the poetry of the past becomes significant merely as cultural anthropology, and the poetry of the present, merely as a political, or religious, or moral instrument. If one consults the typical practice in teaching literature and the behavior of the more popular critics, particularly through the war years, he will find plenty of evidence for the truth of this statement.

The whole matter bears very definitely on the much advertised demise of the Humanities. This book does not claim to make any special contribution to the rapidly increasing literature that demands the resuscitation of the Humanities and tells how that resuscitation is to be effected. But the question as to whether the critic can make normative judgments does touch the heart of the matter; so too, the related question as to whether a poem represents anything more universal than the expression of the particular values of its time.

The men whose poems are considered in this book evidently thought that they were able to transcend the limitations of their own generation. As one of them put it:

> *Or who [Time's] spoil of beauty can forbid?*
> *O none, unless this miracle have might*
> *That in black ink my love may still shine bright.*

We live in an age in which miracles of all kinds are suspect, including the kind of miracle of which the poet speaks. The positivists have tended to explain the miracle away in a general process of reduction which hardly stops short of reducing the "poem" to the ink itself. But the "miracle of communication," as a student of language terms it in a recent book, remains. We had better not ignore it, or try to "reduce" it to a level that distorts it. We had better begin with it, by making the closest possible examination of what the poem says as a poem.

CONTENTS

THE WELL WROUGHT URN

CHAPTER ONE
THE LANGUAGE OF PARADOX

Few of us are prepared to accept the statement that the language of poetry is the language of paradox. Paradox is the language of sophistry, hard, bright, witty; it is hardly the language of the soul. We are willing to allow that paradox is a permissible weapon which a Chesterton may on occasion exploit. We may permit it in epigram, a special subvariety of poetry; and in satire, which though useful, we are hardly willing to allow to be poetry at all. Our prejudices force us to regard paradox as intellectual rather than emotional, clever rather than profound, rational rather than divinely irrational.

Yet there is a sense in which paradox is the language appropriate and inevitable to poetry. It is the scientist whose truth requires a language purged of every trace of paradox; apparently the truth which the poet utters can be approached only in terms of paradox. I overstate the case, to be sure; it is possible that the title of this chapter is itself to be treated as merely a paradox. But there are reasons for thinking that the overstatement which I propose may light up some elements in the nature of poetry which tend to be overlooked.

The case of William Wordsworth, for instance, is instructive on this point. His poetry would not appear to promise many examples of the language of paradox. He usually prefers the direct attack. He insists on

3

simplicity; he distrusts whatever seems sophistical. And yet the typical Wordsworth poem is based upon a paradoxical situation. Consider his celebrated

> *It is a beauteous evening, calm and free,*
> *The holy time is quiet as a Nun*
> *Breathless with adoration. . . .*

The poet is filled with worship, but the girl who walks beside him is not worshiping. The implication is that she should respond to the holy time, and become like the evening itself, nunlike; but she seems less worshipful than inanimate nature itself. Yet

> *If thou appear untouched by solemn thought,*
> *Thy nature is not therefore less divine:*
> *Thou liest in Abraham's bosom all the year;*
> *And worship'st at the Temple's inner shrine,*
> *God being with thee when we know it not.*

The underlying paradox (of which the enthusiastic reader may well be unconscious) is nevertheless thoroughly necessary, even for that reader. Why does the innocent girl worship more deeply than the self-conscious poet who walks beside her? Because she is filled with an unconscious sympathy for *all* of nature, not merely the grandiose and solemn. One remembers the lines from Wordsworth's friend, Coleridge:

> *He prayeth best, who loveth best*
> *All things both great and small.*

Her unconscious sympathy is the unconscious worship. She is in communion with nature "all the year," and her devotion is continual whereas that of the poet is sporadic and momentary. But we have not done with the paradox yet. It not only underlies the poem, but something of the paradox informs the poem, though, since this is Wordsworth, rather timidly. The compari-

son of the evening to the nun actually has more than
one dimension. The calm of the evening obviously
means "worship," even to the dull-witted and insensi-
tive. It corresponds to the trappings of the nun, visible
to everyone. Thus, it suggests not merely holiness, but,
in the total poem, even a hint of Pharisaical holiness,
with which the girl's careless innocence, itself a symbol
of her continual secret worship, stands in contrast.

Or consider Wordsworth's sonnet, "Composed upon
Westminster Bridge." I believe that most readers will
agree that it is one of Wordsworth's most successful
poems; yet most students have the greatest difficulty in
accounting for its goodness. The attempt to account
for it on the grounds of nobility of sentiment soon
breaks down. On this level, the poem merely says: that
the city in the morning light presents a picture which
is majestic and touching to all but the most dull of
soul; but the poem says very little more about the
sight: the city is beautiful in the morning light and
it is awfully still. The attempt to make a case for the
poem in terms of the brilliance of its images also
quickly breaks down: the student searches for graphic
details in vain; there are next to no realistic touches.
In fact, the poet simply huddles the details together:

> *silent, bare,*
> *Ships, towers, domes, theatres, and temples lie*
> *Open unto the fields. . . .*

We get a blurred impression—points of roofs and pin-
nacles along the skyline, all twinkling in the morning
light. More than that, the sonnet as a whole contains
some very flat writing and some well-worn comparisons.

The reader may ask: Where, then, does the poem
get its power? It gets it, it seems to me, from the para-
doxical situation out of which the poem arises. The
speaker is honestly surprised, and he manages to get

some sense of awed surprise into the poem. It is odd to the poet that the city should be able to "wear the beauty of the morning" at all. Mount Snowden, Skiddaw, Mont Blanc—these wear it by natural right, but surely not grimy, feverish London. This is the point of the almost shocked exclamation:

> *Never did sun more beautifully steep*
> *In his first splendour,* valley, rock, *or* hill . . .

The "smokeless air" reveals a city which the poet did not know existed: man-made London is a part of nature too, is lighted by the sun of nature, and lighted to as beautiful effect.

> *The river glideth at his own sweet will* . . .

A river is the most "natural" thing that one can imagine; it has the elasticity, the curved line of nature itself. The poet had never been able to regard this one as a real river—now, uncluttered by barges, the river reveals itself as a natural thing, not at all disciplined into a rigid and mechanical pattern: it is like the daffodils, or the mountain brooks, artless, and whimsical, and "natural" as they. The poem closes, you will remember, as follows:

> *Dear God! the very houses seem asleep;*
> *And all that mighty heart is lying still!*

The city, in the poet's insight of the morning, has earned its right to be considered organic, not merely mechanical. That is why the stale metaphor of the sleeping houses is strangely renewed. The most exciting thing that the poet can say about the houses is that they are *asleep*. He has been in the habit of counting them dead—as just mechanical and inanimate; to say they are "asleep" is to say that they are alive, that they participate in the life of nature. In the same way, the tired old metaphor which sees a great city as a pulsating heart of empire becomes revivified. It is only when the poet sees the city under the semblance of death that he can see it as actually alive—quick with the only life which he can accept, the organic life of "nature."

It is not my intention to exaggerate Wordsworth's own consciousness of the paradox involved. In this poem, he prefers, as is usual with him, the frontal attack. But the situation is paradoxical here as in so many of his poems. In his preface to the second edition of the *Lyrical Ballads* Wordsworth stated that his general purpose was "to choose incidents and situations from common life" but so to treat them that "ordinary things should be presented to the mind in an unusual aspect." Coleridge was to state the purpose for him later, in terms which make even more evident Wordsworth's exploitation of the paradoxical: "Mr. Wordsworth . . . was to propose to himself as his object, to give the charm of novelty to things of every day, and to excite a feeling analogous to the supernatural, by awakening the mind's attention from the lethargy of custom, and directing it to the loveliness and the wonders of the world before us . . ." Wordsworth, in short, was consciously attempting to show his audience that the common was really uncommon, the prosaic was really poetic.

Coleridge's terms, "the charm of novelty to things of every day," "awakening the mind," suggest the Romantic preoccupation with wonder—the surprise, the revelation which puts the tarnished familiar world in a new light. This may well be the *raison d'être* of most Romantic paradoxes; and yet the neo-classic poets use paradox for much the same reason. Consider Pope's lines from "The Essay on Man":

In doubt his Mind or Body to prefer;
Born but to die, and reas'ning but to err;
Alike in ignorance, his Reason such,
Whether he thinks too little, or too much . . .

Created half to rise, and half to fall;
Great Lord of all things, yet a Prey to all;
Sole Judge of Truth, in endless Error hurl'd;
The Glory, Jest, and Riddle of the world!

Here, it is true, the paradoxes insist on the irony, rather than the wonder. But Pope too might have claimed that he was treating the things of everyday, man himself, and awakening his mind so that he would view himself in a new and blinding light. Thus, there is a certain awed wonder in Pope just as there is a certain trace of irony implicit in the Wordsworth sonnets. There is, of course, no reason why they should not occur together, and they do. Wonder and irony merge in many of the lyrics of Blake; they merge in Coleridge's *Ancient Mariner*. The variations in emphasis are numerous. Gray's "Elegy" uses a typical Wordsworth "situation" with the rural scene and with peasants contemplated in the light of their "betters." But in the "Elegy" the balance is heavily tilted in the direction of irony, the revelation an ironic rather than a startling one:

Can storied urn or animated bust
Back to its mansion call the fleeting breath?
Can Honour's voice provoke the silent dust?
Or Flatt'ry sooth the dull cold ear of Death?

But I am not here interested in enumerating the possible variations; I am interested rather in our seeing that the paradoxes spring from the very nature of the poet's language: it is a language in which the connotations play as great a part as the denotations. And I do not mean that the connotations are important as supplying some sort of frill or trimming, something external to the real matter in hand. I mean that the poet does not use a notation at all—as the scientist may properly be said to do so. The poet, within limits, has to make up his language as he goes.

T. S. Eliot has commented upon "that perpetual slight alteration of language, words perpetually juxtaposed in new and sudden combinations," which occurs in poetry. It *is* perpetual; it cannot be kept out of the poem; it can only be directed and controlled. The tendency of science is necessarily to stabilize terms, to freeze them into strict denotations; the poet's tendency is by contrast disruptive. The terms are continually modifying each other, and thus violating their dictionary meanings. To take a very simple example, consider the adjectives in the first lines of Wordsworth's evening sonnet: *beauteous, calm, free, holy, quiet, breathless.* The juxtapositions are hardly startling; and yet notice this: the evening is like a nun breathless with adoration. The adjective "breathless" suggests tremendous excitement; and yet the evening is not only quiet but *calm.* There is no final contradiction, to be sure: it is *that* kind of calm and *that* kind of excitement, and the two states may well occur together. But the poet has no one term. Even if he had a polysyllabic technical term, the term would not provide the solution for his problem. He must work by contradiction and qualification.

We may approach the problem in this way: the poet has to work by analogies. All of the subtler states of emotion, as I. A. Richards has pointed out, necessarily demand metaphor for their expression. The poet must work by analogies, but the metaphors do not lie in the same plane or fit neatly edge to edge. There is a continual tilting of the planes; necessary overlappings, dis-

crepancies, contradictions. Even the most direct and
simple poet is forced into paradoxes far more often
than we think, if we are sufficiently alive to what he
is doing.

But in dilating on the difficulties of the poet's task,
I do not want to leave the impression that it is a task
which necessarily defeats him, or even that with his
method he may not win to a fine precision. To use
Shakespeare's figure, he can

> *with assays of bias*
> *By indirections find directions out.*

Shakespeare had in mind the game of lawnbowls in
which the bowl is distorted, a distortion which allows
the skillful player to bowl a curve. To elaborate the
figure, science makes use of the perfect sphere and its
attack can be direct. The method of art can, I believe,
never be direct—is always indirect. But that does not
mean that the master of the game cannot place the
bowl where he wants it. The serious difficulties will
only occur when he confuses his game with that of
science and mistakes the nature of his appropriate in-
strument. Mr. Stuart Chase a few years ago, with a
touching naïveté, urged us to take the distortion out
of the bowl—to treat language like notation.

I have said that even the apparently simple and
straightforward poet is forced into paradoxes by the
nature of his instrument. Seeing this, we should not be
surprised to find poets who consciously employ it to
gain a compression and precision otherwise unobtain-
able. Such a method, like any other, carries with it its
own perils. But the dangers are not overpowering; the
poem is not predetermined to a shallow and glittering
sophistry. The method is an extension of the normal
language of poetry, not a perversion of it.

I should like to refer the reader to a concrete case.

Donne's "Canonization" ought to provide a sufficiently extreme instance.* The basic metaphor which underlies the poem (and which is reflected in the title) involves a sort of paradox. For the poet daringly treats profane love as if it were divine love. The canonization is not that of a pair of holy anchorites who have renounced the world and the flesh. The hermitage of each is the other's body; but they do renounce the world, and so their title to sainthood is cunningly argued. The poem then is a parody of Christian sainthood; but it is an intensely serious parody of a sort that modern man, habituated as he is to an easy yes or no, can hardly understand. He refuses to accept the paradox as a serious rhetorical device; and since he is able to accept it only as a cheap trick, he is forced into this dilemma. Either: Donne does not take love seriously; here he is merely sharpening his wit as a sort of mechanical exercise. Or: Donne does not take sainthood seriously; here he is merely indulging in a cynical and bawdy parody.

Neither account is true; a reading of the poem will show that Donne takes both love and religion seriously; it will show, further, that the paradox is here his inevitable instrument. But to see this plainly will require a closer reading than most of us give to poetry.

The poem opens dramatically on a note of exasperation. The "you" whom the speaker addresses is not identified. We can imagine that it is a person, perhaps a friend, who is objecting to the speaker's love affair. At any rate, the person represents the practical world which regards love as a silly affectation. To use the metaphor on which the poem is built, the friend repre-

* This poem, along with seven other poems discussed in this book, may be found in Appendix Three. The texts of the two other poems discussed, *Macbeth* and *The Rape of the Lock,* are too lengthy to be included, but the passages examined in most detail are quoted in full.

sents the secular world which the lovers have renounced.

Donne begins to suggest this metaphor in the first stanza by the contemptuous alternatives which he suggests to the friend:

> . . . *chide my palsie, or my gout,*
> *My five gray haires, or ruin'd fortune flout.* . . .

The implications are: (1) All right, consider my love as an infirmity, as a disease, if you will, but confine yourself to my other infirmities, my palsy, my approaching old age, my ruined fortune. You stand a better chance of curing those; in chiding me for this one, you are simply wasting your time as well as mine. (2) Why don't you pay attention to your own welfare—go on and get wealth and honor for yourself. What should you care if I do give these up in pursuing my love.

The two main categories of secular success are neatly, and contemptuously epitomized in the line

> *Or the Kings reall, or his stamped face* . . .

Cultivate the court and gaze at the king's face there, or, if you prefer, get into business and look at his face stamped on coins. But let me alone.

This conflict between the "real" world and the lover absorbed in the world of love runs through the poem; it dominates the second stanza in which the torments of love, so vivid to the lover, affect the real world not at all—

> *What merchants ships have my sighs drown'd?*

It is touched on in the fourth stanza in the contrast between the word "Chronicle" which suggests secular history with its pomp and magnificence, the history of kings and princes, and the word "sonnets" with its suggestions of trivial and precious intricacy. The conflict appears again in the last stanza, only to be resolved when the unworldly lovers, love's saints who have given up the world, paradoxically achieve a more intense world. But here the paradox is still contained in, and supported by, the dominant metaphor: so does the holy anchorite win a better world by giving up this one.

But before going on to discuss this development of the theme, it is important to see what else the second stanza does. For it is in this second stanza and the third, that the poet shifts the tone of the poem, modulating from the note of irritation with which the poem opens into the quite different tone with which it closes.

Donne accomplishes the modulation of tone by what may be called an analysis of love-metaphor. Here, as in many of his poems, he shows that he is thoroughly self-conscious about what he is doing. This second stanza, he fills with the conventionalized figures of the Petrarchan tradition: the wind of lovers' sighs, the floods of lovers' tears, etc.—extravagant figures with which the contemptuous secular friend might be expected to tease the lover. The implication is that the poet himself recognizes the absurdity of the Petrarchan love metaphors. But what of it? The very absurdity of the jargon which lovers are expected to talk makes for his argument: their love, however absurd it may appear to the world, does no harm to the world. The practical friend need have no fears: there will still be wars to fight and lawsuits to argue.

The opening of the third stanza suggests that this vein of irony is to be maintained. The poet points out to his friend the infinite fund of such absurdities which can be applied to lovers:

> *Call her one, mee another flye,*
> *We're Tapers too, and at our owne cost die. . . .*

For that matter, the lovers can conjure up for themselves plenty of such fantastic comparisons: *they* know what the world thinks of them. But these figures of the third stanza are no longer the threadbare Petrarchan conventionalities; they have sharpness and bite. The last one, the likening of the lovers to the phoenix, is fully serious, and with it, the tone has shifted from ironic banter into a defiant but controlled tenderness.

The effect of the poet's implied awareness of the lovers' apparent madness is to cleanse and revivify metaphor; to indicate the sense in which the poet accepts it, and thus to prepare us for accepting seriously the fine and seriously intended metaphors which dominate the last two stanzas of the poem.

The opening line of the fourth stanza,

> *Wee can dye by it, if not live by love,*

achieves an effect of tenderness and deliberate resolution. The lovers are ready to die to the world; they are committed; they are not callow but confident. (The basic metaphor of the saint, one notices, is being carried on; the lovers in their renunciation of the world, have something of the confident resolution of the saint. By the bye, the word "legend"—

> *. . . if unfit for tombes and hearse*
> *Our legend bee—*

in Donne's time meant "the life of a saint.") The lovers are willing to forego the ponderous and stately chronicle and to accept the trifling and insubstantial "sonnet" instead; but then if the urn be well wrought, it provides a finer memorial for one's ashes than does the pompous and grotesque monument. With the finely contemptuous, yet quiet phrase, "halfe-acre tombes," the world which the lovers reject expands into something gross and vulgar. But the figure works further; the pretty sonnets will not merely hold their ashes as a decent earthly memorial. Their legend, their story, will gain them canonization; and approved as love's saints, other lovers will invoke them.

In this last stanza, the theme receives a final complication. The lovers in rejecting life actually win to the most intense life. This paradox has been hinted at earlier in the phoenix metaphor. Here it receives a powerful dramatization. The lovers in becoming hermits, find that they have not lost the world, but have gained the world in each other, now a more intense, more meaningful world. Donne is not content to treat the lovers' discovery as something which comes to them passively, but rather as something which they actively achieve. They are like the saint, God's athlete:

Who did the whole worlds soule contract, *and* drove
    Into the glasses of your eyes. . . .

The image is that of a violent squeezing as of a powerful hand. And what do the lovers "drive" into each other's eyes? The "Countries, Townes," and "Courtes," which they renounced in the first stanza of the poem. The unworldly lovers thus become the most "worldly" of all.

The tone with which the poem closes is one of triumphant achievement, but the tone is a development contributed to by various earlier elements. One of the more important elements which works toward our acceptance of the final paradox is the figure of the phoenix, which will bear a little further analysis.

The comparison of the lovers to the phoenix is very skillfully related to the two earlier comparisons, that in which the lovers are like burning tapers, and that in which they are like the eagle and the dove. The phoenix comparison gathers up both: the phoenix is a bird, and like the tapers, it burns. We have a selected series of items: the phoenix figure seems to come in a

natural stream of association. "Call us what you will,"
the lover says, and rattles off in his desperation the first
comparisons that occur to him. The comparison to the
phoenix seems thus merely another outlandish one, the
most outrageous of all. But it is this most fantastic one,
stumbled over apparently in his haste, that the poet
goes on to develop. It really describes the lovers best
and justifies their renunciation. For the phoenix is not
two but one, "we two being one, are it"; and it burns,
not like the taper at its own cost, but to live again.
Its death is life: "Wee dye and rise the same . . ." The
poet literally justifies the fantastic assertion. In the
sixteenth and seventeenth centuries to "die" means to
experience the consummation of the act of love. The
lovers after the act are the same. Their love is not ex-
hausted in mere lust. This is their title to canonization.
Their love is like the phoenix.

I hope that I do not seem to juggle the meaning of
die. The meaning that I have cited can be abundantly
justified in the literature of the period; Shakespeare
uses "die" in this sense; so does Dryden. Moreover, I
do not think that I give it undue emphasis. The word
is in a crucial position. On it is pivoted the transition
to the next stanza,

> *Wee can dye by it, if not live by love,*
> *And if unfit for tombes . . .*

Most important of all, the sexual submeaning of "die"
does not contradict the other meanings: the poet is
saying: "Our death is really a more intense life"; "We
can afford to trade life (the world) for death (love),
for that death is the consummation of life"; "After all,
one does not expect to live *by* love, one expects, and
wants, to die *by* it." But in the total passage he is also
saying: "Because our love is not mundane, we can give
up the world"; "Because our love is not merely lust,

we can give up the other lusts, the lust for wealth and power"; "because," and this is said with an inflection of irony as by one who knows the world too well, "because our love can outlast its consummation, we are a minor miracle, we are love's saints." This passage with its ironical tenderness and its realism feeds and supports the brilliant paradox with which the poem closes.

There is one more factor in developing and sustaining the final effect. The poem is an instance of the doctrine which it asserts; it is both the assertion and the realization of the assertion. The poet has actually before our eyes built within the song the "pretty room" with which he says the lovers can be content. The poem itself is the well-wrought urn which can hold the lovers' ashes and which will not suffer in comparison with the prince's "halfe-acre tomb."

And how necessary are the paradoxes? Donne might have said directly, "Love in a cottage is enough." "The Canonization" contains this admirable thesis, but it contains a great deal more. He might have been as forthright as a later lyricist who wrote, "We'll build a sweet little nest,/ Somewhere out in the West,/ And let the rest of the world go by." He might even have imitated that more metaphysical lyric, which maintains, "You're the cream in my coffee." "The Canonization" touches on all these observations, but it goes beyond them, not merely in dignity, but in precision.

I submit that the only way by which the poet could say what "The Canonization" says is by paradox. More direct methods may be tempting, but all of them enfeeble and distort what is to be said. This statement may seem the less surprising when we reflect on how many of the important things which the poet has to say have to be said by means of paradox: most of the language of lovers is such—"The Canonization" is a good example; so is most of the language of religion—

"He who would save his life, must lose it"; "The last shall be first." Indeed, almost any insight important enough to warrant a great poem apparently has to be stated in such terms. Deprived of the character of paradox with its twin concomitants of irony and wonder, the matter of Donne's poem unravels into "facts," biological, sociological, and economic. What happens to Donne's lovers if we consider them "scientifically," without benefit of the supernaturalism which the poet confers upon them? Well, what happens to Shakespeare's lovers, for Shakespeare uses the basic metaphor of "The Canonization" in his *Romeo and Juliet?* In their first conversation, the lovers play with the analogy between the lover and the pilgrim to the Holy Land. Juliet says:

For saints have hands that pilgrims' hands do touch
And palm to palm is holy palmers' kiss.

Considered scientifically, the lovers become Mr. Aldous Huxley's animals, "quietly sweating, palm to palm."

For us today, Donne's imagination seems obsessed with the problem of unity; the sense in which the lovers become one—the sense in which the soul is united with God. Frequently, as we have seen, one type of union becomes a metaphor for the other. It may not be too far-fetched to see both as instances of, and metaphors for, the union which the creative imagination itself effects. For that fusion is not logical; it apparently violates science and common sense; it welds together the discordant and the contradictory. Coleridge has of course given us the classic description of its nature and power. It "reveals itself in the balance or reconcilement of opposite or discordant qualities: of saneness, with difference; of the general, with the concrete; the idea, with the image; the individual, with the representative; the sense of novelty and freshness, with old

and familiar objects; a more than usual state of emo-
tion, with more than usual order. . . ." It is a great
and illuminating statement, but is a series of paradoxes.
Apparently Coleridge could describe the effect of the
imagination in no other way.

Shakespeare, in one of his poems, has given a descrip-
tion that oddly parallels that of Coleridge.

> *Reason in it selfe confounded,*
> *Saw Division grow together,*
> *To themselves yet either neither,*
> *Simple were so well compounded.*

I do not know what his "The Phoenix and the Turtle"
celebrates. Perhaps it *was* written to honor the marriage
of Sir John Salisbury and Ursula Stanley; or perhaps
the Phoenix is Lucy, Countess of Bedford; or perhaps
the poem is merely an essay on Platonic love. But the
scholars themselves are so uncertain, that I think we
will do little violence to established habits of thinking,
if we boldly pre-empt the poem for our own purposes.
Certainly the poem is an instance of that magic power
which Coleridge sought to describe. I propose that we
take it for a moment as a poem about that power;

> *So they loved as love in twaine,*
> *Had the essence but in one,*
> *Two distincts, Division none,*
> *Number there in love was slaine.*
>
> *Hearts remote, yet not asunder;*
> *Distance and no space was seene,*
> *Twixt this* Turtle *and his* Queene;
> *But in them it were a wonder. . . .*
>
> *Propertie was thus appalled,*
> *That the selfe was not the same;*
> *Single Natures double name,*
> *Neither two nor one was called.*

Precisely! The nature is single, one, unified. But the name is double, and today with our multiplication of sciences, it is multiple. If the poet is to be true to his poetry, he must call it neither two nor one: the paradox is his only solution. The difficulty has intensified since Shakespeare's day: the timid poet, when confronted with the problem of "Single Natures double name," has too often funked it. A history of poetry from Dryden's time to our own might bear as its subtitle "The Half-Hearted Phoenix."

In Shakespeare's poem, Reason is "in it selfe confounded" at the union of the Phoenix and the Turtle; but it recovers to admit its own bankruptcy:

> *Love hath Reason, Reason none,*
> *If what parts, can so remaine. . . .*

and it is Reason which goes on to utter the beautiful threnos with which the poem concludes:

> *Beautie, Truth, and Raritie,*
> *Grace in all simplicitie,*
> *Here enclosde, in cinders lie.*
>
> *Death is now the* Phoenix *nest,*
> *And the* Turtles *loyall brest,*
> *To eternitie doth rest. . . .*
>
> *Truth may seeme, but cannot be,*
> *Beautie bragge, but tis not she,*
> *Truth and Beautie buried be.*
>
> *To this urne let those repaire,*
> *That are either true or faire,*
> *For these dead Birds, sigh a prayer.*

Having pre-empted the poem for our own purposes, it may not be too outrageous to go on to make one further observation. The urn to which we are summoned, the urn which holds the ashes of the phoenix, is like the well-wrought urn of Donne's "Canonization" which holds the phoenix-lovers' ashes: it is the poem itself. One is reminded of still another urn, Keats's Grecian urn, which contained for Keats, Truth and Beauty, as Shakespeare's urn encloses "Beautie, Truth, and Raritie." But there is a sense in which all such well-wrought urns contain the ashes of a Phoenix. The urns are not meant for memorial purposes only, though that often seems to be their chief significance to the professors of literature. The phoenix rises from its ashes; or ought to rise; but it will not arise for all our mere sifting and measuring the ashes, or testing them for their chemical content. We must be prepared to accept the paradox of the imagination itself; else "Beautie, Truth, and Raritie" remain enclosed in their cinders and we shall end with essential cinders, for all our pains.

CHAPTER TWO
THE NAKED BABE AND THE
CLOAK OF MANLINESS

The debate about the proper limits of metaphor has perhaps never been carried on in so spirited a fashion as it has been within the last twenty-five years. The tendency has been to argue for a much wider extension of those limits than critics like Dr. Johnson, say, were willing to allow—one wider even than the Romantic poets were willing to allow. Indeed, some alarm has been expressed of late, in one quarter or another, lest John Donne's characteristic treatment of metaphor be taken as the type and norm, measured against which other poets must, of necessity, come off badly. Yet, on the whole, I think that it must be conceded that the debate on metaphor has been stimulating and illuminating—and not least so with reference to those poets who lie quite outside the tradition of metaphysical wit.

Since the "new criticism," so called, has tended to center around the rehabilitation of Donne, and the Donne tradition, the latter point, I believe, needs to be emphasized. Actually, it would be a poor rehabilitation which, if exalting Donne above all his fellow poets, in fact succeeded in leaving him quite as much isolated from the rest of them as he was before. What the new awareness of the importance of metaphor—if it is actually new, and if its character is really that of a freshened awareness—what this new awareness of metaphor results in when applied to poets other than

Donne and his followers is therefore a matter of first importance. Shakespeare provides, of course, the supremely interesting case.

But there are some misapprehensions to be avoided at the outset. We tend to associate Donne with the self-conscious and witty figure—his comparison of the souls of the lovers to the two legs of the compass is the obvious example. Shakespeare's extended figures are elaborated in another fashion. They are, we are inclined to feel, spontaneous comparisons struck out in the heat of composition, and not carefully articulated, self-conscious conceits at all. Indeed, for the average reader the connection between spontaneity and seriously imaginative poetry is so strong that he will probably reject as preposterous any account of Shakespeare's poetry which sees an elaborate pattern in the imagery. He will reject it because to accept it means for him the assumption that the writer was not a fervent poet but a preternaturally cold and self-conscious monster.

Poems are certainly not made by formula and blueprint. One rightly holds suspect a critical interpretation that implies that they are. Shakespeare, we may be sure, was no such monster of calculation. But neither, for that matter, was Donne. Even in Donne's poetry, the elaborated and logically developed comparisons are outnumbered by the abrupt and succinct comparisons —by what T. S. Eliot has called the "telescoped conceits." Moreover, the extended comparisons themselves are frequently knit together in the sudden and apparently uncalculated fashion of the telescoped images; and if one examines the way in which the famous compass comparison is related to the rest of the poem in which it occurs, he may feel that even this elaborately "logical" figure was probably the result of a happy accident.

The truth of the matter is that we know very little

of the various poets' methods of composition, and that what may seem to us the product of deliberate choice may well have been as "spontaneous" as anything else in the poem. Certainly, the general vigor of metaphor in the Elizabethan period—as testified to by pamphlets, sermons, and plays—should warn us against putting the literature of that period at the mercy of our own personal theories of poetic composition. In any case, we shall probably speculate to better advantage—if speculate we must—on the possible significant interrelations of image with image rather than on the possible amount of pen-biting which the interrelations may have cost the author.

I do not intend, however, to beg the case by over-simplifying the relation between Shakespeare's intricate figures and Donne's. There are most important differences; and, indeed, Shakespeare's very similarities to the witty poets will, for many readers, tell against the thesis proposed here. For those instances in which Shakespeare most obviously resembles the witty poets occur in the earlier plays or in *Venus and Adonis* and *The Rape of Lucrece;* and these we are inclined to dismiss as early experiments—trial pieces from the Shakespearean workshop. We demand, quite properly, instances from the great style of the later plays.

Still, we will do well not to forget the witty examples in the poems and earlier plays. They indicate that Shakespeare is in the beginning not too far removed from Donne, and that, for certain effects at least, he was willing to play with the witty comparison. Dr. Johnson, in teasing the metaphysical poets for their fanciful conceits on the subject of tears, might well have added instances from Shakespeare. One remembers, for example, from *Venus and Adonis:*

O, how her eyes and tears did lend and borrow!
Her eyes seen in her tears, tears in her eye;
Both crystals, where they view'd each other's sorrow. . . .

Or, that more exquisite instance which Shakespeare, perhaps half-smiling, provided for the King in *Love's Labor's Lost:*

So sweet a kiss the golden sun gives not
To those fresh morning drops upon the rose,
As thy eye-beams, when their fresh rays have smote
The night of dew that on my cheeks down flows:
Nor shines the silver moon one half so bright
Through the transparent bosom of the deep,
As does thy face through tears of mine give light:
Thou shin'st in every tear that I do weep,
No drop but as a coach doth carry thee:
So ridest thou triumphing in my woe.
Do but behold the tears that swell in me,
And they thy glory through my grief will show:
But do not love thyself—then thou wilt keep
My tears for glasses, and still make me weep.

But Berowne, we know, at the end of the play, foreswears all such

> *Taffeta phrases, silken terms precise,*
> *Three-piled hyperboles, spruce affectation,*
> *Figures pedantical. . . .*

in favor of "russet yeas and honest kersey noes." It is sometimes assumed that Shakespeare did the same thing in his later dramas, and certainly the epithet "taffeta phrases" does not describe the great style of *Macbeth* and *Lear.* Theirs is assuredly of a tougher fabric. But "russet" and "honest kersey" do not describe it either. The weaving was not so simple as that.

The weaving was very intricate indeed—if anything, *more* rather than *less* intricate than that of *Venus and Adonis,* though obviously the pattern was fashioned in accordance with other designs, and yielded other kinds of poetry. But in suggesting that there is a real continuity between the imagery of *Venus and Adonis,* say, and that of a play like *Macbeth,* I am glad to be able to avail myself of Coleridge's support. I refer to the remarkable fifteenth chapter of the *Biographia.*

There Coleridge stresses not the beautiful tapestry-work—the purely visual effect—of the images, but quite another quality. He suggests that Shakespeare was prompted by a secret dramatic instinct to realize, in the imagery itself, that "constant intervention and running comment by tone, look and gesture" ordinarily provided by the actor, and that Shakespeare's imagery becomes under this prompting "a series and never broken chain . . . always vivid and, because unbroken, often minute. . . ." Coleridge goes on, a few sentences later, to emphasize further "the perpetual activity of attention required on the part of the reader, . . . the rapid flow, the quick change, and the playful nature of the thoughts and images."

These characteristics, Coleridge hastens to say, are not in themselves enough to make superlative poetry. "They become proofs of original genius only as far as they are modified by a predominant passion; or by associated thoughts or images awakened by that passion; or when they have the effect of reducing multitude to unity, or succession to an instant; or lastly, when a human and intellectual life is transferred to them from the poet's own spirit."

Of the intellectual vigor which Shakespeare possessed, Coleridge then proceeds to speak—perhaps extravagantly. But he goes on to say: "In Shakespeare's *poems,* the creative power and the intellectual energy wrestle as in a war embrace. Each in its excess of strength seems to threaten the extinction of the other."

I am tempted to gloss Coleridge's comment here, perhaps too heavily, with remarks taken from Chapter XIII where he discusses the distinction between the Imagination and the Fancy—the modifying and creative power, on the one hand, and on the other, that "mode of Memory" . . . "blended with, and modified by . . . Choice." But if in *Venus and Adonis* and *The Rape of Lucrece* the powers grapple "in a war embrace," Coleridge goes on to pronounce: "At length, in the *Drama* they were reconciled, and fought each with its shield before the breast of the other."

It is a noble metaphor. I believe that it is also an accurate one, and that it comprises one of the most brilliant insights ever made into the nature of the dramatic poetry of Shakespeare's mature style. If it is accurate, we shall expect to find, even in the mature poetry, the "never broken chain" of images, "always vivid and, because unbroken, often minute," but we shall expect to find the individual images, not mechanically linked together in the mode of Fancy, but organically related, modified by "a predominant passion," and mutually modifying each other.

T. S. Eliot has remarked that "The difference between imagination and fancy, in view of [the] poetry of wit, is a very narrow one." If I have interpreted Coleridge correctly, he is saying that in Shakespeare's greatest work, the distinction lapses altogether—or rather, that one is caught up and merged in the other. As his latest champion, I. A. Richards, observes: "Coleridge often insisted—and would have insisted still more often had he been a better judge of his reader's capacity for misunderstanding—that Fancy and Imagination are not exclusive of, or inimical to, one another."

I began by suggesting that our reading of Donne

might contribute something to our reading of Shakespeare, though I tried to make plain the fact that I had no design of trying to turn Shakespeare into Donne, or—what I regard as nonsense—of trying to exalt Donne above Shakespeare. I have in mind specifically some such matter as this: that since the *Songs and Sonets* of Donne, no less than *Venus and Adonis,* requires a "perpetual activity of attention . . . on the part of the reader from the rapid flow, the quick change, and the playful nature of the thoughts and images," the discipline gained from reading Donne may allow us to see more clearly the survival of such qualities in the later style of Shakespeare. And, again, I have in mind some such matter as this: that if a reading of Donne has taught us that the "rapid flow, the quick change, and the playful nature of the thoughts and images"—qualities which we are all too prone to associate merely with the fancy—can, on occasion, take on imaginative power, we may, thus taught, better appreciate details in Shakespeare which we shall otherwise dismiss as merely fanciful, or, what is more likely, which we shall simply ignore altogether.

With Donne, of course, the chains of imagery, "always vivid" and "often minute" are perfectly evident. For many readers they are all too evident. The difficulty is not to prove that they exist, but that, on occasion, they may subserve a more imaginative unity. With Shakespeare, the difficulty may well be to prove that the chains exist at all. In general, we may say, Shakespeare has made it relatively easy for his admirers to choose what they like and neglect what they like. What he gives on one or another level is usually so magnificent that the reader finds it easy to ignore other levels.

Yet there are passages not easy to ignore and on which even critics with the conventional interests have been forced to comment. One of these passages occurs in *Macbeth*, Act I, Scene vii, where Macbeth compares the pity for his victim-to-be, Duncan, to

> *a naked new-born babe,*
> *Striding the blast, or heaven's cherubim, hors'd*
> *Upon the sightless couriers of the air . . .*

The comparison is odd, to say the least. Is the babe natural or supernatural—an ordinary, helpless baby, who, as newborn, could not, of course, even toddle, much less stride the blast? Or is it some infant Hercules, quite capable of striding the blast, but, since it is powerful and not helpless, hardly the typical pitiable object?

Shakespeare seems bent upon having it both ways—and, if we read on through the passage—bent upon having the best of both worlds; for he proceeds to give us the option: pity is like the babe "or heaven's cherubim" who quite appropriately, of course, do ride the blast. Yet, even if we waive the question of the legitimacy of the alternative (of which Shakespeare so promptly avails himself), is the cherubim comparison really any more successful than is the babe comparison? Would not one of the great warrior archangels be more appropriate to the scene than the cherub? Does Shakespeare mean for pity or for fear of retribution to be dominant in Macbeth's mind?

Or is it possible that Shakespeare could not make up his own mind? Was he merely writing hastily and loosely, and letting the word "pity" suggest the typically pitiable object, the babe naked in the blast, and then, stirred by the vague notion that some threat to Macbeth should be hinted, using "heaven's cherubim" —already suggested by "babe"—to convey the hint? Is the passage vague or precise? Loosely or tightly organized? Comments upon the passage have ranged all

the way from one critic's calling it "pure rant, and
intended to be so" to another's laudation: "Either like
a mortal babe, terrible in helplessness; or like heaven's
angel-children, mighty in love and compassion. This
magnificent passage . . ."

An even more interesting, and perhaps more disturb-
ing passage in the play is that in which Macbeth de-
scribes his discovery of the murder:

> *Here lay Duncan,*
> *His silver skin lac'd with his golden blood;*
> *And his gash'd stabs, look'd like a breach in nature*
> *For ruin's wasteful entrance: there, the murderers,*
> *Steep'd in the colours of their trade, their daggers*
> *Unmannerly breech'd with gore. . . .*

It is amusing to watch the textual critics, particularly
those of the eighteenth century, fight a stubborn rear-
guard action against the acceptance of "breech'd." War-
burton emended "breech'd" to "reech'd"; Johnson, to
"drench'd"; Seward, to "hatch'd." Other critics argued
that the *breeches* implied were really the handles of
the daggers, and that, accordingly, "breech'd" actually
here meant "sheathed." The Variorum page witnesses
the desperate character of the defense, but the position
has had to be yielded, after all. *The Shakespeare Glos-
sary* defines "breech'd" as meaning "covered as with
breeches," and thus leaves the poet committed to a
reading which must still shock the average reader as
much as it shocked that nineteenth-century critic who
pronounced upon it as follows: "A metaphor must not
be far-fetched nor dwell upon the details of a disgust-
ing picture, as in these lines. There is little, and that
far-fetched, similarity between *gold lace* and *blood,* or
between *bloody daggers* and *breech'd legs.* The slight-
ness of the similarity, recalling the greatness of the dis-
similarity, disgusts us with the attempted comparison."

The two passages are not of the utmost importance, I dare say, though the speeches (of which each is a part) are put in Macbeth's mouth and come at moments of great dramatic tension in the play. Yet, in neither case is there any warrant for thinking that Shakespeare was not trying to write as well as he could. Moreover, whether we like it or not, the imagery is fairly typical of Shakespeare's mature style. Either passage ought to raise some qualms among those who retreat to Shakespeare's authority when they seek to urge the claims of "noble simplicity." They are hardly simple. Yet it is possible that such passages as these may illustrate another poetic resource, another type of imagery which, even in spite of its apparent violence and complication, Shakespeare could absorb into the total structure of his work.

Shakespeare, I repeat, is not Donne—is a much greater poet than Donne; yet the example of his typical handling of imagery will scarcely render support to the usual attacks on Donne's imagery—for, with regard to the two passages in question, the second one, at any rate, is about as strained as Donne is at his most extreme pitch.

Yet I think that Shakespeare's daggers attired in their bloody breeches can be defended as poetry, and as characteristically Shakespearean poetry. Furthermore, both this passage and that about the newborn babe, it seems to me, are far more than excrescences, mere extravagances of detail: each, it seems to me, contains a central symbol of the play, and symbols which we must understand if we are to understand either the detailed passage or the play as a whole.

If this be true, then more is at stake than the merit of the quoted lines taken as lines. (The lines as constituting mere details of a larger structure could, of course, be omitted in the acting of the play without

seriously damaging the total effect of the tragedy—
though this argument obviously cuts two ways. Whole
scenes, and admittedly fine scenes, might also be
omitted—have in fact *been* omitted—without quite
destroying the massive structure of the tragedy.) What
is at stake is the whole matter of the relation of Shake-
speare's imagery to the total structures of the plays
themselves.

I should like to use the passages as convenient points
of entry into the larger symbols which dominate the
play. They *are* convenient because, even if we judge
them to be faulty, they demonstrate how obsessive for
Shakespeare the symbols were—they demonstrate how
far the conscious (or unconscious) symbolism could
take him.

If we see how the passages are related to these sym-
bols, and they to the tragedy as a whole, the main mat-
ter is achieved; and having seen this, if we still prefer
"to wish the lines away," that, of course, is our privi-
lege. In the meantime, we may have learned something
about Shakespeare's methods—not merely of building
metaphors—but of encompassing his larger meanings.

One of the most startling things which has come out
of Miss Spurgeon's book on Shakespeare's imagery is
her discovery of the "old clothes" imagery in *Macbeth*.
As she points out: "The idea constantly recurs that
Macbeth's new honours sit ill upon him, like a loose
and badly fitting garment, belonging to someone else."
And she goes on to quote passage after passage in
which the idea is expressed. But, though we are all in
Miss Spurgeon's debt for having pointed this out, one
has to observe that Miss Spurgeon has hardly explored
the full implications of her discovery. Perhaps her in-
terest in classifying and cataloguing the imagery of the
plays has obscured for her some of the larger and more
important relationships. At any rate, for reasons to be

given below, she has realized only a part of the potentialities of her discovery.

Her comment on the clothes imagery reaches its climax with the following paragraphs:

And, at the end, when the tyrant is at bay at Dunsinane, and the English troops are advancing, the Scottish lords still have this image in their minds. Caithness sees him as a man vainly trying to fasten a large garment on him with too small a belt:

> *He cannot buckle his distemper'd cause*
> *Within the belt of rule;*

while Angus, in a similar image, vividly sums up the essence of what they all have been thinking ever since Macbeth's accession to power:

> *now does he feel his title*
> *Hang loose about him, like a giant's robe*
> *Upon a dwarfish thief.*

This imaginative picture of a small, ignoble man encumbered and degraded by garments unsuited to him, should be put against the view emphasized by some critics (notably Coleridge and Bradley) of the likeness between Macbeth and Milton's Satan in grandeur and sublimity.

Undoubtedly Macbeth . . . is great, magnificently great . . . But he could never be put beside, say, Hamlet or Othello, in nobility of nature; and there *is* an aspect in which he is but a poor, vain, cruel, treacherous creature, snatching ruthlessly over the dead bodies of kinsman and friend at place and power he is utterly unfitted to possess. It is worth remembering that it is thus that Shakespeare, with his unshrinking clarity of vision, repeatedly *sees* him.

But this is to make primary what is only one aspect of the old-clothes imagery! And there is no warrant for interpreting the garment imagery as used by Macbeth's enemies, Caithness and Angus, to mean that *Shakespeare* sees Macbeth as a poor and somewhat comic figure.

The crucial point of the comparison, it seems to me, lies not in the smallness of the man and the largeness of the robes, but rather in the fact that—whether the man be large or small—these are not *his* garments; in Macbeth's case they are actually stolen garments. Macbeth is uncomfortable in them because he is continually conscious of the fact that they do not belong to him. There is a further point, and it is one of the utmost importance; the oldest symbol for the hypocrite is that of the man who cloaks his true nature under a disguise. Macbeth loathes playing the part of the hypocrite— and actually does not play it too well. If we keep this in mind as we look back at the instances of the garment images which Miss Spurgeon has collected for us, we shall see that the pattern of imagery becomes very rich indeed. Macbeth says in Act I:

> *The Thane of Cawdor lives: why do you dress me*
> *In borrow'd robes?*

Macbeth at this point wants no honors that are not honestly his. Banquo says in Act I:

> *New honours come upon him,*
> *Like our strange garments, cleave not to their mould,*
> *But with the aid of use.*

But Banquo's remark, one must observe, is not censorious. It is indeed a compliment to say of one that he wears new honors with some awkwardness. The observation becomes ironical only in terms of what is to occur later.

Macbeth says in Act I:

> *He hath honour'd me of late; and I have bought*
> *Golden opinions from all sorts of people,*

> Which would be worn now in their newest gloss,
> Not cast aside so soon.

Macbeth here is proud of his new clothes: he is happy to wear what he has truly earned. It is the part of simple good husbandry not to throw aside these new garments and replace them with robes stolen from Duncan.

But Macbeth has already been wearing Duncan's garments in anticipation, as his wife implies in the metaphor with which she answers him:

> Was the hope drunk,
> Wherein you dress'd yourself?

(The metaphor may seem hopelessly mixed, and a full and accurate analysis of such mixed metaphors in terms of the premises of Shakespeare's style waits upon some critic who will have to consider not only this passage but many more like it in Shakespeare.) For our purposes here, however, one may observe that the psychological line, the line of the basic symbolism, runs on unbroken. A man dressed in a drunken hope is garbed in strange attire indeed—a ridiculous dress which accords thoroughly with the contemptuous picture that Lady Macbeth wishes to evoke. Macbeth's earlier dream of glory has been a drunken fantasy merely, if he flinches from action now.

But the series of garment metaphors which run through the play is paralleled by a series of masking or cloaking images which—if we free ourselves of Miss Spurgeon's rather mechanical scheme of classification—show themselves to be merely variants of the garments which hide none too well his disgraceful self. He is consciously hiding that self throughout the play.

"False face must hide what the false heart doth know," he counsels Lady Macbeth before the murder

of Duncan; and later, just before the murder of Ban-
quo, he invokes night to "Scarf up the eye of pitiful
day."

One of the most powerful of these cloaking images
is given to Lady Macbeth in the famous speech in
Act I:

> *Come, thick night,*
> *And pall thee in the dunnest smoke of hell,*
> *That my keen knife see not the wound it makes,*
> *Nor heaven peep through the blanket of the dark,*
> *To cry, "Hold, Hold!"*

I suppose that it is natural to conceive the "keen
knife" here as held in her own hand. Lady Macbeth
is capable of wielding it. And in this interpretation,
the imagery is thoroughly significant. Night is to be
doubly black so that not even her knife may see the
wound it makes. But I think that there is good warrant
for regarding her "keen knife" as Macbeth himself.
She has just, a few lines above, given her analysis of
Macbeth's character as one who would "not play false,/
And yet [would] wrongly win." To bring him to the
point of action, she will have to "chastise [him] with
the valour of [her] tongue." There is good reason, then,
for her to invoke night to become blacker still—to
pall itself in the "dunnest smoke of hell." For night
must not only screen the deed from the eye of heaven
—conceal it at least until it is too late for heaven to
call out to Macbeth "Hold, Hold!" Lady Macbeth
would have night blanket the deed from the hesitant
doer. The imagery thus repeats and reinforces the sub-
stance of Macbeth's anguished aside uttered in the
preceding scene:

> *Let not light see my black and deep desires;*
> *The eye wink at the hand; yet let that be*
> *Which the eye fears, when it is done, to see.*

I do not know whether "blanket" and "pall" qualify as garment metaphors in Miss Spurgeon's classification: yet one is the clothing of sleep, and the other, the clothing of death—they are the appropriate garments of night; and they carry on an important aspect of the general clothes imagery. It is not necessary to attempt to give here an exhaustive list of instances of the garment metaphor; but one should say a word about the remarkable passage in II, iii.

Here, after the discovery of Duncan's murder, Banquo says

And when we have our naked frailties hid,
That suffer in exposure, let us meet,
And question this most bloody piece of work—

that is, "When we have clothed ourselves against the chill morning air, let us meet to discuss this bloody piece of work." Macbeth answers, as if his subconscious mind were already taking Banquo's innocent phrase, "naked frailties," in a deeper, ironic sense:

Let's briefly put on manly readiness. . . .

It is ironic; for the "manly readiness" which he urges the other lords to put on, is, in his own case, a hypocrite's garment: he can only pretend to be the loyal, grief-stricken liege who is almost unstrung by the horror of Duncan's murder.

But the word "manly" carries still a further ironic implication: earlier, Macbeth had told Lady Macbeth that he dared

do all that may become a man;
Who dares do more is none.

Under the weight of her reproaches of cowardice, however, he *has* dared do more, and has become less than a man, a beast. He has already laid aside, therefore, one kind of "manly readiness" and has assumed another: he has garbed himself in a sterner composure than that which he counsels to his fellows—the hard and inhuman "manly readiness" of the resolved murderer.

The clothes imagery, used sometimes with emphasis on one aspect of it, sometimes, on another, does pervade the play. And it should be evident that the daggers "breech'd with gore"—though Miss Spurgeon does not include the passage in her examples of clothes imagery —represent one more variant of this general symbol. Consider the passage once more:

> *Here lay Duncan,*
> *His silver skin lac'd with his golden blood;*
> *And his gash'd stabs look'd like a breach in nature*
> *For ruin's wasteful entrance: there, the murderers,*
> *Steep'd in the colours of their trade, their daggers*
> *Unmannerly breech'd with gore. . . .*

The clothes imagery runs throughout the passage; the body of the king is dressed in the most precious of garments, the blood royal itself; and the daggers too are dressed—in the same garment. The daggers, "naked" except for their lower parts which are reddened with blood, are like men in "unmannerly" dress —men, naked except for their red breeches, lying beside the red-handed grooms. The figure, though vivid, is fantastic; granted. But the basis for the comparison is *not* slight and adventitious. The metaphor fits the real situation on the deepest levels. As Macbeth and Lennox burst into the room, they find the daggers wearing, as Macbeth knows all too well, a horrible masquerade. They have been carefully "clothed" to play a part. They are not honest daggers, honorably naked in readiness to guard the king, or, "mannerly" clothed in their own sheaths. Yet the disguise which they wear will enable Macbeth to assume the robes of Duncan—robes to which he is no more entitled than are the daggers to the royal garments which they now wear, grotesquely.

The reader will, of course, make up his own mind as to the value of the passage. But the metaphor in question, in the light of the other garment imagery, cannot be dismissed as merely a strained ingenuity, irrelevant to the play. And the reader who *does* accept it as poetry will probably be that reader who knows the play best, not the reader who knows it slightly and regards Shakespeare's poetry as a rhetoric more or less loosely draped over the "content" of the play.

And now what can be said of pity, the "naked newborn babe"? Though Miss Spurgeon does not note it (since the governing scheme of her book would have hardly allowed her to see it), there are, by the way, a great many references to babes in this play—references which occur on a number of levels. The babe appears sometimes as a character, such as Macduff's child; sometimes as a symbol, like the crowned babe and the bloody babe which are raised by the witches on the occasion of Macbeth's visit to them; sometimes, in a metaphor, as in the passage under discussion. The number of such references can hardly be accidental; and the babe turns out to be, as a matter of fact, perhaps the most powerful symbol in the tragedy.

But to see this fully, it will be necessary to review the motivation of the play. The stimulus to Duncan's murder, as we know, was the prophecy of the Weird Sisters. But Macbeth's subsequent career of bloodshed stems from the same prophecy. Macbeth was to have the crown, but the crown was to pass to Banquo's children. The second part of the prophecy troubles Macbeth from the start. It does not oppress him, however, until the crown has been won. But from this point on, the effect of the prophecy is to hurry Macbeth into action and more action until he is finally precipitated into ruin.

We need not spend much time in speculating on whether Macbeth, had he been content with Duncan's murder, had he tempted fate no further, had he been willing to court the favor of his nobles, might not have died peaceably in bed. We are dealing, not with history, but with a play. Yet, even in history the usurper sometimes succeeds; and he sometimes succeeds on the stage. Shakespeare himself knew of, and wrote plays about, usurpers who successfully maintained possession of the crown. But, in any case, this much is plain: the train of murders into which Macbeth launches aggravates suspicions of his guilt and alienates the nobles.

Yet, a Macbeth who could act once, and then settle down to enjoy the fruits of this one attempt to meddle with the future would, of course, not be Macbeth. For it is not merely his great imagination and his warrior courage in defeat which redeem him for tragedy and place him beside the other great tragic protagonists: rather, it is his attempt to conquer the future, an attempt involving him, like Oedipus, in a desperate struggle with fate itself. It is this which holds our imaginative sympathy, even after he has degenerated into a bloody tyrant and has become the slayer of Macduff's wife and children.

To sum up, there can be no question that Macbeth stands at the height of his power after his murder of Duncan, and that the plan—as outlined by Lady Macbeth—has been relatively successful. The road turns toward disaster only when Macbeth decides to murder Banquo. Why does he make this decision? Shakespeare has pointed up the basic motivation very carefully:

> *Then prophet-like,*
> *They hail'd him father to a line of kings.*
> *Upon my head they plac'd a fruitless crown,*
> *And put a barren sceptre in my gripe,*
> *Thence to be wrench'd with a unlineal hand,*
> *No son of mine succeeding. If't be so,*
> *For Banquo's issue have I fil'd my mind;*
> *For them the gracious Duncan have I murder'd;*
> *Put rancours in the vessel of my peace*
> *Only for them; and mine eternal jewel*
> *Given to the common enemy of man,*
> *To make them kings, the seed of Banquo kings!*

Presumably, Macbeth had entered upon his course from sheer personal ambition. Ironically, it is the more human part of Macbeth—his desire to have more than a limited personal satisfaction, his desire to found a line, his wish to pass something on to later generations —which prompts him to dispose of Banquo. There is, of course, a resentment against Banquo, but that resentment is itself closely related to Macbeth's desire to found a dynasty. Banquo, who has risked nothing, who has remained upright, who has not defiled himself, will have kings for children; Macbeth, none. Again, ironically, the Weird Sisters who have given Macbeth, so he has thought, the priceless gift of knowledge of the future, have given the real future to Banquo.

So Banquo's murder is decided upon, and accomplished. But Banquo's son escapes, and once more, the future has eluded Macbeth. The murder of Banquo thus becomes almost meaningless. This general point may be obvious enough, but we shall do well to note some of the further ways in which Shakespeare has pointed up the significance of Macbeth's war with the future.

When Macbeth, at the beginning of Scene vii, Act I, contemplates Duncan's murder, it is the future over which he agonizes:

> *If it were done, when 'tis done, then 'twere well*
> *It were done quickly; if the assassination*
> *Could trammel up the consequence, and catch*
> *With his surcease success; that but this blow*
> *Might be the be-all and the end-all here. . . .*

But the continuum of time cannot be partitioned off; the future is implicit in the present. There is no net strong enough to trammel up the consequence—not even in this world.

Lady Macbeth, of course, has fewer qualms. When Macbeth hesitates to repudiate the duties which he owes Duncan—duties which, by some accident of imagery perhaps—I hesitate to press the significance— he has earlier actually called "children"—Lady Macbeth cries out that she is willing to crush her own child in order to gain the crown:

> *I have given suck, and know*
> *How tender 'tis to love the babe that milks me;*
> *I would, while it was smiling in my face,*
> *Have pluck'd my nipple from his boneless gums*
> *And dash'd the brains out, had I so sworn as you*
> *Have done to this.*

Robert Penn Warren has made the penetrating observation that all of Shakespeare's villains are rationalists. Lady Macbeth is certainly of their company. She knows what she wants; and she is ruthless in her consideration of means. She will always "catch the nearest way." This is not to say that she ignores the problem of scruples, or that she is ready to oversimplify psychological complexities. But scruples are to be used to entangle one's enemies. One is not to become tangled in the mesh of scruples himself. Even though she loves her husband and though her ambition for herself is a part of her ambition for him, still she seems willing to consider even Macbeth at times as pure instrument, playing upon his hopes and fears and pride.

Her rationalism is quite sincere. She is apparently thoroughly honest in declaring that

> *The sleeping and the dead*
> *Are but as pictures; 'tis the eye of childhood*
> *That fears a painted devil. If he do bleed,*
> *I'll gild the faces of the grooms withal,*
> *For it must seem their guilt.*

For her, there is no moral order: *guilt* is something like *gilt*—one can wash it off or paint it on. Her pun is not frivolous and it is deeply expressive.

Lady Macbeth abjures all pity; she is willing to unsex herself; and her continual taunt to Macbeth, when he falters, is that he is acting like a baby—not like a man. This "manhood" Macbeth tries to learn. He is a dogged pupil. For that reason he is almost pathetic when the shallow rationalism which his wife urges upon him fails. His tone is almost one of puzzled bewilderment at nature's unfairness in failing to play the game according to the rules—the rules which have applied to other murders:

> *the time has been,*
> *That, when the brains were out, the man would die,*
> *And there an end; but now they rise again. . . .*

Yet, after the harrowing scene, Macbeth can say, with a sort of dogged weariness:

> *Come, we'll to sleep. My strange and self-abuse*
> *Is the initiate fear that wants hard use:*
> *We are yet but young in deed.*

Ironically, Macbeth is still echoing the dominant metaphor of Lady Macbeth's reproach. He has not yet attained to "manhood"; that *must* be the explanation. He has not yet succeeded in hardening himself into something inhuman.

Tempted by the Weird Sisters and urged on by his wife, Macbeth is thus caught between the irrational and the rational. There is a sense, of course, in which every man is caught between them. Man must try to predict and plan and control his destiny. That is man's fate; and the struggle, if he is to realize himself as a man, cannot be avoided. The question, of course, which has always interested the tragic dramatist involves the terms on which the struggle is accepted and the protagonist's attitude toward fate and toward himself. Macbeth in his general concern for the future is typical—is Every Man. He becomes the typical tragic protagonist when he yields to pride and *hybris*. The occasion for temptation is offered by the prophecy of the Weird Sisters. They offer him knowledge which cannot be arrived at rationally. They offer a key—if only a partial key—to what is otherwise unpredictable. Lady Macbeth, on the other hand, by employing a ruthless clarity of perception, by discounting all emotional claims, offers him the promise of bringing about the course of events which he desires.

Now, in the middle of the play, though he has not lost confidence and though, as he himself says, there can be no turning back, doubts have begun to arise; and he returns to the Weird Sisters to secure unambiguous answers to his fears. But, pathetically and ironically for Macbeth, in returning to the Weird Sisters, he is really trying to impose rationality on what sets itself forth plainly as irrational: that is, Macbeth would force a rigid control on a future which, by definition—by the very fact that the Weird Sisters already know it—stands beyond his manipulation.

It is because of his hopes for his own children and his fears of Banquo's that he has returned to the witches for counsel. It is altogther appropriate, therefore, that two of the apparitions by which their counsel is revealed should be babes, the crowned babe and the bloody babe.

For the babe signifies the future which Macbeth would control and cannot control. It is the unpredictable thing itself—as Yeats has put it magnificently, "The uncontrollable mystery on the bestial floor." It is the one thing that can justify, even in Macbeth's mind, the murders which he has committed. Earlier in the play, Macbeth had declared that if the deed could "trammel up the consequence," he would be willing to "jump the life to come." But he cannot jump the life to come. In his own terms he is betrayed. For it is idle to speak of jumping the life to come if one yearns to found a line of kings. It is the babe that betrays Macbeth—his own babes, most of all.

The logic of Macbeth's distraught mind, thus, forces him to make war on children, a war which in itself reflects his desperation and is a confession of weakness. Macbeth's ruffians, for example, break into Macduff's castle and kill his wife and children. The scene in which the innocent child prattles with his mother about his absent father, and then is murdered, is typical Shakespearean "fourth act" pathos. But the pathos is not adventitious; the scene ties into the inner symbolism of the play. For the child, in its helplessness, defies the murderers. Its defiance testifies to the force which threatens Macbeth and which Macbeth cannot destroy.

But we are not, of course, to placard the child as The Future in a rather stiff and mechanical allegory. *Macbeth* is no such allegory. Shakespeare's symbols are richer and more flexible than that. The babe signifies not only the future; it symbolizes all those enlarging purposes which make life meaningful, and it symbolizes, furthermore, all those emotional and—to Lady Macbeth—irrational ties which make man more than a machine—which render him human. It signifies preeminently the pity which Macbeth, under Lady Macbeth's tutelage, would wean himself of as something "unmanly." Lady Macbeth's great speeches early in the play become brilliantly ironical when we realize that Shakespeare is using the same symbol for the unpredictable future that he uses for human compassion. Lady Macbeth is willing to go to any length to grasp the future: she would willingly dash out the brains of her own child if it stood in her way to that future. But this is to repudiate the future, for the child is its symbol.

Shakespeare does not, of course, limit himself to the symbolism of the child: he makes use of other symbols of growth and development, notably that of the plant. And this plant symbolism patterns itself to reflect the development of the play. For example, Banquo says to the Weird Sisters, early in the play:

> *If you can look into the seeds of time,*
> *And say which grain will grow and which will not,*
> *Speak then to me. . . .*

A little later, on welcoming Macbeth, Duncan says to him:

> *I have begun to plant thee, and will labour*
> *To make thee full of growing.*

After the murder of Duncan, Macbeth falls into the same metaphor when he comes to resolve on Banquo's death. The Weird Sisters, he reflects, had hailed Banquo as

> . . . *father to a line of kings.*
> *Upon my head they placed a fruitless crown,*
> *And put a barren sceptre in my gripe. . . .*

Late in the play, Macbeth sees himself as the winter-stricken tree:

> *I have liv'd long enough: my way of life*
> *Is fall'n into the sear, the yellow leaf. . . .*

The plant symbolism, then, supplements the child symbolism. At points it merges with it, as when Macbeth ponders bitterly that he has damned himself.

> *To make them kings, the seed of Banquo kings!*

And, in at least one brilliant example, the plant symbolism unites with the clothes symbolism. It is a crowning irony that one of the Weird Sisters' prophecies on which Macbeth has staked his hopes is fulfilled when Birnam Wood comes to Dunsinane. For, in a sense, Macbeth is here hoist on his own petard. Macbeth, who has invoked night to "Scarf up the tender eye of pitiful day," and who has, again and again, used the "false face" to "hide what the false heart doth know," here has the trick turned against him. But the garment which cloaks the avengers is the living green of nature itself, and nature seems, to the startled eyes of his sentinels, to be rising up against him.

But it is the babe, the child, that dominates the symbolism. Most fittingly, the last of the prophecies in which Macbeth has placed his confidence, concerns the child: and Macbeth comes to know the final worst when Macduff declares to him that he was not "born of woman" but was from his "mother's womb/ Untimely ripp'd." The babe here has defied even the thing which one feels may reasonably be predicted of him—his time of birth. With Macduff's pronouncement, the

unpredictable has broken through the last shred of
the net of calculation. The future cannot be tram-
melled up. The naked babe confronts Macbeth to pro-
nounce his doom.

The passage with which we began this essay, then, is
an integral part of a larger context, and of a very rich
context:

> *And pity, like a naked new-born babe,*
> *Striding the blast, or heaven's cherubim, hors'd*
> *Upon the sightless couriers of the air,*
> *Shall blow the horrid deed in every eye,*
> *That tears shall drown the wind.*

Pity is like the naked babe, the most sensitive and
helpless thing; yet, almost as soon as the camparison
is announced, the symbol of weakness begins to turn
into a symbol of strength; for the babe, though new-
born, is pictured as "Striding the blast" like an ele-
mental force—like "heaven's cherubim, hors'd/ Upon
the sightless couriers of the air." We can give an an-
swer to the question put earlier: is Pity like the human
and helpless babe, or powerful as the angel that rides
the winds? It is both; and it is strong because of its
very weakness. The paradox is inherent in the situa-
tion itself; and it is the paradox that will destroy the
overbrittle rationalism on which Macbeth founds his
career.

For what will it avail Macbeth to cover the deed
with the blanket of the dark if the elemental forces
that ride the winds will blow the horrid deed in every
eye? And what will it avail Macbeth to clothe himself
in "manliness"—to become bloody, bold, and resolute,
—if he is to find himself again and again, viewing his
bloody work through the "eye of childhood/ That fears
a painted devil"? Certainly, the final and climactic ap-
pearance of the babe symbol merges all the contra-

dictory elements of the symbol. For, with Macduff's statement about his birth, the naked babe rises before Macbeth as not only the future that eludes calculation but as avenging angel as well.

The clothed daggers and the naked babe—mechanism and life—instrument and end—death and birth—that which should be left bare and clean and that which should be clothed and warmed—these are facets of two of the great symbols which run throughout the play. They are not the only symbols, to be sure; they are not the most obvious symbols: darkness and blood appear more often. But with a flexibility which must amaze the reader, the image of the garment and the image of the babe are so used as to encompass an astonishingly large area of the total situation. And between them— the naked babe, essential humanity, humanity stripped down to the naked thing itself, and yet as various as the future—and the various garbs which humanity assumes, the robes of honer, the hypocrite's disguise, the inhuman "manliness" with which Macbeth endeavors to cover up his essential humanity—between them, they furnish Shakespeare with his most subtle and ironically telling instruments.

CHAPTER THREE
THE LIGHT SYMBOLISM IN
"L'ALLEGRO-IL PENSEROSO"

The most amusing and at the same time probably the most penetrating comment on "L'Allegro-Il Penseroso" has to be credited to Dr. Samuel Johnson. True, Johnson sometimes seems brutally obvious as when he points out that "the gaiety [of L'Allegro does not spring] from the pleasures of the bottle." We scarcely need to be warned against attempting to visualize Milton's demure and academic Platonist tippling his way through the morning landscape. Some of Johnson's other comments seem quite as pointless without having the merit of seeming amusing. For example, Johnson tells us that "the *pensive* man never loses himself in crowds." To be sure, he does not; and if he does not, what of it? Yet it has remained for Dr. Johnson to point out the essential character of the speaker in the two poems, and several of the pertinent passages are worth quoting:

Both Mirth and Melancholy are solitary, silent inhabitants of the breast, that neither receive nor transmit communication; no mention is therefore made of a philosophical friend, or a pleasant companion. The seriousness does not arise from any participation of calamity, nor the gaiety from the pleasures of the bottle . . . but [the cheerful man] mingles [as] a mere spectator. . . .

The *pensive* man never loses himself in crowds. . . .

His Cheerfulness is without levity, and his Pensiveness without asperity. . . .

No mirth can, indeed, be found in his melancholy; but I am afraid that I always meet some melancholy in his mirth. They are two noble efforts of imagination.

The passage ends with what is apparently one of the most astonishing *non sequiturs* in criticism. What have the facts given above to do with the fact that the two poems are "noble efforts of imagination"?

Actually they have a great deal to do with it, but Dr. Johnson did not see fit to point out why, and with the critical tools at his disposal, he may very well have had difficulty in doing so. It is characteristic of his honesty and his bluntness that he penetrated so far into the secret, and then rather clumsily appended his concluding judgment.

But Johnson is definitely about the critic's proper job. He inspects the poems—he does not emote over them. And for his failure to connect his observations on the poems with his judgment of their nobility, I hazard the following explanation: Milton is using in these poems something which looks curiously like symbolism, and a symbolism too delicate and indeterminate to be treated in terms of the coarser modes of it such as allegory, for example, with which Dr. Johnson was acquainted.

The typical critic since Johnson has done little more than express his appreciation of the delicious quality of the double poem, feeling perhaps that the beauty of the poem was so obvious as to require no further comment, and the effect given so simple as to render any consideration of architectonics a mere intrusion. This view is based upon a sound consideration of the effectiveness of the poem; but great art is never so simple that it will not repay careful reading, and the result has been that except for communication between admirers of the poem, the "criticism" has been quite useless. Confronted with the skeptic or the honest ignoramus, the admirer has frequently found himself embarrassed in attempting to demonstrate that the poem is so fine, or in explaining its difference from the numerous eighteenth-century imitations of it, which, though filled with the same details of landscape, are so wooden and dull.

Professor Tillyard has got much nearer the point in those of his comments which emphasize the element of tone: the poems, he says, are characterized by a "subtle friendliness of tone," and further, Milton displays in them "a perfect social tone." Tillyard has even gone so far as to suggest that the opening passage in "L'Allegro" represents conscious burlesque on Milton's part: "what possessed him," Tillyard asks, "that he should write such bombast? By what strange anticipation did he fall into the manner of the worst kind of eighteenth-century ode? If Milton meant to be noble, he failed dreadfully. If, however, he knew what he was doing, he can only have meant to be funny. And if he meant to be funny, to what end? There is nothing in the rest of the poem that suggests humour—at least of the burlesque sort."

This is all very shrewd. But Professor Tillyard, in his preoccupation with the problem of dating the poems —a matter that has its own importance, certainly—has hardly followed up the implications of his surmise. The alleged burlesque is justified by Tillyard on what are really extrapoetic grounds: the poems were written for an academic audience and the parody on the high-flown style, meant for their amusement, "can perhaps be justified" as the "high spirits of a young man." Tillyard does not relate the justification to the tone of the rest of the double poem, nor to its total effect.

With regard to the symbolism of the poem also, Tillyard has come close to the main matter. In pointing out the close connections between "L'Allegro-Il Penseroso" and Milton's First Prolusion ("Whether Day or Night is the more excellent"), he has indicated how important the day-night contrasts are in determining the general architecture of the poem. But he has not seen that the light-shade imagery amounts to a symbolism and that this symbolism is related ultimately to the "meaning" of the poem, including its tone.

Precisely how these symbols work—how Milton gives the illusion of full day, dawn, noon, and night, and yet manages to keep both poems bathed in their special quality of coolness, is a matter to be discussed in detail a little later on. For the moment, it is sufficient to prepare for such a discussion by examining a little further Dr. Johnson's observation that the protagonist of both poems is a mere spectator who avoids crowds and who has no companion, and the further observation that mirth and melancholy in this poem "are solitary, silent inhabitants of the breast."

Mirth and melancholy need not be solitary—mirth in particular need not be. Dr. Johnson's reference to the pleasures of the bottle is definitely *not* beside the point; for, if Milton had intended to exploit mere contrast, "L'Allegro" would have been sociable; "Il Penseroso," solitary; "L'Allegro," boisterous; "Il Penseroso," prim and sober. A little consideration, however, will show that Milton could not afford to exploit mere contrast. If he had, the two halves would have been driven poles apart. They would have ceased to be twin halves of *one* poem, for the sense of unity in variety would have been lost. We are almost justified in putting the matter in this way: by choosing the obvious contrast between mirth and melancholy, Milton obligated himself to bring them as close together as possible in their effect on the mind. For the tension between the two choices depends upon their presentation as choices which can appeal to the same mind;

and the element of choice is worth emphasizing. Such pleasures and such sorrows as are intruded upon the character—"public," convivial mirth, or "public" melancholy, a funeral in the family—deprive the protagonist of conscious choice and render him chosen rather than choosing. Milton, one feels, is quite as emphatic in his belief that the aesthetic requires a deliberate act of will as was Immanuel Kant in insisting that the ethical involves deliberate choice.

It is not for nothing that the "Mountain Nymph, sweet Liberty" presides over "L'Allegro" and that the "Cherub Contemplation" dominates "Il Penseroso." Yet, as a matter of fact, the "Mountain Nymph" and the "Cherub," as we shall see, tend to merge into the same figure.

If, under the influence of Milton's later political career, we tend to give Liberty any political significance, we find her in "L'Allegro" in very strange company, consorting with

> Jest and youthful Jollity,
> Quips and Cranks, and wanton Wiles,
> Nods, and Becks, and Wreathed Smiles . . .
> Sport that wrincled Care derides,
> And Laughter holding both his sides.

The petition to Mirth

> To live with her, and live with thee,
> In unreproved pleasures free . . .

indicates, of course, plainly enough why Liberty walks at the right hand of Mirth: the pleasures are those which are unreproved. They are, moreover, the pleasures which can be had for the asking—the pleasure of drifting through the landscape or through the city, and watching the varying beauties of the landscape or the pageantry of men. But such pleasures pertain to liberty in another sense also: they depend upon one's freedom from business appointments and dinner engagements. One must be able to move along, unhurried and undetained, or the spell is broken. The necessity for being at a particular place at a particular time would wreck the cheerful man's day as described in the poem quite as completely as it would the day of the pensive man.

Dr. Johnson, always on the alert to ruffle up at the presence of Milton's somewhat aggressively republican goddess, does not betray any irritation at the presence of Liberty here. Perhaps he recognized in her, in spite of the mountain-nymph disguise, the same deity who presided over some of his own most delightful rambles. And if we find it difficult to associate Dr. Johnson, whose pleasures were uncompromisingly eighteenth-century, with either of Milton's cool and leisurely observers, we might recall such a passage as the following, in which Boswell describes a typical Johnsonian jaunt: "We landed at the Old Swan, and walked to Billingsgate, where we took oars, and moved smoothly along the silver Thames. It was a very fine day. We were entertained with the immense number and variety of ships that were lying at anchor, and with the beautiful country on each side of the river." The parallelism is at once destroyed when talkative Boswell, "the philosophical friend, or . . . pleasant companion," begins again to draw the great man out. But the delight in moving through a busy and fascinating world, leisurely and aimlessly, himself unbusied, was one which Johnson found most attractive. If the indulgence in such pleasures sometimes caused the rigid moralist to reprove himself for idleness, still, idle with such an idleness, he remained to the end. For all their differences over "liberty," the great republican and the great tory find themselves in close agreement here.

I have remarked that the mountain nymph and the cherub tend to merge into the same figure. One can easily see why. The more serious pleasures of Il Penseroso are so obviously "unreproved pleasures free" that the poet does not even need to point out that they are unreproved; yet, on the other hand, they are hardly more "contemplative" than those which delight L'Allegro. The happy man, too, is the detached observer, gliding through his world, a spectator of it, and preserving a certain aesthetic distance between it and himself. It is true that the spectator as the happy man emphasizes the spontaneity, the effortless freedom of his pleasures; and that the more austere observer is more consciously the man dedicated to the contemplative life. But here, as elsewhere in these poems, Milton's oppositions tend to come together.

The cheerful man's day is balanced by the pensive man's day at every point: a cheery dawn scene played off against a somber evening scene; Elizabethan comedy balanced against Greek tragedy; Lydian airs in antithesis to

> Such notes as warbled to the string,
> Drew Iron tears down Pluto's cheek. . . .

There is no need to detail them here; they are charming, and everyone knows them. What may be more to the point is to note that the tendency for these opposites to merge comes out even here. Both music passages, for example, refer to Orpheus; in "L'Allegro," to an Orphean strain which might have won Eurydice completely; in "Il Penseroso," to the Orphean strain played when Orpheus won her only to lose her. Or, to take another instance, the reference to supernatural lore in the one case involves Faery Mab, the most charming and harmless of folklores; in the other, the "unsphering" of

> *The spirit of Plato to unfold*
> *What Worlds, or what vast Regions hold*
> *The immortal mind that hath forsook*
> *Her mansion in this fleshly nook:*
> *And of those Dæmons that are found*
> *In fire, air, flood, or under ground. . . .*

But in neither case are we dealing with vulgar superstition—with the person in terror of spooks. In "L'Allegro" the superstition is reduced to a charming and poetic fancy; in "Il Penseroso," it has been elevated to the level of the philosophical imagination.

Even more striking is the tendency for the opposed items to cross over from their usual antitheses in a fashion which associates the same object with both mirth and melancholy. Here, the network of patternings is less obvious, and the instances given here may well be thought to be merely trivial. Perhaps they are; and yet in poetry so rich and cunningly contrived as this, we shall probably err less in putting down apparent relationships as meant and meaningful than in assuming that Milton threw materials into the double poem "every which way," and that the relations among them have no part in the total effect because we do not consciously associate them with the effect.

In "Il Penseroso," one of the finest passages is that in which Milton describes his Platonist toiling on at his studies:

> *Or let my Lamp at midnight hour,*
> *Be seen in som high lonely Towr,*
> *Where I may oft out-watch the Bear . . .*

Yet if "high" and "lonely" seem inevitably associated with the tower, and the tower itself, the inevitable symbol of the meditative, ascetic life, one remembers that towers are to be found all through "L'Allegro"—yet they're associated with anything but lonely solitude. The lark scares away the dull night by singing "From his watch-towre in the skies." And again, the next tower that appears is one which is "Boosom'd high in tufted Trees." "Boosom'd" is almost shockingly un-ascetic. (One is tempted to pursue the parallel with the "Il Penseroso" passage further. There, in the tower he outwatches the stars of the Bear; here the tower contains the "star" which all watch, for "Cyno-sure" is the constellation of the Lesser Bear.)

Lastly, "Towred" is the adjective which Milton chooses to apply to the cities to which the cheerful man will turn at nightfall after his day in the country—

> *Towred Cities please us then,*
> *And the busie humm of men. . . .*

Or, take another example. The most sociable and crowded scene that occurs in "L'Allegro" is perhaps that in which

> *. . . throngs of Knights and Barons bold,*
> *In weeds of Peace high triumphs hold,*
> *With store of Ladies, whose bright eies*
> *Rain influence, and judge the prise. . . .*

It is a court scene of some pomp and circumstance. But the only parallel to it in "Il Penseroso"—and Milton has of course provided a parallel—is one of the most poignant of the melancholy delights. The knights have been shifted out of reality into Spenser's Faeryland:

> *And if ought els, great* Bards *beside,*
> *In sage and solemn tunes have sung,*
> *Of Turneys and of Trophies hung;*
> *Of Forests, and inchantments drear,*
> *Where more is meant than meets the ear.*

But the most important device used to bring the patterns of opposites together—to build up an effect of unity in variety—is the use of a basic symbolism involving light. The symbolism never becomes quite explicit, but it is most important, nevertheless, and in the use of it Milton brings all the oppositions of the poem together, and orders and unifies them. I have said that Milton never declares his symbolism explicitly, but he comes very close to it in the preamble of each poem: Melancholy is born "of . . . blackest midnight"; the fancies of Mirth are like the "gay motes that people the Sun Beams." This is more than a broad hint; and to have "L'Allegro" begin with a dawn scene and "Il Penseroso," with an evening scene, emphasizes it.

But "L'Allegro," as we know, is not consistently a daylight poem, just as "Il Penseroso" is not consistently a night poem. The day, for both the cheerful man and the pensive man, embraces the whole round of the twenty-four hours. If both poems are characterized by a leisurely flowing movement as the spectator in each case drifts from pleasure to pleasure, and if in both poems he *is the detached spectator*—not the participant in the world he wanders through—in neither of the poems do we get the flaring sunbeam in which the dust motes swim or the unrelieved blackness of midnight. In both poems the spectator moves through what are predominantly cool half-lights. It is as if the half-light were being used in both poems as a sort of symbol of the aesthetic distance which the cheerful man, no less than the pensive man, consistently maintains. The full glare of the sun would then symbolize the actual workaday world over which neither the "Mountain Nymph, sweet Liberty" nor the "Cherub Contemplation" presides.

I have said that in this symbolism all the problems of the double poem head up. Let me mention a specific one: the landscape through which the spectator (as cheerful or pensive) moves must seem—even in its variety—cool, inviting, delightful. It must seem subdued to a mood; but more than that, it must present, when seen from every varying vantage-point, an aesthetic object. Yet even in a poem which skirts the *tour de force* as narrowly as this one does, it must seem *real*. It must be a world in which a real sun glares and real people sweat at their work; otherwise, it will seem a reduced world, or even an unreal, paper-thin world. The point is highly important. Milton must not merely, through his selection of materials, rule out the unpleasant or ugly. That is easy enough to do on the mechanical level. His selectivity must operate on a much higher plane: Milton must give the illusion of a real world, and of a full life—the whole round of the day—while at the same time presenting a world which meets at every point L'Allegro's cheer or Il Penseroso's melancholy.

To see how important this is, it is only necessary to recall the "Miltonic" landscapes of Akenside or the Wartons, poets who tend to heap up mechanically the characteristic details of Milton's poem, and yet fail of the characteristic atmosphere.

Since the progression of both "L'Allegro" and "Il Penseroso" is based upon the chronology of the day, Milton's light symbolism comes in naturally (and apparently inevitably), for the clock of the day is the sun; and the allusions to morning, noon, twilight, and moonlight provide Milton all the opportunities which he could wish to develop his symbolism of light and shade.

After the somewhat rhetorical exorcism of Melancholy, "Of *Cerberus,* and blackest midnight born,"

Mirth comes in with the morning. The first scene is a dawn scene—sunrise and people going to work: the plowman, the milkmaid, the mower, and the shepherd. But though we see people going to work, we never see them *at* their work, just as we do not ever feel the full glare of the sun. Even after the cottage dinner, when we are told of Phillis that

> . . . *then in haste her Bowre she leaves,*
> *With* Thestylis *to bind the Sheaves;*
> *Or if the earlier season lead*
> *To the tann'd Haycock in the Mead.* . . .

we do not accompany them to the haycock, nor do we feel the sun which "tans" it. Instead, with "secure delight" we slip with the observer over to one of the "up-land Hamlets" where we watch

> . . . *many a youth, and many a maid,*
> *Dancing in the Chequer'd shade;*
> *And young and old com forth to play*
> *On a Sunshine Holyday,*
> *Till the live-long day-light fail.* . . .

There is the illusion of a real world and of a daylight world; but the basic scenes of the daylight sequence in "L'Allegro" are dominated by the whistling plowman, the rustics at their noon meal, and the dancing in the "Chequer'd shade." The sunshine is that of a "Sunshine Holyday." Nobody sweats in the world of "L'Allegro" —except the goblin:

> *Tells how the drudging* Goblin *swet,*
> *To ern his Cream-bowle duly set,*
> *When in one night, ere glimps of morn,*
> *His shadowy Flale hath thresh'd the Corn.* . . .

(Perhaps it is overingenious to suggest that in this scene—the only depiction of strenuous activity in the poem—Milton has "cooled" it off by making the flail "shadowy," by presenting it as part of a night scene, and by making the laborer, not a flesh-and-blood man, but a goblin. And yet the scene has been carefully patterned: it is balanced by the passage in "Il Penserso," where the spectator having taken refuge from the sun, listens

> *While the Bee with Honied thie,*
> *. . . at her flowry work doth sing. . . .*

Goblins and bees are the only creatures presented "at work" in the two poems.)

If we get merely holiday sunshine in the country-scene sequence of "L'Allegro," we get, of course, no sunshine at all in the city sequence. But Milton has attended very carefully to the lighting of the scene displayed. The "high triumphs" of the knights and barons are presided over by the "bright eies" of the ladies, eyes which "Rain influence." "Rain influence" suggests a star metaphor: the stars were supposed to rain influence and determine events. The court ceremonial is succeeded by a wedding ceremony presided over by Hymen with his "Taper clear." The light in these scenes, then, is starlight or candlelight, not, to be sure, presented as the actual physical lighting of the scenes, but certainly insinuated into the mood of the scenes. The "thronged" scenes of "L'Allegro" are thus softened—the aesthetic distance from which they are viewed is thus indicated—just as the scenes of physical work have been softened and pushed back from the immediate presence of the observer.

The common-sense reader who distrusts the ingenious and wants his poetry to be explicit, declared, and forthright, may well ask why, if all this elaborate handling of the lighting is going on, Milton has to handle it so indirectly. Why doesn't Milton declare himself? But

Milton does—at least with regard to the central element of the symbol, the association of the raw glare of the sun with the workaday world. In "Il Penseroso," when the showery morning has passed and the sun has broken forth, the speaker says:

> *And when the Sun begins to fling*
> *His flaring beams, me Goddes bring*
> *To arched walks of twilight groves,*
> *And shadows brown that* Sylvan *loves*
> *Of Pine, or monumental Oake,*
> *Where the rude Ax with heaved stroke,*
> *Was never heard the Nymphs to daunt,*
> *Or fright them from their hallow'd haunt.*
> *There in close covert by som Brook,*
> *Where no profaner eye may look,*
> *Hide me from Day's garish eie. . . .*

We are not told in so many words that the sun ("Day's . . . eie") is one of the "profaner" eyes; but it is "garish"; and it is associated definitely with the "heaved stroke." The pensive man withdraws from both—to the "twilight groves" where he may hear only the "work" of the bee—"flowry work," at which the bee sings—labor which is a part of nature itself. But the cheerful man too, as we have seen, has been kept out of "Day's garish eie" almost as completely as has Il Penseroso himself.

On the other hand, "Il Penseroso" avoids "blackest midnight" too. And at this point we are prepared to take up Tillyard's point about the burlesque style of the passage in which Melancholy is dismissed. The reprehension of Melancholy as loathsome, and the identification of her with the blackness of midnight are associated with a consciously stilted rhetoric which forms an ironical contrast with the freer and more casual rhythms in which the pensive man's actual ex-

perience of melancholy is expressed. It is the most
delicate kind of qualification that a poet can give.
For those who feel with Tillyard that the opening *is*
bombastic, the presence of the bombast thus becomes
meaningful. Melancholy as actually experienced by
the pensive man is not a monstrosity at all. In contrast
to her "literary" and abstract caricature, the actual
goddess moves in a solid and "real" world, a beautiful
world, and not a world of midnight black.

The poem has her come in with evening into a scene
dominated by the moon. But even when the pensive
man goes within doors and the moonlight is shut out,
there are the "glowing Embers" which "Teach light
to counterfeit a gloom." Midnight itself, when it is
mentioned, is relieved by the speaker's studious lamp,
and above the tower the stars are shining:

> *Or let my Lamp at midnight hour,*
> *Be seen in som high lonely Towr,*
> *Where I may oft out-watch the* Bear. . . .

The night scene here balances the starlight and candle-
light of its companion scene in "L'Allegro," with star-
light and lamplight—though the stars here are not the
eyes of brilliant women which "Rain influence, and
judge the prise" but the cold, watchful stars of Ursa
Major.

More important still, the sequence which follows,
with its references to Plato, "Gorgeous Tragedy,"
Chaucer, and the other "great *Bards,*" emphasizes the
light accorded to the "inward eye," and thus provides
a concrete realization of the paradox hinted at earlier
in the poem: that the black of night, "staid Wisdoms
hue," is merely a necessary veil to conceal a brightness
which is in reality too intense for human sight.

This, of course, is the point which Milton was to

make years later when he wrote his *Paradise Lost*, where, addressing the celestial light, he says:

> *Shine inward, and the mind through all her powers*
> *Irradiate, there plant eyes, all mist from thence*
> *Purge and disperse, that I may see and tell*
> *Of things invisible to mortal sight.*

When "Il Penseroso" was being written, that day was far in the future, and it is not my purpose to suggest that the poem gives a calculated foresight of that sterner time to come. What one may fairly say, however, is that the light symbolism, used so powerfully, though unobtrusively, in these earlier poems, was perfectly consonant with Milton's thinking, and was to emerge later in the great poem quite explicitly.

Actually, the connection of the life of contemplation with the higher life, and of the shades associated with melancholy with the brightest visions (though unearthly visions) is made quite explicitly at the end of "Il Penseroso." This concluding passage, by the way, has no parallel in the twin poem: "Il Penseroso" is twenty-four lines longer than its companion piece.

Here the secular life is made to pass over into the religious—the semipaganism of the "Genius of the Wood" frankly gives way to Christianity, and the measure of aesthetic distance with which the world has been consistently viewed is extended into the hermit's avowed withdrawal from the secular world altogether. The light symbolism accommodates itself to the change:

> *. . . storied Windows richly dight,*
> *Casting a dimm religious light.*

The pensive man is now bathed neither in midnight nor in the moted sunbeam. The daylight of the senses, dimmed and enriched by the storied windows, has been brought nearer to darkness, and yet at the same time prepared for the vision of the inward eye:

> *Dissolve me into extasies,*
> *And bring all Heav'n before mine eyes.*

Is the light "dimm" because religious, or religious because "dimm"? Or is it paradoxically dim, though religious—dim to the physical eye, though actually the proper light for one who would have the vision too insupportably bright for human sight to receive? To unravel these questions is to recapitulate the entire symbolism of the two poems. Suffice it to say that the collocation, if it seems inevitable, seems so because of Milton's cunning development of the light passages throughout the poems.

CHAPTER FOUR
WHAT DOES POETRY COMMUNICATE?

The question of what poetry communicates, if any-thing, has been largely forced upon us by the advent of "modern" poetry. Some of that poetry is admittedly highly difficult—a very great deal of it is bound to *appear* difficult to the reader of conventional reading habits, even in spite of the fact—actually, in many cases, *because* of the fact—that he is a professor of lit-erature.

For this reason, the difficult moderns are often rep-resented as untraditional and generally irresponsible. (The War, incidentally, has encouraged the tendency: critics who ought to know better lend themselves to the popular plea that we should go back to the good old days when a poet meant what he said and there was no nonsense about it.)

The question, however, allows only one honest an-swer: modern poetry (if it is really poetry, and, at its best, it is really poetry) communicates whatever any other poetry communicates. The fact is that the ques-tion is badly asked. What does traditional poetry com-municate? What does a poem like Herrick's "Corinna's going a-Maying" communicate? The example is a fair one: the poem has been long praised, and it is not noted for its difficulty.

The textbook answer is easy: the poem is a state-ment of the *carpe diem* theme. So it is, of course. But what does the poem do with the theme—specifically: Does the poet accept the theme? How seriously does he accept it? Within what context? etc., etc. These are questions of the first importance, a point that becomes obvious when we come to deal with such a matter as the following: after describing the joys of the May-day celebration, the poet prefaces his final invitation to Corinna to accept these joys by referring to them as "the harmlesse follie of the time." Unless we are absent-mindedly dictating a stock answer to an indifferent freshman, we shall certainly feel constrained to go further in describing what the poem "says."

Well, let us try again. Herrick's poem says that the celebration of nature is a beautiful but harmless folly, and his invitation to Corinna, thus, is merely playful, not serious. The Anglican parson is merely pretending for the moment that he is Catullus and that his Corinna is a pagan nymph. The poem is a pretense, a masquerade.

But there are the closing lines of the poem:

> Our life is short; and our dayes run
> As fast away as do's the Sunne:
> And as a vapour, or a drop of raine
> Once lost, can ne'er be found againe:
> So when or you or I are made
> A fable, song, or fleeting shade;
> All love, all liking, all delight
> Lies drown'd with us in endlesse night.
> Then while time serves, and we are but decaying;
> Come, my Corinna, come, let's goe a-Maying.

Obviously, there is a sense in which the invitation is thoroughly serious.

Confronted with this apparent contradiction, we can conclude, if we like, that Herrick is confused; or, softening the censure, we can explain that he was concerned only with providing some sort of framework for a description of the Devonshire spring. But if Herrick is confused about what he is saying in the poem, he behaves very strangely for a man in that plight. Far from being unconscious of the contradictory elements in the poem, he quite obviously has them in mind. Indeed, he actually takes pains to stress the clash between the Christian and pagan world views; or, rather, while celebrating the pagan view, he refuses to suppress references to the Christian. For instance, for all the dew-besprinkled description of the morning, he makes the ominous, unpagan word "sin" run throughout the poem. While the flowers are rejoicing and the birds are singing their hymns of praise, it is a "sin" and a "profanation" for Corinna to remain within doors. In the second stanza, the clash between paganism and Christianity becomes quite explicit: Corinna is to be "briefe in praying:/ Few Beads are best" on this morning which is dedicated to the worship of the nature god. And in the third stanza, paganism becomes frankly triumphant. Corinna is to

. . . sin no more, as we have done, by staying. . . .

Moreover, a great deal that is usually glossed over as decoration or atmosphere in this poem is actually used by the poet to point up this same conflict. Herrick persists (with a shrewdness worthy of Sir James Frazer) in seeing the May-day rites as religious rites, though, of course, those of a pagan religion. The flowers, like worshipers, bow to the east; the birds sing "Mattens" and "Hymnes"; and the village itself, bedecked with greenery, becomes a cluster of pagan temples:

> *Devotion gives each House a Bough,*
> *Or Branch: Each Porch, each doore, ere this,*
> *An Arke a Tabernacle is. . . .*

The religious terms—"devotion," "ark," "tabernacle" —appear insistently. Corinna is actually being reproached for being late to church—the church of nature. The village itself has become a grove, subject to the laws of nature. One remembers that the original sense of "pagan" was "country-dweller" because the worship of the old gods and goddesses persisted longest there. On this May morning, the country has come into the village to claim it, at least on this one day, for its own. Symbolically, the town has disappeared and its mores are superseded.

I cannot see how we can avoid admitting that all this is communicated by the poem. Here it is in the poem. And its repercussions on the theme (if we still want to view the poem as a communication of a theme) are important. Among other things, they qualify the theme thus: the poem is obviously not a brief for the acceptance of the pagan ethic so much as it is a statement that the claims of the pagan ethic—however much they may be overlaid—exist, and on occasion emerge, as on this day.

The description of Corinna herself supplies another important qualification of the theme. The poet suggests that she properly falls under the dominion of nature as do the flowers and birds and trees. Notice the opening of the second stanza:

> *Rise; and put on your Foliage. . . .*

And this suggestion that she is a part of nature, like a plant, is reinforced throughout the poem. The trees drenched in dew will shake down dew-drops on her hair, accepting her as a companion and equal. Her human companions, the boys and girls of the village, likewise are plants—

> *There's not a budding Boy, or Girle, this day,*
> *But is got up, and gone to bring in May.*

Indeed, as we go through the first three stanzas of the poem, the old relationships gradually dissolve: the street itself turns into a park, and the boys and girls returning with their arms loaded with branches of white-thorn, merge into the plants themselves. Corinna, like them, is subject to nature, and to the claims of nature; and the season of springtime cannot, and ought not, to be denied. Not to respond is to "sin" against nature itself.

All this is "communicated" by the poem, and must be taken into account when we attempt to state what the poem "says." No theory of communication can deny that this is part of what the poem communicates, however awkwardly a theory of communication may be put to it to handle the problem.

We have still not attempted to resolve the conflict between the Christian and pagan attitudes in the poem, though the qualification of each of them, as Herrick qualifies each in the poem, may make it easier to discover possible resolutions which would have appealed to Herrick the Anglican parson who lived so much of his life in Devonshire and apparently took so much interest, not only in the pagan literature of Rome and Greece, but in the native English survivals of the old fertility cults.

Something of the nature of the poet's reconcilement of the conflicting claims of paganism and Christianity —and this, again, is part of what the poem communicates—is foreshadowed in the fourth stanza. The paganism with which the poem is concerned is clearly not an abstract and doctrinaire paganism. It comes to terms with the authoritative Christian mores, casually and without undue thought about the conflict—at least the paganism in action does: the village boys and the girls with their grass-stained gowns, coming to the priest to receive the blessing of the church.

And some have wept, and woo'd, and plighted Troth,
And chose their Priest, ere we can cast off sloth. . . .

After the poet's teasing play between attitudes in the
first three stanzas, we are apparently approaching some
kind of viable relation between them in this most
realistic stanza of the poem with its

> *Many a jest told of the Keyes betraying*
> *This night, and Locks pickt. . . .*

The explicit resolution, of course, is achieved, with a
change of tone, in the last stanza, with its

> *Come, let us goe, while we are in our prime;*
> *And take the harmlesse follie of the time.*
> *We shall grow old apace, and die . . .*

I shall not try to indicate in detail what the resolu-
tion is. Here one must refer the reader to the poem
itself. Yet one can venture to suggest the tone. The
tone would be something like this: All right, let's be
serious. Dismiss my pagan argument as folly. Still, in a
sense, we are a part of nature, and are subject to its
claims, and participate in its beauty. Whatever may be
true in reality of the life of the soul, the body does de-
cay, and unless we make haste to catch some part of
that joy and beauty, that beauty—whatever else may
be true—is lost.

If my clumsy paraphrase possesses any part of the
truth, then this is still another thing which the poem
communicates, though I shall hardly be able to "prove"
it. As a matter of fact, I do not care to insist upon this
or any other paraphrase. Indeed it is just because I am
suspicious of such necessarily abstract paraphrases that
I think our initial question, "What does the poem com-
municate?" is badly asked. It is not that the poem com-
municates nothing. Precisely the contrary. The poem

communicates so much and communicates it so richly and with such delicate qualifications that the thing communicated is mauled and distorted if we attempt to convey it by any vehicle less subtle than that of the poem itself.

This general point is reinforced if we consider the function of particular words and phrases within the poem. For instance, consider

> *Our life is short; and our dayes run*
> *As fast away as do's the Sunne:*
> *And as a vapour, or a drop of raine*
> *Once lost, can ne'er be found againe. . . .*

Why does the rain-drop metaphor work so powerfully? It is hardly because the metaphor is startlingly novel. Surely one important reason for its power is the fact that the poet has filled the first two stanzas of his poem with references to the dew. And the drops of dew have come to stand as a symbol of the spring and early dawn and of the youth of the lovers themselves. The dew-drops are the free gift of nature, spangling every herb and tree; they sparkle in the early light like something precious, like gems; they are the appropriate decoration for the girl; but they will not last—Corinna must hasten to enjoy them if she is to enjoy them at all. Thus, in the context of the poem they become a symbol heavily charged with meanings which no dictionary can be expected to give. When the symbol is revived at the end of the poem, even though in somewhat different guise, the effect is powerful; for the poet has made the little globule of moisture come to stand for the brief beauty of youth. And this too is part of what the poem says, though it is said indirectly, and the dull or lazy reader will not realize that it has been said at all.

The principle of rich indirection applies even to the individual word. Consider

Then while times serves, and we are but decaying;
Come, my Corinna, *come, let's goe a-Maying.*

"While time serves" means loosely "while there is yet
time," but in the full context of the poem it also means
"while time serves us," while time is still servant, not
master—before we are mastered by time. Again, mere
recourse to the dictionary will not give us this powerful
second meaning. The poet is exploiting the potentiali-
ties of language—indeed, as all poets must do, he is
remaking language.

To sum up: our examination of the poem has not
resulted in our locating an idea or set of ideas which
the poet has communicated with certain appropriate
decorations. Rather, our examination has carried us
further and further into the poem itself in a process
of exploration. As we have made this exploration, it has
become more and more clear that the poem is not only
the linguistic vehicle which conveys the thing com-
municated most "poetically," but that it is also the sole
linguistic vehicle which conveys the things communi-
cated accurately. In fact, if we are to speak exactly, the
poem itself is the *only* medium that communicates the
particular "what" that is communicated. The conven-
tional theories of communication offer no easy solution
to our problem of meanings: we emerge with nothing
more enlightening than this graceless bit of tautology:
the poem says what the poem says.

There is a further point that comes out of our ex-
amination: our examination tends to suggest that not
only our reading of the poem is a process of explora-
tion, but that Herrick's process of making the poem
was probably a process of exploration too. To say that
Herrick "communicates" certain matters to the reader
tends to falsify the real situation. The old description
of the poet was better and less dangerous: the poet is

a maker, not a communicator. He explores, consolidates, and "forms" the total experience that is the poem. I do not mean that he fashions a replica of his particular experience of a certain May morning like a detective making a moulage of a footprint in wet clay. But rather, out of the experiences of many May mornings, and out of his experience of Catullus, and possibly out of a hundred other experiences, he fashions, probably through a process akin to exploration, the total experience which is the poem.

This experience is *communicable*, partially so, at least. If we are willing to use imaginative understanding, we can come to know the poem as an object—we can share in the experience. But the poet is most truthfully described as a *poietes* or maker, not as an expositor or communicator. I do not mean to split hairs. It is doubtless possible to elaborate a theory of communication which will adequately cover these points. I believe that I. A. Richards, if I understand him correctly, has attempted to qualify his theory in precisely this way. At any rate, the net effect of his criticism has been to emphasize the need of a more careful reading of poetry and to regard the poem as an organic thing.

But most proponents of poetry as communication have been less discerning, and have used this view of poetry to damn the modern poets. I refer to such typical critics as Max Eastman and F. L. Lucas. But perhaps the most hard-bitten and vindictive of all the adherents of the theory is a man to whom the phrase "theory of communication" may seem novel and unfamiliar: I mean the average English professor. In one form or another, whether in a conception which makes poetry a romantic raid on the absolute, or in a conception of more didactic persuasion which makes poetry an instrument of edification, some form of the theory of communication is to be found deeply embedded in the average teacher's doctrine of poetry. In many contexts it does little or no harm; but it can emerge to becloud the issues thoroughly when one confronts poetry which is unfamiliar or difficult.

Much modern poetry is difficult. Some of it may be difficult because the poet is snobbish and definitely wants to restrict his audience, though this is a strange vanity and much rarer than Mr. Eastman would have us think. Some modern poetry is difficult because it is bad—the total experience remains chaotic and incoherent because the poet could not master his material and give it a form. Some modern poetry is difficult because of the special problems of our civilization. But a great deal of modern poetry is difficult for the reader simply because so few people, relatively speaking, are accustomed to reading *poetry as poetry*. The theory of communication throws the burden of proof upon the poet, overwhelmingly and at once. The reader says to the poet: Here I am; it's your job to "get it across" to me—when he ought to be assuming the burden of proof himself.

Now the modern poet has, for better or worse, thrown the weight of the responsibility upon the reader. The reader must be on the alert for shifts of tone, for ironic statement, for suggestion rather than direct statement. He must be prepared to accept a method of indirection. He is further expected to be reasonably well acquainted with the general tradition —literary, political, philosophical, for he is reading a poet who comes at the end of a long tradition and who can hardly be expected to write honestly and with full integrity and yet ignore this fact. But the difficulties are not insuperable, and most of them can be justified in principle as the natural results of the poet's employment of his characteristic methods. For example, surely there can be no objection to the poet's placing emphasis on methods characteristic of poetry—the use of symbol rather than abstraction, of suggestion rather than explicit pronouncement, of metaphor rather than direct statement.

In stressing such methods, it is true, the modern poet has not produced a poetry which easily yields manageable abstractions in the way that some of the older poetry seems to do. But this is scarcely a conclusion that is flattering to the antagonists of modern poetry. What does an "older poem" like "Corinna's going a-Maying" say? What does this poem communicate? If we are content with the answer that the poem says that we should enjoy youth before youth fades, and if we are willing to write off everything else in the poem as "decoration," then we can properly censure Eliot or Auden or Tate for not making poems so easily tagged. But in that case we are not interested in poetry; we are interested in tags. Actually, in a few years, when time has wrought its softening changes, and familiarity has subdued the modern poet's frightful mien, and when the tags have been obligingly supplied, we may even come to terms with our difficult moderns.

Postscript:

In a recent essay, Arthur Mizener connects the reference to "the god unshorn" in the first lines of Herrick's poem with a comparable passage in Spenser.

At last the golden Orientall gate
  Of greatest heauen gan to open faire,
  And Phoebus *fresh, a bridegrome to his mate,*
  Came dauncing forth, shaking his deawie haire:
  And hurled his glistring beames through gloomy aire.
  Which when the wakeful Elf perceiu'd streight way
  He started vp, and did him selfe arraye:
  In svn-bright armes, and battailovs array:
For with that Pagan proud he combat will that day.

"There is," Mizener comments, "a nice fusion, if, to our tastes, not a complete ordering of Pagan and Christian elements here. Phoebus, fresh as the Psalmist's bridegroom, comes dancing (with, I suppose, both a pagan grace and the rejoicing of a strong man to run a race) from the gate of a heaven which is actually felt simultaneously in terms of the clear and lovely classical fantasy on nature and in terms of a Christian vision of the metaphysical source of the meaning of life." And a little later in the essay Mizener goes on to say: "Certainly the Red Cross Knight's 'sun-bright armes' ('the armour of a Christian man') are intended to be compared to the 'glistring beames' with which Apollo attacks the darkness, as the virtuous and enlightened Elf is about to attack the darkly evil Pagan. And it is tempting to suppose that since the strength of Holiness is that of the sun, of 'the god unshorn,' the references to Apollo's hair and to the bridegroom's energy are also significant."

Later still in his essay, Mizener quotes the following passage from *Paradise Lost*:

> . . . *nor appear'd*
> *Less than Arch Angel ruin'd, and th' excess*
> *Of Glory obscur'd: As when the Sun new ris'n*
> *Looks through the Horizontal misty Air*
> *Shorn of his Beams, or from behind the Moon*
> *In dim Eclipse disastrous twilight sheds*
> *On half the Nations, and with fear of change*
> *Perplexes Monarchs.*

"By the first of these sun comparisons," Mizener points out, "the archangel ruined is the sun deprived of its power to dispel with its beams the foul mists of winter and make the earth fruitful once more; the fallen angel is Apollo, shorn. . . . Nor is it easy to believe the epithet insignificant here; with all his learning Milton must certainly have known how common a symbol of virility the hair was among the Greeks. Herrick, a much less learned man, knew this, as his use of it in 'Corinna's going a-Maying' clearly shows:

> *Get up, get up, for shame, the Blooming Morn*
> *Upon her wings presents the god unshorne."*

It is unfair, of course, to quote from Mizener's essay without reference to his general thesis, and to quote only those bits of it which bear directly upon the dawn passage in Herrick's poem. (The essay, by the way, should be read in entirety and for its own sake: "Some Notes on the Nature of English Poetry," *The Sewanee Review,* Winter, 1943.) Even so, the passage quoted may be of value in demonstrating to the skeptical reader, suspicious that too much is being "read into" Herrick's innocent poem, how other poets of the same general period used the sun figure.

In Herrick's poem, "the god unshorne" is obviously the prepotent bridegroom of nature, the fertility god himself, toward whom the plants bow in adoration and whose day is now to be celebrated.

CHAPTER FIVE
THE CASE OF
MISS ARABELLA FERMOR

Aldous Huxley's lovers, "quietly sweating, palm to palm," may be conveniently taken to mark the nadir of Petrarchianism. The mistress is no longer a goddess —not even by courtesy. She is a congeries of biological processes and her too evident mortality is proclaimed at every pore. But if we seem to reach, with Huxley's lines, the end of something, it is well to see what it is that has come to an end. It is not the end of a naïve illusion.

The Elizabethans, even those who were immersed in the best tradition of Petrarchianism, did not have to wait upon the advent of modern science to find out that women perspired. They were thoroughly aware that woman was a biological organism, but their recognition of this fact did not prevent them from asserting, on occasion, that she was a goddess, nevertheless. John Donne, for instance, frequently has it both ways: in-deed, some of the difficulty which the modern reader has with his poems may reside in the fact that he some-times has it both ways in the same poem. What is relevant to our purposes here is not the occurrence of a line like "Such are the sweat drops of my Mistres breast" in one of the satiric "elegies," but the occur-rence of lines like

> *Our hands were firmly cimented*
> *With a fast balme, which thence did spring*

in a poem like "The Ecstasy"! The passage quoted, one may argue, glances at the very phenomenon which Huxley so amiably describes; but Donne has transmuted it into something else.

But if Donne could have it both ways, most of us, in this latter day, cannot. We are disciplined in the tradition of either-or, and lack the mental agility—to say nothing of the maturity of attitude—which would allow us to indulge in the finer distinctions and the more subtle reservations permitted by the tradition of both-and. Flesh *or* spirit, merely a doxy or purely a goddess (or alternately, one and then the other), is more easily managed in our poetry, and probably, for that matter, in our private lives. But the greater poems of our tradition are more ambitious in this matter: as a consequence, they come perhaps nearer the truth than we do with our ordinary hand-to-mouth insights. In saying this, however, one need by no means confine himself to the poetry of Donne. If we are not too much blinded by our doctrine of either-or, we shall be able to see that there are many poems in the English tradition which demonstrate a thorough awareness of the problem and which manage, at their appropriate levels, the same kinds of synthesis of attitudes which we associate characteristically with Donne.

Take Pope's *Rape of the Lock,* for instance. Is Belinda a goddess, or is she merely a frivolous tease? Pope himself was, we may be sure, thoroughly aware of the problem. His friend Swift penetrated the secrets of the lady's dressing room with what results we know. Belinda's dressing table, of course, is bathed in a very different atmosphere; yet it may be significant that Pope is willing to allow us to observe his heroine at her dressing table at all. The poet definitely means to give us scenes from the greenroom, and views from the wings, as well as a presentation "in character" on the lighted stage.

Pope, of course, did not write *The Rape of the Lock* because he was obsessed with the problem of Belinda's divinity. He shows, indeed, that he was interested in a great many things: in various kinds of social satire, in a playful treatment of the epic manner, in deflating some of the more vapid clichés that filled the love poetry of the period, and in a dozen other things. But we are familiar with Pope's interest in the mock-epic as we are not familiar with his interest in the problem of woman as goddess; and moreover, the rather lurid conventional picture of Pope as the "wicked wasp of Twickenham"—the particular variant of the either-or theory as applied to Pope—encourages us to take the poem as a dainty but rather obvious satire. There is some justification, therefore, for emphasizing aspects of the poem which have received little attention in the past, and perhaps for neglecting other aspects of the poems which critics have already treated in luminous detail.

One further point should be made: if Pope in this account of the poem turns out to be something of a symbolist poet, and perhaps even something of what we call, in our clumsy phrase, a "metaphysical poet" as well, we need not be alarmed. It matters very little whether or not we twist some of the categories which the literary historian jealously (and perhaps properly) guards. It matters a great deal that we understand Pope's poem in its full richness and complexity. It would be an amusing irony (and one not wholly undeserved) if we retorted upon Pope some of the brittleness and inelasticity which we feel that Pope was inclined to impose upon the more fluid and illogical poetry which preceded him. But the real victims of the maneuver, if it blinded us to his poem, would be ourselves.

Pope's own friends were sometimes guilty of oversimplifying and reducing his poem by trying to make it accord with a narrow and pedantic logic. For example, Bishop Warburton, Pope's friend and editor, finds an error in the famous passage in which Belinda and her maid are represented as priestesses invoking the goddess of beauty. Warburton feels forced to comment as follows: "There is a small inaccuracy in these lines. He first makes his Heroine the chief Priestess, then the Goddess herself." The lines in question run as follows:

> *First, rob'd in White, the Nymph intent adores*
> *With Head uncover'd, the Cosmetic Pow'rs.*
> *A heav'nly Image in the Glass appears,*
> *To that she bends, to that her Eyes she rears. . . .*

It is true that Pope goes on to imply that Belinda is the chief priestess (by calling her maid the "inferior Priestess"), and that, a few lines later, he has the maid deck the goddess (Belinda) "with the glitt'ring Spoil." But surely Warburton ought not to have missed the point: Belinda, in worshiping at the shrine of beauty, quite naturally worships herself. Whose else is the "heav'nly Image" which appears in the mirror to which she raises her eyes? The violation of logic involved is intended and is thoroughly justified. Belinda *is* a goddess, but she puts on her divinity at her dressing table; and, such is the paradox of beauty-worship, she can be both the sincere devotee and the divinity herself. We shall certainly require more sensitive instruments than Bishop Warburton's logic if we are to become aware of some of the nicest effects in the poem.

But to continue with the dressing-table scene:

The Fair each moment rises in her Charms,
Repairs her Smiles, awakens ev'ry Grace,
And calls forth all the Wonders of her Face;
Sees by Degrees a purer Blush arise,
And keener Lightnings quicken in her Eyes.

It is the experience which the cosmetic advertisers take at a level of dead seriousness, and obviously Pope is amused to have it taken seriously. And yet, is there not more here than the obvious humor? Belinda is, after all, an artist, and who should be more sympathetic with the problems of the conscious artist than Pope himself? In our own time, William Butler Yeats, a less finicky poet than Pope, could address a "young beauty" as "dear fellow artist."

In particular, consider the "purer Blush." Why purer? One must not laugh too easily at the purity of the blush which Belinda is engaged in painting upon her face. After all, may we not regard it as a blush "recollected in tranquillity," and therefore a more ideal blush than the spontaneous actual blush which shame or hauteur on an actual occasion might bring? If we merely read "purer" as ironic for its opposite, "impurer"—that is, unspontaneous and therefore unmaidenly—we shall miss not only the more delightful aspects of the humor, but we shall miss also Pope's concern for the real problem. Which is, after all, the more maidenly blush? That will depend, obviously, upon what one considers the essential nature of maidens to be; and Belinda, we ought to be reminded, is not the less real nor the less feminine because she fails to resemble Whittier's robust heroine, Maude Muller.

One is tempted to insist upon these ambiguities and complexities of attitude, not with any idea of overturning the orthodox reading of Pope's irony, but rather to make sure that we do not conceive it to be more brittle and thin than it actually is. This fact, at least, should be plain: regardless of what we may make of the "purer Blush," it is true that Belinda's dressing table does glow with a special radiance and charm, and that Pope, though amused by the vanity which it represents, is at the same time thoroughly alive to a beauty which it actually possesses.

There is a further reason for feeling that we shall not err in taking the niceties of Pope's descriptions quite seriously. One notices that even the metaphors by which Pope characterizes Belinda are not casual bits of decoration, used for a moment, and then forgotten. They run throughout the poem as if they were motifs. For instance, at her dressing table Belinda is not only a priestess of "the Sacred Rites of Pride," but she is also compared to a warrior arming for the fray. Later in the poem she is the warrior once more at the card table in her conquest of the two "adventrous Knights"; and again, at the end of the poem, she emerges as the heroic conqueror in the epic encounter of the beaux and belles.

To take another example, Belinda, early in the poem, is compared to the sun. Pope suggests that the sun recognizes in Belinda a rival, and fears her:

> Sol *thro' white Curtains shot a tim'rous Ray,*
> *And op'd those Eyes that must eclipse the Day.*

But the sun's fear of Belinda has not been introduced merely in order to give the poet an opportunity to mock at the polite cliché. The sun comparison appears again at the beginning of Canto II:

> *Not with more Glories, in th' Etherial Plain,*
> *The Sun first rises o'er the purpled Main,*
> *Than issuing forth, the Rival of his Beams*
> *Lanch'd on the Bosom of the silver Thames.*

Belinda is like the sun, not only because of her bright eyes, and not only because she dominates her special world ("But ev'ry Eye was fix'd on her alone"). She is like the sun in another regard:

> Bright as the Sun, her Eyes the Gazers strike,
> And, like the Sun, they shine on all alike.

Is this general munificence on the part of Belinda a fault or a virtue? Is she shallow and flirtatious, giving her favors freely to all; or, does she distribute her largesse impartially like a great prince? Or, is she simply the well-bred belle who knows that she cannot play favorites if she wishes to be popular? The sun comparison is able to carry all these meanings, and therefore goes past any momentary jest. Granting that it may be overingenious to argue that Belinda in Canto IV (the gloomy Cave of Spleen) represents the sun in eclipse, still the sun comparison does appear once more in the poem, and quite explicitly. As the poem closes, Pope addresses Belinda thus:

> When those fair Suns shall sett, as sett they must,
> And all those Tresses shall be laid in Dust;
> This Lock, the Muse shall consecrate to Fame,
> And mid'st the stars inscribe Belinda's Name!

Here, one notices that the poet, if he is forced to concede that Belinda's eyes are only metaphorical suns after all, still promises that the ravished lock shall have a celestial eternity, adding, like the planet Venus, "new Glory to the shining Sphere!" And here Pope, we may be sure, is not merely playful in his metaphor. Belinda's name has been inscribed in the only heaven in which a poet would care to inscribe it. If the skeptic still has any doubts about Pope's taking Belinda very seriously, there should be no difficulty in convincing him that Pope took his own work very seriously indeed.

We began by raising the question of Belinda's status as a goddess. It ought to be quite clear that Pope's attitude toward Belinda is not exhausted in laughing away her claims to divinity. The attitude is much more complicated than that. Belinda's charm is not viewed uncritically, but the charm is real: it can survive the poet's knowledge of how much art and artifice have gone into making up the charm. The attitude is not wholly unrelated to that of Mirabell toward Millamant in Congreve's *The Way of the World*. Mirabell knows that his mistress has her faults, but as he philosophically remarks: ". . . I like her with all her faults; nay, like her for her faults. Her follies are so natural, or so artful, that they become her. . . . she once used me with that insolence, that in revenge I took her to pieces, sifted her, and separated her failings; I studied 'em, and got 'em by rote. . . . They are now grown as familiar to me as my own frailties; and in all probability, in a little time longer, I shall like 'em as well." The relation of author to creation can be more philosophical still: and though Pope's attitude toward his heroine has a large element of amused patronage in it, I find no contempt. Rather, Pope finds Belinda charming, and expects us to feel her charm.

To pursue the matter of attitude further still, what, after all, is Pope's attitude toward the iridescent little myth of the sylphs which he has provided to symbolize the polite conventions which govern the conduct of maidens? We miss the whole point if we dismiss the sylphs as merely "supernatural machinery." In general, we may say that the myth represents a qualification of the poet's prevailingly naturalistic interpretation. More specifically, it represents his attempt to do justice to the intricacies of the feminine mind. For, in spite of Pope's amusement at the irrationality of that mind, Pope acknowledges its beauty and its power.

In making this acknowledgement, he is a good realist —a better realist, indeed, than he appears when he tries to parade the fashionable ideas of the Age of Reason as in his "Essay on Man." He is good enough realist to know that although men in their "Learned Pride" may say that it is Honor which protects the chastity of maids, actually it is nothing of the sort: the belles are not kept chaste by any mere abstraction. It is the sylphs, the sylphs with their interest in fashion notes and their knowledge of the feminine heart:

With varying Vanities, from ev'ry Part,
They shift the moving Toyshop of their Heart;
Where Wigs with Wigs, with Sword-knots Sword-knots
*   strive,*
Beaus banish Beaus, and Coaches Coaches drive.

Yet the myth of the sylphs is no mere decoration to this essentially cynical generalization. The sylphs do represent the supernatural, though the supernatural reduced, of course, to its flimsiest proportions. The poet has been very careful here. Even Belinda is not made to take their existence too seriously. As for the poet, he very modestly recuses himself from rendering any judgment at all by ranging himself on the side of "Learned Pride":

Some secret Truths from Learned Pride conceal'd,
To Maids alone and Children are reveal'd:
What tho' no Credit doubting Wits may give?
The Fair and Innocent shall still believe.

In the old wives' tale or the child's fairy story may lurk an item of truth, after all. Consider the passage carefully.

"Fair" and "Innocent" balance "Maids" and "Children." Yet they act further to color the whole passage. Is "fair" used merely as a synonym for "maids"—*e.g.,* as in "the fair"? Or, is it that beauty is easily flattered? The doctrine which Ariel urges Belinda to accept is certainly flattering: "Hear and believe! thy own Importance know/ . . . unnumber'd Spirits round thee fly. . . ." Is "innocent" to be taken to mean "guiltless," or does it mean "naïve," perhaps even "credulous"? And how do "fair" and "innocent" influence each other? Do the fair believe in the sylphs because they are still children? (Ariel, one remembers, begins by saying: "If e'er one Vision touch'd thy *infant* Thought . . .") Pope is here exploiting that whole complex of associations which surround "innocence" and connect it on the one hand with more than worldly wisdom and, on the other, with simple gullibility.

Pope, as we now know, was clearly unjust in suggesting that Addison's advice against adding the machinery of the sylphs was prompted by any desire to prevent the improvement of the poem. Addison's caution was "safe" and natural under the circumstances. But we can better understand Pope's pique if we come to understand how important the machinery was to become in the final version of the poem. For it is Pope's treatment of the sylphs which allows him to develop, with the most delicate modulation, his whole attitude toward Belinda and the special world which she graces. It is precisely the poet's handling of the supernatural— the level at which he is willing to entertain it—the amused qualifications which he demands of it—that makes it possible for him to state his attitude with full complexity.

The sylphs are, as Ariel himself suggests, "honor," though honor rendered concrete and as it actually functions, not honor as a dry abstraction. The sylphs' concern for good taste allows little range for critical perspective or a sense of proportion. To Ariel it will really be a dire disaster whether it is her honor or her new brocade that Belinda stains. To stain her honor will certainly constitute a breach of good taste—whatever else it may be—and that for Ariel is enough. Indeed, it is enough for the rather artificial world of manners with which Pope is concerned.

The myth of the sylphs is, thus, of the utmost utility to Pope: it allows him to show his awareness of the absurdities of a point of view which, nevertheless, is charming, delightful, and filled with a real poetry. Most important of all, the myth allows him to suggest that the charm, in part at least, springs from the very absurdity. The two elements can hardly be separated in Belinda; in her guardian, Ariel, they cannot be separated at all.

In this connection, it is well to raise specifically the question of Pope's attitude toward the "rape" itself. We certainly underestimate the poem if we rest complacently in the view that Pope is merely laughing at a tempest in a teapot. There is such laughter, to be sure, and late in the poem, Pope expresses his own judgment of the situation, employing Clarissa as his mouthpiece. But the tempest, ridiculous though it is when seen in perspective, is a real enough tempest and related to very real issues. Indeed, Pope is able to reduce the incident to its true importance, precisely because he recognizes clearly its hidden significance. And nowhere is Pope more careful to take into account all the many sides of the situation than just here in the loss of the lock itself.

For one thing, Pope is entirely too clear-sighted to allow that the charming Belinda is merely the innocent victim of a rude assault. Why has she cherished the lock at all? In part at least, "to the Destruction of Mankind," though mankind, of course, in keeping with the convention, wishes so to be destroyed. Pope suggests that the Baron may even be the victim rather than the aggressor—it is a moot question whether he has seized the lock or been ensnared by it. Pope does this very skillfully, but with great emphasis:

> *Love in these Labyrinths his Slaves detains,*
> *And mighty Hearts are held in slender Chains.*
> *With hairy Sprindges we the Birds betray,*
> *Slight Lines of Hair surprize the Finny Prey,*
> *Fair Tresses Man's Imperial Race insnare,*
> *And Beauty draws us with a single Hair.*

Indeed, at the end of the poem, the poet addresses his heroine not as victim but as a "murderer":

> *For, after all the Murders of your Eye,*
> *When, after Millions slain, your self shall die. . . .*

After all, does not Belinda want the Baron (and young men in general) to covet the lock? She certainly does not want to retain possession of the lock forever. The poet naturally sympathizes with Belinda's pique at the way in which the Baron obtains the lock. He must, in the war of the sexes, coax her into letting him have it. Force is clearly unfair, though blandishment is fair. If she is an able warrior, she will consent to the young man's taking the lock, though the lock still attached to her head—and on the proper terms, honorable marriage. If she is a weak opponent, she will yield the lock, and herself, without any stipulation of terms, and will thus become a ruined maid indeed. Pope has absolutely no illusions about what the game is, and is certainly not to be shocked by any naturalistic interpretation of the elaborate and courtly conventions under which Belinda fulfills her natural function of finding a mate.

On the other hand, this is not at all to say that Pope is anxious to do away with the courtly conventions as a pious fraud. He is not the romantic anarchist who would abolish all conventions because they are artificial. The conventions not only have a regularizing function: they have their own charm. Like the rules of the card game in which Belinda triumphs, they may at points be arbitrary; but they make the game possible, and with it, the poetry and pageantry involved in it, in which Pope very clearly delights.

The card game itself, of course, is another symbol of the war of the sexes. Belinda must defeat the men; she must avoid that debacle in which

The Knave *of* Diamonds *tries his wily Arts,*
And wins (oh shameful Chance!) the Queen *of* Hearts.

She must certainly avoid at every cost becoming a ruined maid. In the game as played, there is a moment in which she is "Just in the Jaws of Ruin, and *Codille*," and gets a thrill of delicious excitement at being in so precarious a position.

If the reader objects that the last comment suggests a too obviously sexual interpretation of the card game, one must hasten to point out that a pervasive sexual symbolism informs, not only the description of the card game, but almost everything else in the poem, though here, again, our tradition of either-or may cause us to miss what Pope is doing. We are not forced to take the poem as either sly bawdy *or* as delightful fantasy. But if we are to see what Pope actually makes of his problem, we shall have to be alive to the sexual implications which are in the poem.

They are perfectly evident—even in the title itself; and the poem begins with an address to the Muse in which the sexual implications are underscored:

Say what strange Motive, Goddess! cou'd compel
A well-bred Lord t'assault a gentle Belle?
Oh say what stranger Cause, yet unexplor'd,
Cou'd make a gentle Belle *reject a* Lord?

True, we can take *assault* and *reject* in their more general meanings, not in their specific Latin senses, but the specific meanings are there just beneath the surface. Indeed, it is hard to believe, on the evidence of the poem as a whole, that Pope would have been in the least surprised by Sir James Frazer's later commentaries on the ubiquity of hair as a fertility symbol. In the same way, one finds it hard to believe, after some of the material in the "Cave of Spleen" section ("And Maids turn'd Bottels, call aloud for Corks"), that Pope would have been too much startled by the theories of Sigmund Freud.

The sexual implications become quite specific after the "rape" has occurred. Thalestris, in inciting Belinda to take action against the Baron, cries:

> *Gods! shall the Ravisher display your Hair,*
> *While the Fops envy, and the Ladies stare!*

Even if we take *ravisher* in its most general sense, still the sexual symbolism lurks just behind Thalestris' words. Else why should honor be involved as it is? Why should the Baron desire the lock, and why should Belinda object so violently, not as to an act of simple rudeness, but to losing "honor" and becoming a "degraded Toast"? The sexual element is involved at least to the extent that Belinda feels that she cannot afford to suffer the Baron, without protest, to take such a "liberty."

But a deeper sexual importance is symbolized by the whole incident. Belinda's anguished exclamation—

> *Oh hadst thou, Cruel! been content to seize*
> *Hairs less in sight, or any Hairs but these!*

carries on, unconsciously, the sexual suggestion. The lines indicate, primarily, of course, Belinda's exasperation at the ruining of her coiffure. The principal ironic

effect, therefore, is one of bathos: her angry concern for
the prominence of the lock deflates a little her protests
about honor. (Something of the bathos carries over to
the sexual parallel: it is hinted, perhaps, that the worst
thing about a real rape for the belle would be that it
could not be concealed.) But though Belinda's vehe-
mence gives rise to these ironies, the exclamation itself
is dramatically appropriate; and Belinda would doubt-
less have blushed to have her emphasis on "any" in-
terpreted literally and rudely. In her anger, she is ob-
viously unconscious of the *faux pas*. But the fops whose
admiring and envious comments on the exposed trophy
Thalestris can predict—"Already hear the horrid
things they say"—would be thoroughly alive to the
unconscious *double entendre*. Pope's friend, Matthew
Prior, wrote a naughty poem in which the same *double
entendre* occurs. Pope himself, we may be sure, was
perfectly aware of it.

In commenting on Pope's attitude toward the rape,
we have suggested by implication his attitude toward
chastity. Chastity is one of Belinda's most becoming
garments. It gives her her retinue of airy guardians. As
a proper maiden, she will keep from staining it just as
she will keep from staining her new brocade. Its very
fragility is part of its charm, and Pope becomes some-
thing of a symbolist poet in suggesting this. Three
times in the poem he refers to the breaking of a frail
china jar, once in connection with the loss of chastity,
twice in connection with the loss of "honor" suffered
by Belinda in the "rape" of the lock:

Whether the Nymph shall break Diana's *Law,*
Or some frail China *Jar receive a Flaw. . . .*

Or when rich China *Vessels, fal'n from high,*
In glittring Dust and painted Fragments lie!

> *Thrice from my trembling hands the* Patch-box *fell;*
> *The tott'ring* China *shook without a Wind. . . .*

Pope does not say, but he suggests, that chastity is, like the fine porcelain, something brittle, precious, useless, and easily broken. In the same way, he has hinted that honor (for which the sylphs, in part, stand) is something pretty, airy, fluid, and not really believed in. The devoted sylph who interposes his "body" between the lock and the closing shears is clipped in two, but honor suffers little damage:

> *Fate urg'd the Sheers, and cut the* Sylph *in twain,*
> (*But Airy Substance soon unites again*).

It would be easy here to turn Pope into a cynic; but to try to do this is to miss the point. Pope does not hold chastity to be of no account. He definitely expects Belinda to be chaste; but, as a good humanist, he evidently regards virginity as essentially a negative virtue, and its possession, a temporary state. He is very far from associating it with any magic virtue as Milton does in his *Comus*. The only magic which he will allow it is a kind of charm—a *je-ne-sais-quoi* such as the sylphs possess.

Actually, we probably distort Pope's views by putting the question in terms which require an explicit judgment at all. Pope accepts in the poem the necessity for the belle to be chaste just as he accepts the necessity for her to be gracious and attractive. But in accepting this, he is thoroughly alive to the cant frequently talked about woman's honor, and most of all, he is ironically, though quietly, resolute in putting first things first. This, I take it, is the whole point of Clarissa's speech. When Clarissa says:

> *Since painted, or not painted, all shall fade,*
> *And she who scorns a Man, must die a Maid,*

we need not assume with Leslie Stephen that Pope is expressing a smug masculine superiority, with the implication that, for a woman, spinsterhood is the worst of all possible ills. (There is actually no reason for supposing that Pope thought it so.) The real point is that, for Belinda, perpetual spinsterhood *is* the worst of all possible ills. In her own terms, it would be a disaster to retain her locks forever—locks turned to gray, though still curled with a pathetic hopefulness, unclaimed and unpossessed by any man. Belinda does not want *that;* and it is thus a violation of good sense to lose sight of the fact that the cherished lock is finally only a means to an end—one weapon to be used by the warrior in the battle, and not the strongest weapon at that.

Clarissa is, of course, promptly called a prude, and the battle begins at once in perfect disregard of the "good sense" that she has spoken. Pope is too fine an artist to have it happen otherwise. Belinda *has* been sorely vexed—and she, moreover, remains charming, even as an Amazon. After all, what the poet has said earlier is sincerely meant:

> *If to her share some Female Errors fall,*
> *Look on her Face, and you'll forget 'em all.*

Though Pope obviously agrees with Clarissa, he is neither surprised nor particularly displeased with his heroine for flying in the face of Clarissa's advice.

The battle of the sexes which ensues parodies at some points the combat in the great epic which Milton fashioned on the rape of the apple. But the absurdity of a battle in which the contestants cannot be killed is a flaw in Milton's great poem, whereas Pope turns it to beautiful account in his. In *Paradise Lost,* the great archangels single each other out for combat in the best Homeric style. But when Michael's sword cleaves the side of Lucifer, the most that Milton can do with the incident is to observe that Lucifer feels pain, for his premises force him to hurry on to admit that

> . . . *th'Ethereal substance clos'd*
> *Not long divisible.* . . .

Lucifer is soon back in the fight, completely hale and formidable as ever. We have already seen how delightfully Pope converts this cabbage into a rose in the incident in which the sylph, in a desperate defense of the lock, is clipped in two by the shears.

The absurdity of a war fought by invulnerable opponents gives an air of unreality to the whole of Milton's episode. There is a bickering over rules. Satan and his followers cheat by inventing gunpowder. The hosts under Michael retort by throwing the celestial hills at the enemy; and the Almighty, to put a stop to the shameful rumpus, has the Son throw the troublemakers out. But if the fight were really serious, a fight to the death, why does the heavenly host not throw the hills in the first place? Or, why does not the Almighty cast out the rebels without waiting for the three days of inconclusive fighting to elapse? The prevailing atmosphere of a game—a game played by good little boys and by unmannerly little ruffians, a game presided over by the stern schoolmaster, haunts the whole episode. The advantage is wholly with Pope here. By frankly recognizing that the contest between his beaux and belles is a game, he makes for his basic intention.

The suspicion that Pope in this episode is glancing at Milton is corroborated somewhat by Pope's general use of his celestial machinery. The supernatural guardians in *The Rape of the Lock* are made much of, but their effectiveness is hardly commensurate with their zeal. The affinities of the poem on this point are again with *Paradise Lost,* not with the *Iliad.* In Mil-

ton's poem, the angels are carefully stationed to guard
Adam and Eve in their earthly home, but their pro-
tection proves, in the event, to be singularly ineffectual.
They cannot prevent Satan from finding his way to
the earth; and though they soar the Garden, their
"radiant Files,/ Daz'ling the Moon," they never strike
a blow. Even when they discover Satan, and prepare
to engage him in combat, God, at the last moment, pre-
vents the fight. Indeed, for all their numbers and for
all their dazzling splendor, they succeed in determining
events not at all. They can merely, in the case of
Raphael, give the human pair advice and warning.
Milton, though he loved to call their resonant names,
and evidently tried to provide them with a realistic
function, was apparently so fearful lest he divert atten-
tion from Adam's own freely made decision that he suc-
ceeds in giving them nothing to do.

If this limitation constitutes another ironical defect,
perhaps, in Milton's great epic, it fits Pope's purposes
beautifully. For, as we have seen, Pope's supernatural
machinery is as airy as gossamer, and the fact that Ariel
can do no more than Raphael, advise and warn—for
all his display of zeal—makes again for Pope's basic
intention. The issues in Pope's poem are matters of
taste, matters of "good sense," and the sylphs do not
violate the human limitations of this world which Pope
has elected to describe and in terms of which judg-
ments are to be made. Matters of morality—still less,
the ultimate sanctions of morality—are never raised.

One more of the numerous parallels between *The
Rape of the Lock* and *Paradise Lost* ought to be men-
tioned here, even though it may well be one of which
Pope was unconscious. After the Fall has taken place,
Michael is sent to prepare Adam for his expulsion from
the happy garden. The damage has been done, the

apple has been plucked and eaten, the human pair must prepare to go out into the "real" world, the "fallen" world of our ordinary human experience. Yet, Michael promises that Adam can create within his own breast "A Paradise . . . happier farr." Clarissa's advice to Belinda makes the same point. For better or worse, the lock has been lost. That fact must be accepted. In suggesting Belinda's best course under the circumstances, Clarissa raises quite explicitly Belinda's status as a divinity:

Say, why are Beauties prais'd and honour'd most . . .
Why Angels call'd, and Angel-like ador'd?

The divine element cannot reside in mere beauty alone, painted cheeks, bright eyes, curled locks. All human beauty is tainted with mortality: true "angelhood" resides in a quality of mind, and therefore can survive the loss of mere mortal beauty—can survive the loss of the lock, even the destruction of its beauty by the shears of time. The general parallel between the two speeches is almost complete. Belinda's true divinity, like Adam's happier paradise, is to be found within her. Pope, like Milton, can thus rationalize the matter in terms which allow him to dismiss the supernatural machinery and yet maintain the presence of a qualified supernatural in the midst of a stern and rational world in which no longer one may expect "God or Angel Guest/ With Man, as with his Friend, familiar us'd/ To sit indulgent"—an altered world in which Belinda will expect no more intimate communications from Ariel, and where she, like Adam and Eve, must rely on an inner virtue for advice and protection.

Indeed, one is tempted to complete the parallel by suggesting that Belinda is, at this point, like Adam, being prepared to leave her happy garden world of innocence and maidenly delight for a harsher world, the world of human society as it is and with the poetic illusions removed.

To return to the battle between the beaux and belles: here Pope beautifully unifies the various motifs of the poem. The real nature of the conventions of polite society, the heroic pretensions of that society as mirrored in the epic, the flattering clichés which society conventionally employs—all come in for a genial ragging. Indeed, the clichés of the ardent lover become the focal point of concentration. For the clichés, if they make the contention absurd and pompous, do indicate, by coming alive on another level, the true, if unconscious, nature of the struggle.

> *No common Weapons in their Hands are found,*
> *Like Gods they fight, nor dread a mortal Wound.*

"Like Gods they fight" should mean, in the epic framework, "with superhuman energy and valor." And "nor dread a mortal Wound" logically completes "Like Gods they fight"—until a yet sterner logic asserts itself and deflates the epic pomp. A fight in which the opponents cannot be killed is only a sham fight. Yet, this second meaning is very rich after all, and draws "Like Gods they fight" into its own orbit of meanings: there may be an extra zest in the fighting because it *is* an elaborate game. One can make godlike gestures because one has the invulnerability of a god. The contest is godlike, after all, because it is raised above the dust and turmoil of real issues. Like an elaborate dance, it symbolizes real issues but can find room for a grace and poetry which in a more earnest struggle are lost.

I have said earlier that Pope, by recognizing the real issues involved, is able to render his mock-epic battle meaningful. For the beaux of Hampton Court, though in truth they do not need to dread a mortal wound, can, and are prepared to, die. We must remember that "to die" had at this period, as one of its submeanings, to experience the consummation of the sexual act. Pope's invulnerable beaux rush bravely forward to achieve such a death; for the war of the sexes, when fought seriously and to the death, ends in such an act.

The elegant battleground resounds with the cries of those who die "in *Metaphor*, and . . . in *Song*." In some cases, little more is implied than a teasing of the popular clichés about bearing a "living Death," or being burnt alive in Cupid's flames. But few will question the sexual implications of "die" in the passage in which Belinda overcomes the Baron:

> *Nor fear'd the Chief th'unequal Fight to try,*
> *Who sought no more than on his Foe to die.*
> *"Boast not my Fall" (he cry'd) "insulting Foe!*
> *Thou by some other shalt be laid as low. . . ."*

The point is not that Pope is here leering at bawdy meanings. In the full context of the poem, they are not bawdy at all—or, perhaps we put the matter more accurately if we say that Pope's *total* attitude, as reflected in the poem, is able to absorb and digest into itself the incidental bawdy of which Pope's friends, and obviously Pope himself, were conscious. The crucial point is that Pope's interpretation of Belinda's divinity does not need to flinch from bawdy interpretations. The further meanings suggested by the naughty *double entendres* are not merely snickering jibes which contradict the surface meaning: rather those further meanings constitute the qualifying background against which Belinda's divinity is asserted. Pope's testimony to Belinda's charm is not glib; it is not thin and one-sided. It is qualified by, though not destroyed by, a recognition of all the factors involved—even of those factors which seem superficially to negate it. The touch is light, to be sure; but the poem is not flimsy, not mere froth. The tone is ironical, but the irony is not that of a narrow and acerb satire; rather it is an irony which accords with a wise recognition of the total situation. The "form" of the poem is, therefore, much more than the precise regard for a set of rules and conventions mechanically apprehended. It is, finally, the delicate balance and reconciliation of a host of partial interpretations and attitudes.

It was observed earlier that Pope is able to reduce the "rape" to its true insignificance because he recognizes, as his characters do not, its real significance. Pope knows that the rape has in it more of compliment than of insult, though he naturally hardly expects Belinda to interpret it thus. He does not question her indignation, but he does suggest that it is, perhaps, a more complex response than Belinda realizes. Pope knows too how artificial the social conventions really are and he is thoroughly cognizant of the economic and biological necessities which underlie them—which the conventions sometimes seem to mask and sometimes to adorn. He is therefore not forced to choose between regarding them as either a hypocritical disguise or as a poetic and graceful adornment. Knowing their true nature, he can view this outrage of the conventions with a wise and amused tolerance, and can set it in its proper perspective.

Here the functional aspect of Pope's choice of the epic framework becomes plain. The detachment, the amused patronage, the note of aloof and impartial judgment—all demand that the incident be viewed with a large measure of aesthetic distance. Whatever incidental fun Pope may have had with the epic conventions, his choice of the mock-epic fits beautifully his general problem of scaling down the rape to its proper insignificance. The scene is reduced and the characters become small and manageable figures whose actions can always be plotted against a larger background.

How large that background is has not always been noticed. Belinda's world is plainly a charming, artificial world; but Pope is not afraid to let in a glimpse of the real world which lies all about it:

> *Mean while declining from the Noon of Day,*
> *The Sun obliquely shoots his burning Ray;*
> *The hungry Judges soon the Sentence sign,*
> *And Wretches hang that Jury-men may Dine;*
> *The Merchant from th'*Exchange *returns in Peace,*
> *And the long Labours of the* Toilette *cease—*
> Belinda *now . . .*

It is a world in which business goes on and criminals are hanged for all that Belinda is preparing to sit down to omber. This momentary glimpse of the world of serious affairs, of the world of business and law, of the world of casualness and cruelty, is not introduced merely to shrivel the high concerns of polite society into ironical insignificance, though its effect, of course, is to mock at the seriousness with which the world of fashion takes its affairs. Nor is the ironical clash which is introduced by the passage uncalculated and unintentional: it is not that Pope himself is unconsciously callous—without sympathy for the "wretches." The truth is that Pope's own perspective is so scaled, his totality of view so honest, that he can afford to embellish his little drama as lovingly as he likes without for a moment losing sight of its final triviality. A lesser poet would either have feared to introduce an echo of the "real" world lest the effect prove to be too discordant, or would have insisted on the discord and moralized, too heavily and bitterly, the contrast between the gay and the serious. Pope's tact is perfect. The passage is an instance of the complexity of tone which the poem possesses.

For readers who insist that great poetry can make use of "simple eloquence"—a straightforward treatment of "poetic" material, free from any of the glozings of rhetoric—"Elegy written in a Country Churchyard" must seem the classical instance. And by the same token, the "Elegy" would appear to be the most difficult poem to subsume under the theory of poetic structure maintained in this book.

In Gray's poem, the imagery does seem to be intrinsically poetic; the theme, true; the "statement," free from ambiguity, and free from irony. Indeed, I. A. Richards is able to use the first stanza of the "Elegy" as an example of what he says "we are apt to regard as the normal standard case" where "the prose-sense appears to be the source of the rest of our response," in contrast to that type of poetic structure (which Richards illustrates by Blake's "Memory, hither come") in which the "prose-sense" has little or nothing to do with the reader's response.

It is noteworthy, however, that Richards writes "appears to be the source," for we can conceive of the prose-sense as the *exclusive* source of the poetic effect only as a limiting case. In no actual poem is the reader's response determined solely by the prose-sense. Still, what the "Elegy" "says" as poetry does seem so close to what the prose-sense manages to say, that the reader is

tempted to think of the prose-sense as the poetic con-
tent, a content which in this poem is transmitted, essen-
tially unqualified, to the reader by means of the poetic
form, which, in this case, merely supplies a discreet
decoration to the content.

There are a number of evidences, however, which
ought to put us on our guard against accepting so
simple an account of the relation of form to content,
even in this poem. For example, there are the Milton
references with which the poem, as has frequently been
pointed out, is suffused. The rude forefathers of the
village not only have in their company "mute inglori-
ous Miltons." They are conceived of as young Miltonic
swains: "How jocund did they drive their team afield"
—just as, "Under the opening eye-lids of the morn,"
Lycidas and his companion "drove a field." Or consider
the famous "Full many a gem" stanza. I suspect that the
gem which "the dark unfathom'd caves of ocean bear"
and the flower "born to blush unseen" derive ultimately
from the great speech of Comus with its "unsought
diamonds" from "the Deep" and, ten lines down, its
"neglected rose" that "withers on the stalk"—though
Gray himself may well have been unconscious of the
Miltonic echo.

Some of the echoes Gray was plainly conscious of, as
his specification of some of them in his notes would
indicate; and many of them are from Milton, though
many others are not. One of the non-Miltonic echoes
which seems clearly resonant to me but which Gray
does not mention (and of which perhaps he was not
conscious) is that of the "Dying Emperor Hadrian to
his Soul." In Prior's translation it runs:

Poor little, pretty, flutt'ring Thing,
　　Must We no longer live together?
And dost Thou preene thy trembling Wing,
　　To take the Flight Thou know'st not whither?

Thy humorous Vein, thy pleasing Folly
  Lyes all neglected, all forgot:
And pensive, wav'ring, melancholy,
  Thou dread'st and hop'st Thou know'st not what.

One may compare:

> *For who, to dumb Forgetfulness a prey,*
> *This pleasing anxious being e'er resigned,*
> *Left the warm precincts of the chearful day,*
> *Nor cast one longing ling'ring look behind.*

The "Elegy" is thus—like *The Waste Land*—a tissue of allusions and half-allusions. If the materials of which it is composed are "poetic," they have been made poetic by other poets. The point is not, surely, that as we read the "Elegy" we are to be fully conscious of all the references. But the audience for which Gray wrote and which gave its admiration to the poem was aware of many of them. We had therefore better not discount the effect of such allusions on an appreciation of the poem, even though it may be difficult to assess the particular function of each of them in detail. (How important they are may be judged by the response to the poem made by an audience which is *really* completely unaware of them: our public school system, it may be said, is rapidly providing such an audience for the purposes of making such a test.)

Yet, let me repeat, the precise modifications made by these allusions are difficult to assess and more difficult to prove. A better way to get at the alleged simplicity and directness of the "Elegy" is through an examination of its use of the conventional. Why is the poem rich and meaningful instead of merely trite and "conventional"? Do the conventional "materials" remain conventional, or are they somehow rendered dramatic and moving? And if they are rendered dramatic, how is this accomplished?

One can touch upon this question at an obvious level by considering the personifications. There are many of them in the "Elegy." Do they weigh the poem down beneath a clutter of lifeless eighteenth-century ornament, or do they come alive as convincing metaphors which carry the poem on the tide of their energy? Some of them, it must be confessed—"Let not Ambition mock their useful toil"—seem vulnerable to Coleridge's charge that they have acquired little more of the *persona* than can be accorded by a capital letter.

The personifications, I think, can, as a matter of fact, be justified. But they cannot be justified in the conventional account. They are certainly not vivid and fresh metaphors. The personifications indeed furnish perhaps the sharpest instance of the general problem which the conventional accounts of the poem fail to solve. Such accounts of the poem cannot explain why the "large and general truths" of this poem, when expressed quite as clearly in other poems, and decorated there with materials out of the same poetic wardrobe, fail as the "Elegy" does not fail. On this point indeed the success of past criticism has not been so notable as to preclude another sort of account.

In the first place, it may be of interest to note that very little description is lavished upon the churchyard itself. There is stanza four, of course: "Beneath those rugged elms, etc." There are also, later in the poem, passing allusions to the "short and simple annals of the poor," to "this neglected spot," to the "frail memorial[s]" with their "uncouth rhimes"—but these later references tend to be general, not specific. What the attention is focused on, even in the first stanzas, is not' the graveyard itself, but what can be seen by a man standing in the graveyard: "the lowing herd [winding] slowly o'er the lea," the fading landscape, the ivy-mantled tower from which the owl hoots.

Even the dead, when the poet recurs to them specifically, are described in terms of what they were—the village (in the churchyard of which they lie) as it was when the men were alive. It is primarily a village at dawn ("The breezy call of incense-breathing Morn") or a village at noon ("Oft did the harvest to their sickle yield"), not the night-shrouded village on which the speaker now looks out. And the one reference in this passage to the village at evening is to the village of the past when the "blazing hearth" burned for the return of the men who are now dead.

These points are perhaps too obvious to seem worth making. But there must be no mistake as to what is going on: the poem is not a simple mood piece, centered on the description of the churchyard itself. Certainly, the poem does not derive its vitality from either a "realistic" or a "poetic" description of the churchyard as such. (This is not to say that the "graveyard imagery" is not typical of the century, or that it does not have its importance. It *is* to say that the "graveyard imagery" does not, by its mere presence, convert the "Elegy" into a poem.)

Indeed, one can go further. The churchyard is described for the most part, not directly, but by contrast with its opposite: the great abbey church. And there are actually more references to the details of the abbey church as a burial place than to the details of the country churchyard itself.

This becomes plain when we see that the personifications are actually the allegoric figures, beloved by the eighteenth century, which clutter a great abbey church such as that at Bath or at Westminster. It is true that Gray does not restrict himself to the sculptured figures of Memory, Honor, Knowledge; and it is true that he calls some of them by their less flattering names: Ambition, Grandeur, Flattery, Luxury, Pride. But we recognize them clearly enough, even so. They wear the glazed "disdainful smile" of eighteenth-century mortu-ary sculpture. They take up the conventional attitudes of such sculpture: one leans to soothe the ear—one unrolls the lettered scroll. They are to be met with

> *Where thro' the long-drawn isle and fretted vault*
> *The pealing anthem swells the note of praise.*

The marks of their identification seem plain enough. Even so, some readers may hesitate to accept it. Was Gray actually conscious of such a purpose? Is not such a device too witty, too ingenious for a poet of Gray's sensibility? But this is, if not to beg the question, at least to ask the question badly: for the self-conscious-ness of the artist is not necessarily involved. The ap-peal is to be made to the poem itself.

The rural graveyard in its simplicity calls up for the speaker memories of another kind of burial-place, one in which heraldry visibly makes its boast, and one filled with "storied urn" and "animated bust." "Honour," at least, it must be granted, is treated as one of the personifications on an allegorical monument:

> *Can storied urn or animated bust*
> *Back to its mansion call the fleeting breath?*
> *Can Honour's voice provoke the silent dust . . .*

But whether we treat the personifications as sculp-tures, or as terms used in the grandiloquent epitaphs, or merely as the poet's own projections of the pomp implied by the ornate burial-place—in any case, they are used ironically. That is to say, they are contrasted with the humble graves of the country churchyard, and they are meant, in contrast, to seem empty, flat, and lifeless. For "Honour" to possess more vitality as a metaphor would run counter to the intention of the poem. We can put the matter in this way: the more richly and dramatically realized Honour becomes, the more plausible it would be to feel that "Honour" could "provoke the silent dust." Conversely, the more fully dead, the more flatly abstract Flatt'ry is, the more absurdly ironical becomes its attempt to "sooth the dull cold ear of Death." (There is, of course, here a further level of irony: Flatt'ry attempts what it cannot perform; but further, it is witless in its attempt to do what has already been done: the ear has been fully "soothed" already.)

Once we see that the purpose of the poem demands that the personifications be used ironically, one is allowed to see some of the supporting ironical devices. They are rich, and some of them are intricate. For example, the speaker asks Ambition not to mock the rustics' "homely joys." "Homely" would mean primarily "concerned with the home"—the children running to "lisp their sire's return"—with which the speaker has dealt in an earlier stanza. But "homely" probably still had the meanings (still preserved in America though it has died out in England) of "plain," unadorned. (Milton used it in this sense, and Shakespeare clearly employs it.)

Grandeur is not to smile at the "short and simple annals of the poor." Properly speaking, of course, the poor do not have "annals." Kingdoms have annals, and so do kings, but the peasantry does not. The choice of the term is ironical, and yet the "short and simple" records of the poor are their "annals"—the important records for them.

A more important and brilliant example of such irony occurs in the eleventh stanza. An "animated" bust would presumably be one into which the breath of life had been breathed—a speaking likeness, endowed by the chisel of the sculptor with the soul itself. But the most "animated" bust (*anima* = breath, soul) cannot call the fleeting *anima* of the dead man back to its "mansion." And the mansion receives its qualification in the next line: it is no more than silent dust.

Mr. William Empson has commented on the function of the images in the famous fourteenth stanza:

What this means, as the context makes clear, is that eighteenth-century England had no scholarship system or *carrière ouverte aux talents*. This is stated as pathetic, but the reader is put into a mood in which one would not try to alter it. (It is true that Gray's society, unlike a possible machine society, was necessarily based on manual labour, but it might have used a man of special ability wherever he was born.) By comparing the social arrangement to Nature he makes it seem inevitable, which it was not, and gives it a dignity which was undeserved. Furthermore, a gem does not mind being in a cave and a flower prefers not to be picked; we feel that the man is like the flower, as short-lived, natural, and valuable, and this tricks us into feeling that he is better off without opportunities. The sexual suggestion of *blush* brings in the Christian idea that virginity is good in itself, and so that any renunciation is good; this may trick us into feeling it is lucky for the poor man that society keeps him unspotted from the World. The tone of melancholy claims that the poet understands the considerations opposed to aristocracy, though he judges against them; the truism of the reflections in the churchyard, the universality and impersonality this gives to the style, claim as if by comparison that we ought to accept the injustice of society as we do the inevitability of death.

As a counterpoise to the conventional view which sees in the gem-flower comparison only "decoration," this is excellent. But Empson, in his anxiety to establish the "latent political ideas," has extended the implications a little further than the total context of the whole poem warrants. How the implications of the jewel-flower metaphors are qualified by the total context will be discussed a little later.

For the present it will be better to consider the further development which the metaphors receive in the next stanza. The arrangement of the three instances is more subtle than it may at first glance seem. The "prose-sense," of course, is clear enough: a village-Hampden is a Hampden *in petto;* a mute Milton, a man with the potentialities of a Milton without Milton's achievement; and the Cromwell of the case, one who had the potentialities of a Cromwell but who did not realize Cromwell's crimes. But the stanza suggests much more, and qualifies the prose-sense greatly. As we have already remarked, the three names really form a very cunningly contrived scale. We easily accept the "village-Hampden," for his case is proved, and the comparison involved is a rather obvious one. He protests against tyranny, and thus is a petty Hampden, a "village" Hampden. We accept it the more readily because the implication that the village-Hampden might have, had fate placed him on a larger stage, been Hampden himself, is not pressed. But our acceptance of this case carries over to the next where it may help to secure conviction for the claim that the "mute inglorious Milton" might possibly have achieved Milton's glory had "Chill Penury" not "repress'd" his "noble rage"—though here there is no achievement—merely potential achievement, to be accepted on faith. The Cromwell example is, of course, the boldest item and makes most demand upon our acceptance. Here not even potentiality is stressed, but rather the negative virtues, the freedom from the Cromwellian crimes. We are asked to accept the fact that "the guiltless Cromwell" might have realized the virtues *because* the non-realization of the crimes is proved.

The last line goes on to suggest the essentially ironical observation that there can be no *real* Cromwell without blood-guilt. This last point is very pertinent to the argument which the following stanzas make: that the village Hampdens and Cromwells, had not "Their lot forbad," might well have indulged in the worst of "heroic" crimes—waded through slaughter to a throne —or, that the mute inglorious Miltons might have committed the worst of artistic sins—might have heaped

> . . . the shrine of Luxury and Pride
> With incense kindled at the Muse's flame.

It is true, of course, that the speaker does not insist that this would have been the inevitable course that they must have taken had not their "lot forbad." The speaker has admitted that they possessed "growing virtues" to be "circumscrib'd" as well as "crimes" to be "confin'd." Yet the implied judgment is severely realistic: many of the "rude Forefathers" would have ended in cruelty and empty vanity had they "learn'd to stray" into the "paths of glory." The paths of glory lead but to the grave, but so does the path along which the "plowman homeward plods his weary way." The graves are different, as we have seen. But both are graves—the fact of death cannot be glossed over—this is the matter on which Gray's irony exerts its force: not on the sentimental matter which would try to make of the plowman's "narrow cell" something less than a grave.

One last point before we leave this subject of what the "rude Forefathers" might have become. The poet says that "Their sober wishes never *learn'd* to stray." This constitutes a careful inversion of the usual terms. One expects straying to be "natural," not something to be learned. One "learns" to *refrain* from straying. Knowledge has therefore conferred a favor, whatever her intentions, in refusing to unroll "to their eyes her ample page." For what Knowledge has to give is associated with madness, not sobriety. The rustics' wishes need no sobering discipline—they are already sober;

"knowledge" would drive them into ignoble competition with the rest of the "madding crowd." The description of the page of Knowledge as "Rich with the spoils of time" is not literary decoration. It is appropriate and it distinguishes Knowledge as most men know it from the Science which we shall meet with at the close of the poem.

Yet we misread the poem if we conclude that Gray is here merely anxious to insist for the villagers as for the Eton schoolboys, that where "Ignorance is bliss/ 'Tis folly to be wise." He has not overly insisted upon their joys. The portrayal of them has been realistic, not sentimental. And it has been impossible for them to be wise: it has not been a matter of volition at all: "Their lot forbad . . ." We shall not come to an instance of choice until we come to the case which concludes the poem.

But if the poem thus far has tended to contrast the country churchyard and the abbey tombs, with the twentieth stanza the two are drawn together once more. The contrast gives perspective to the rustic churchyard, but the comparison is used fairly. The abbey burial ground is, in its turn, humanized by the churchyard Even the extravagancies on which the poet has looked sardonically are rooted finally in something so deep that it can be found in the country churchyard too: the churchyard has its memorials, though "frail," its rhimes, though "uncouth," and its sculpture, though "shapeless." If the passage carries on the contrast between the sumptuous magnificence of the ornate tombs and those other tombs of "this neglected" spot, and thus adds to the pathos of the rustic graves, it tends to account for the ornate tombs by making them, after all, the expression of a basic human impulse. The "Proud," thus, partake of the pathos in a queer, ironical fashion. For their attempts to hold on to "the warm precincts of the chearful day"—attempts which the speaker has shown to be ineffectual—appear the more desperate in proportion as their luxury exceeds the simple tomb.

The Miltonic inversion of the twenty-second stanza supports the effect very nicely. "For who, to dumb Forgetfulness a prey," etc., can mean: for what man, having forgotten himself completely, ever left the cheerful day without casting back a look of regret. Actually most of us will read it as meaning: for what man ever resigned this being as a prey to oblivion without casting back one look of regret. But, on reflection, the two meanings tend to coalesce. To forget one's human nature sufficiently to be able cheerfully to leave the "warm precincts of the chearful day" makes a demand as heroic as that of cheerfully resigning oneself to being forgotten by other men. In either case, one becomes the prey to "dumb Forgetfulness." The general commentary on death (which ends with line ninety-two) has thus brought the proud and the humble together in a common humanity. The impulse to hold on to life—to strive against the encompassing oblivion—is to be found under the "yew-tree's shade" as well as beneath the "fretted vault." If the one has been treated with more pathos, the other with more irony, still neither can be effectual, and both in their anguish of attempt are finally deeply human.

The poet, it seems to me, carries very fairly here between both groups. To press, with Empson, the poet's complacency in seeming to accept the fate of the humble is to ignore these elements in the poem. (Thomas Gray, as a man, may or may not have been guilty of such complacency. But we are not dealing with Gray's political ideas. We are dealing with what the "Elegy" "says"—something that is not quite the same thing.)

Any doubt as to this last point should be dissipated by a consideration of the resolution of the poem. For what is the *speaker's* choice? After all, if the rude Forefathers of the village could not choose, since Knowledge did not unroll her ample page to them, *he* at least can choose. "Fair Science frown'd not on his humble birth." He *need* not be buried in the churchyard in which he actually wishes to be buried.

But before one goes on to examine the significance of his choice, it is well to begin with the first lines of the "resolution." With line ninety-three the speaker comes to apply the situation to himself. He should, therefore, be saying

> *For* me, *who, mindful of th' unhonour'd Dead*
> *Do in these lines their artless tale relate;*
> *If chance, by lonely contemplation led,*
> *Some kindred Spirit shall inquire* my *fate, etc.*

(In the first stanza the speaker was willing to say *me*: "And leaves the world to darkness and to me.") Dramatically, what has happened is that the meditation has gone on so fervently that in talking to himself, the speaker has lost his identity as an ego. The commentary which has been going on, though it has begun as that of the solitary observer, has become more general, more external. It would be a nice point to determine precisely *who* does speak this twenty-fourth stanza: the spirit of the place, the Muse, Melancholy, one side of the speaker's own nature? Presumably, the speaker is a part of the observer's own nature; but in any case, the observer is willing to be addressed in the second person: he is willing to see himself as he shall be, merely one with the others in the country churchyard.

We have said that this last section of the poem is to be considered the resolution of the poem: first, we have had the case of those who could not choose, the "rude

Forefathers of the hamlet"; next, the Proud, who chose, but chose in vanity; lastly, there is the present case, the man who is able to choose, and chooses the "neglected spot" after all. But though his choice is a kind of vindication of the lot forced upon the rustics—a point which Empson's discussion of the poet's attitude fails to take into account—still, it will not do to insist upon the speaker's conscious choice lest it seem too smugly heroic; or to make his identification with the rustics too easy, lest it seem unrealistic. It is better that the "I" to be buried should treat that self as passive, as he does. Moreover, stanza twenty-four grows out of the preceding stanza: it is human for the parting soul to wish for an understanding friend:

> *E'en from the tomb the voice of Nature cries,*
> *E'en in our Ashes live their wonted Fires.*

The speaker does not attempt to sustain an inhumanly heroic role. He too yearns for "Some kindred Spirit" who shall inquire his fate; and he provides an epitaph to be read by that unknown friend.

Furthermore, he sees clearly that his motives in keeping himself in obscurity—in confining himself to "the cool sequester'd vale of life"—will hardly be understood by the unlettered companions who accompany him through the vale. Their "sober wishes [have] never learn'd" the vanity of straying from it; his, sobered by wisdom, have learned the folly of straying from it. They, saved by ignorance, cannot comprehend his saving knowledge. It is a nice touch, therefore, which has the observer envisage with complete realism the account of him which the "hoary-headed Swain" would necessarily give to the inquirer. To the Swain, he will be a creature pathetically inexplicable, and perhaps crazy:

'Now drooping, woeful wan, like one forlorn,
'Or crazed with care, or crossed in hopeless love.

It is significant that the hoary-headed Swain cannot
read the epitaph which might explain the observer's
conduct and his choice. But even if he could read the
epitaph, it is evident that he still could not understand
it, for the implication is that only a "kindred Spirit"
could understand. In its way, then, his own epitaph
will be more lonely than the other epitaphs about it—
those on which the name and years "spelt by th' un-
letter'd muse,/ The place of fame and elegy supply."

And what of the epitaph itself? Does it furnish a
proper climax for the poem? Or is it, after all, trite, flat,
with an eighteenth-century tameness? Landor regarded
it as a tin-kettle tied to the tail of an otherwise noble
poem; and certainly the epitaph has come in for very
little praise ever since the poem was published. But
before one undertakes to defend the epitaph as poetry,
it is better to make sure first that we understand it—
in itself, and in its relation to the rest of the poem.

To take up the first question (for the silence of the
commentators here warns us that the explication had
better not be taken for granted): what does the epitaph
say in itself? In the first place, it implies the choice of
which we have spoken in its very first line. His head
will be laid upon the "lap of Earth"—the grave will
be in the churchyard, not within the church. And the
lines that follow have to do with the choice further:
he will be unknown, but not because his "lot forbad."
Fair Science did *not* frown upon his humble birth, as
she has upon the humble birth of his companions in
the churchyard. Why does the poet not go on to write:
"But Melancholy . . ."? This would be an easier read-
ing: that is, he had the knowledge requisite for enter-
ing into the competition for fame, but he was incapaci-

tated by Melancholy. But the poet's choice of the con-
junction "and" compels the richer reading: Melancholy
is something more than a disease which rendered him
unfit for the "madding crowd's ignoble strife." It is
associated with "Fair Science," which in turn is differ-
entiated by the association from the earlier "Knowl-
edge" with which we might have been tempted to
identify it. Melancholy becomes thus, in association
with Science, a kind of wisdom which allows him to
see through the vanities which delude the Proud.

"Large was his bounty. . . ." How? Because, like the
widow's mite, what he gave to Misery represented his
all. How did Heaven render him as largely prosperous?
Because Heaven gave him everything that he could
possibly wish. Are the oppositions here merely pertly
ironical? If we take the epitaph in isolation, perhaps
they are. But the ironies of this stanza have the whole
of the poem behind them. This epitaph, which the
speaker contemplates as one to which the kindred
Spirit may be directed by the hoary-headed swain, is
to be read in the light of the commentary already made
upon those which recite the short and simple annals
of the poor, and those others which are dictated by
"the pomp of pow'r." This epitaph commemorates one
of the literally poor ("all he had, a tear") but it claims
to be the epitaph of a man who was rich—in his bounty
to the miserable, and in the possessions which Heaven
has showered upon him. (If, again, the paradox seem
too easy, too brittle, we must in fairness take the stanza
in terms of the context already established: there, it
has certainly been implied that a true friend is the
rarest of things. The trophies which Memory raises
over the tombs of the proud admit Flattery to their
company.)

And now for the last stanza: is it modesty which re-
quests the reader to seek no farther "his merits to dis-

close." Two of the "merits" have already been disclosed. Have these two been chosen because they are modest and ordinary, or because they are in reality superlatively rare? If we are alive to the context, we can use both these answers: generosity to the poor and the proofs of Heaven's favor (in accomplishment, in achievement) are the common matter of epitaphs. In this sense, the speaker's imagined epitaph is thus typical and conventional. Yet these "merits" are more often boasted of rather than exemplified.

But there is a better reason still for the choice: the merits disclosed are those which have special reference to the opinion of the world: what Heaven bestowed, and what the recipient himself bestowed to the needy. Thus far the imagined epitaph complies with the demands of the world; for the rest, "his other merits" and his frailties—these have another reference. Knowledge of them is already possessed by the only Being who can judge them and thus the only Being to whom they are pertinent.

Even so, the reader may not be altogether convinced, as I am not altogether convinced, that the epitaph with which the poem closes is adequate. But surely its intended function is clear, and it is a necessary function if the poem is to have a structure and is not to be considered merely a loose collection of poetic passages.

Moreover, it ought to be equally clear that the epitaph is not to be judged in isolation. It is part of a context, and a very rich context. We have to read it in terms of the conditions for a certain dramatic propriety which the context sets up. Among those conditions are these: it must be a recognizable epitaph, even a humble epitaph, modest in what it says, and modest, perhaps, even as an example of art. For it is the epitaph, after all, of a "Youth to Fortune and to Fame unknown." It must be closely related to the evening meditation in the churchyard, for it is an outgrowth of that meditation.

But what, then, of the "kindred Spirit" who may some day read it? How is he, coming upon the epitaph, and reading it, naked of the context of the whole meditation—what is he to be expected to make of it? It is all very well to treat the poem as a dramatic structure, but if we do, then will the epitaph for the "kindred Spirit" incorporate within itself enough of a qualifying context? Or will it not seem to him rather flat and bare? But the poet has evidently taken this question into account. The "kindred Spirit" must presumably know something of the youth, though "tc Fortune and to Fame unknown," if he is to be able to inquire about his fate at all. He will come to the epitaph possessed by a proper mood, led to this spot by "lonely contemplation." And the fact that he is a "kindred Spirit" will supply for him much of the context which the poet has elaborately built up for us in the poem itself. Indeed, the poet has prepared us, the readers, to be the "kindred Spirit" if we wish. The poet has been too good a poet, in his practice at least, for him to rely here upon the "prose-sense" of the epitaph as such. Whatever its merit (or lack of merit) as a poem in its own right, it is not the "Elegy written in a Country Churchyard," nor is the reader brought to it in isolation as the "kindred Spirit" may be, nor is Gray merely identical with the youth in the poem who is "to Fortune and to Fame unknown."

In the poem, as we have seen, the epitaph is set over against the "shapeless sculpture" of the churchyard and also over against the "storied urn" of the abbey church. We have tried to see what its relation to each is. But when we come to Gray himself, it is the whole "Elegy" that is *his* storied urn—it is the poem itself, the "lines" in which he relates the "artless tale" of the villagers—all the lines of the poem, the whole poem, taken as a poetic structure. As for the urn which stands beside the "animated bust," its "stories" are supposed to be the material proper to art, and surely, as the speaker of the poem envisages the storied urn, they have been treated artfully—in all the senses of that ambiguous word. By contrast, the "tale" which the speaker of the poem undertakes to relate is, on the other hand, admittedly "artless." It is conventionally regarded as matter which cannot be turned into art. It is artless in this sense because the men whose tale it is were themselves *artless*—too innocent, too simple to have a significant story. Their story is merely a tale; it is no more properly a set of "annals" than the tale of Donne's lovers is properly a "chronicle."

But is Gray's telling of the "artless tale" really artless? The tale is simple enough, to be sure; but is the telling simple: is the structure of the poem simple? Not, most of us will agree, in the sense that it lacks art—not in the sense that it is either a casual collection of poetic "materials" or in the sense that it is the "artless" rendition of a set of poetic truths. The "Elegy" has a structure which we neglect at our peril if we mean to pass judgment on it as a poem, or, even if we are merely to point to it as a poem. It is a "storied urn," after all, and, many of us will conclude that, like Donne's, it is a "well wrought urne," superior to the half-acre tombs of the Proud.

Wordsworth's great "Intimations" ode has been for so long intimately connected with Wordsworth's own autobiography, and indeed, Wordsworth's poems in general have been so consistently interpreted as documents pertaining to that autobiography, that to consider one of his larger poems as an object in itself may actually seem impertinent. Yet to do so for once at least is not to condemn the usual mode of procedure and it may, in fact, have positive advantages.

Wordsworth's spiritual history is admittedly important: it is just possible that it is ultimately the important thing about Wordsworth. And yet the poems are structures in their own right; and, finally, I suppose, Wordsworth's spiritual biography has come to have the importance which it has for us because he is a poet.

At any rate, it may be interesting to see what happens when one considers the "Ode" as a poem, as an independent poetic structure, even to the point of forfeiting the light which his letters, his notes, and his other poems throw on difficult points. (That forfeiture, one may hasten to advise the cautious reader, need not, of course, be permanent.) But to enforce it for the moment will certainly avoid confusion between what the poem "says" and what Wordsworth in general may have meant; and it may actually surprise some readers to see how much the poem, strictly considered in its own right, manages to say, as well as precisely what it says.

If we consider the "Ode" in these terms, several observations emerge. For one thing, the poem will be seen to make more use of paradox than is commonly supposed. Of some of these paradoxes, Wordsworth himself must obviously have been aware; but he was probably not aware, the reader will conjecture, of the extent to which he was employing paradox.

The poem, furthermore, displays a rather consistent symbolism. This may be thought hardly astonishing. What may be more surprising is the fact that the symbols reveal so many ambiguities. In a few cases, this ambiguity, of which Wordsworth, again, was apparently only partially aware, breaks down into outright confusion. Yet much of the ambiguity is rich and meaningful in an Empsonian sense, and it is in terms of this ambiguity that many of the finest effects of the poem are achieved.

There are to be found in the "Ode" several varieties of irony; and some of the themes which Wordsworth treats in the poem are to be successfully related only through irony. Yet the principal defect of the "Ode" results from the fact that Wordsworth will not always accept the full consequences of some of his ironical passages.

Lastly, as may be surmised from what has already been remarked, the "Ode" for all its fine passages, is not entirely successful as a poem. Yet, we shall be able to make our best defense of it in proportion as we recognize and value its use of ambiguous symbol and paradoxical statement. Indeed, it might be maintained that, failing to do this, we shall miss much of its power as poetry and even some of its accuracy of statement.

It is tempting to interpret these propositions as proof of the fact that Wordsworth wrote the "Ode" with the "dark" side of his mind—that the poem welled up from his unconscious and that his conscious tinkering with it which was calculated to blunt and coarsen some of the finest effects was, in this case, held to a minimum. But it hardly becomes a critic who has just proposed to treat the poem strictly as a poem, apart from its reflections of Wordsworth's biography, to rush back into biographical speculation. It is far more important to see whether the generalizations proposed about the nature of the poem are really borne out by the poem itself. This is all the more true when one reflects that to propose to find in the poem ambiguities, ironies, and paradoxes will seem to many a reader an attempt to fit the poem to a Procrustean bed—in fine, the bed in which John Donne slept comfortably enough but in which a Romantic poet can hardly be supposed to find any ease.

In reading the poem, I shall emphasize the imagery primarily, and the success or relative failure with which Wordsworth meets in trying to make his images carry and develop his thought. It is only fair to myself to say that I am also interested in many other things, the metrical pattern, for example, though I shall necessarily have to omit detailed consideration of this and many other matters.

In the "Ode" the poet begins by saying that he has lost something. What is it precisely that he has lost? What does the poem itself say? It says that things uncelestial, the earth and every common sight, once seemed apparelled in celestial light. The word "apparelled" seems to me important. The light was like a garment. It could be taken off. It was not natural to the earth; it *has* been taken off. And if the celestial light is a garment, the earth must have been clad with the garment by someone (the garment motif, by the way, is to appear later with regard to the child: "trailing clouds of glory do we come").

The earth, which has had to be apparelled in the garment of light, is counterbalanced by the celestial bodies like the sun, moon, and stars of the next stanza. These are lightbearers capable of trailing clouds of glory themselves, and they clothe the earth in light of various sorts. One is tempted here to say that the poles of the basic comparison are already revealed in these first two stanzas: the common earth on which the glory has to be conferred, and the sun or moon, which confers glory. We can even anticipate the crux of the poem in these terms: has the child been clothed with light? Or does he himself clothe the world about him in light? But more of this later.

This celestial apparel, the garment of light, had, the speaker says, the glory and the freshness of a dream. A dream has an extraordinary kind of vividness often associated with strong emotional coloring. It frequently represents familiar objects, even homely ones, but with the familiarity gone and the objects endowed with strangeness. But the dream is elusive, it cannot be dissected and analyzed. (Even if Wordsworth could have been confronted with Dr. Freud, he would, we may surmise, have hardly missed seeing that Freud's brilliant accounts of dreams resemble science less than they do poems—"Odes on the Intimations of all too human humanity from unconscious recollections of early childhood.") Moreover, the phrase, taken as a whole, suggests that the glory has the unsubstantial quality of a dream. Perhaps this is to overload an otherwise innocent phrase. But I should like to point out as some warrant for this suggestion of unsubstantiality that "dream" is rhymed emphatically with "To me did *seem*," and that it is immediately followed by

"It is not now as it hath been of yore." The dream quality, it seems to me, is linked definitely with the transience of the experience. Later in the poem, the dream is to be connected with "visionary gleam," is to be qualified by the adjective "fugitive," and finally is to be associated with "Those shadowy recollections."

The ambiguous character of the child's vision as remembered by the man is implicit, therefore, in the first stanza of the poem. What the speaker has lost, it is suggested, is something which is fleeting, shadowy, and strange, but something which possesses a quality of insight and wholeness which no amount of other perception—least of all patient analysis—will duplicate. It is *visionary;* that is, like a vision, a revelation. But visionary perhaps also suggests something impractical, not completely real. Perhaps most interesting of all, the speaker, a little later in the "Ode," has it fade into the light of common day, which is inimical to both its freshness and its glory. The vision which has been lost is at once more intense and less intense than common daylight.

The second stanza, I think, is very important in defining further the relation of the visionary gleam to the man and to the earth. Ostensibly, this second stanza simply goes on to define further the nature of the thing lost: it is not mere beauty; nature is still beautiful, but a special quality has been lost. Yet the imagery seems to me to be doing something else beneath this surface statement, and something which is very important. In contrast to the earth, we have the rainbow, the moon, the stars, and the sun—all examples of celestial light; and to these we may add the rose by the sort of extension, not too difficult to be sure, by which Cowley treats it as light in his "Hymn to Light." Wordsworth says that the rainbow and the rose are beautiful. We expect him to go on to say the same of the moon. But here, with one of the nicest touches in the poem, he reverses the pattern to say, "The moon doth with delight/ Look round her when the heavens are bare." The moon is treated as if she were the speaker himself in his childhood, seeing the visionary gleam as she looks round her with joy. The poet cannot see the gleam, but he implies that the moon can see it, and suggests how she can: she sheds the gleam herself; she lights up and thus creates her world. This seems to me a hint which Wordsworth is to develop later more explicitly, that it is the child, looking round him with joy, who is at once both the source and the recipient of the vision. In this stanza even the sunshine (though as the source of common day it is to be used later in the poem as the antithesis of the visionary gleam) participates in the glory—"The sunshine is a glorious birth." The word *birth,* by the way, suggests that it is a dawn scene: it is the childhood of the sun's course, not the maturity. Like the moon, the sun joyfully creates its world. The poet is giving us here, it seems to me, some very important preparation for Stanza V, in which he is to say "Our birth is but a sleep and a forgetting:/ The Soul that rises with us, our life's Star,/ Hath had elsewhere its setting . . ." Surely, it is perfectly clear here that the child, coming upon the world, trailing his clouds of glory, is like the sun or moon which brings its radiance with it, moonlight or starlight or dawn light.

I shall not try to prove here that Wordsworth consciously built up the imagery of Stanza II as preparation for Stanza V. In one sense I think the question of whether or not Wordsworth did this consciously is irrelevant. What I am certain of is this: that the lines

> *The Moon doth with delight*
> *Look round her . . .*

strike any sensitive reader as fine to a degree which their value as decoration will not account for. Certainly it is a testimony of many readers that the famous passage "Our birth is but a sleep, etc." has registered with a special impact, with more impact than the mere "beauty" of the images will account for. The relation of both passages to the theme, and their mutual interrelations seem to me one way of accounting for their special force.

This relation of both passages to the theme is so important, however, that I should like for the moment to pass over consideration of Stanzas III and IV in order to pursue further the central symbolism of light as treated in Stanza V. The basic metaphor from line sixty-seven onward has to do with the child's moving away from heaven, his home—the shades of the prison house closing about him—the youth's progress further and further from the day-spring in the east. We should, however, if the figure were worked out with thorough consistency, expect him to arrive at darkness or near darkness, the shades of the prison house having closed round the boy all but completely—the youth having traveled into some darkened and dismal west. Yet the tantalizing ambiguity in the symbol which we have noticed earlier, continues. The climax of the process is not darkness but full daylight: "At length the Man perceives it die away,/ And fade into the light of common day." We have a contrast, then, between prosaic daylight and starlight or dawn light—a contrast between kinds of light, not between light and darkness. There is a further difficulty in the symbolism: the sunlight, which in Stanza II was a glorious birth, has here become the symbol for the prosaic and the common and the mortal.

I point out the ambiguities, not to convict the poet of confusion, but to praise him for his subtlety and accuracy. I suggest that the implied comparison of the child to the sun or the moon is still active here, and that Wordsworth is leaning on his earlier figure more heavily than most of his critics have pointed out, or than, perhaps, he himself realized. If the sun, at his glorious birth, lights up a world with the glory and freshness of a dream, with a light which persists even after he has begun to ascend the sky, yet the sun gradually becomes the destroyer of his earlier world and becomes his own prisoner. Indeed it is very easy to read the whole stanza as based on a submerged metaphor of the sun's progress: the soul is like our life's star, the sun, which has had elsewhere its setting. It rises upon its world, not in utter nakedness. The trailing clouds of glory suggest the sunrise. The youth is like the sun, which, as it travels farther from the east, leaves the glory more and more behind it, and approaches prosaic daylight. But it is the sun itself which projects the prosaic daylight, just as the man projects the common day which surrounds him, and upon which he now looks without joy.

I do not insist that we have to read the stanza as a consistent parallelism between the growing boy and the rising sun. Certainly other metaphors intrude: that of the darkening prison house, for example. But whether or not we bring the dominant symbolism to the surface, there is no question, I think, that it is at work within the stanza. And it *is* a symbolism: we are not permitted to pick up the metaphors when we please and drop them when we please. Light plays throughout the poem, and the "Ode," one must remember, closes with another scene in which sunlight again figures prominently:

> *The Clouds that gather round the setting sun*
> *Do take a sober colouring from an eye*
> *That hath kept watch o'er man's mortality. . . .*

Here, by the way, the hint that it is the child who confers the "gleam" upon the world becomes explicit. The clouds take their sober coloring from the eye. Even if we make "eye" refer to the sun as the eye of day, we have but brought the basic metaphors into closer relationship. If the sun, the eye of heaven, after it has watched over mortality, is sobered, so is the eye of the man who has kept the same watch. The parallel between the sun and the developing child which we noticed in Stanza V is completed.

To some readers, however, the occurrence of the word "shades" may still render such an interpretation bizarre. But such a reader will have to prepare himself to face another even more startling ambiguity in the central symbol. Blindness and darkness in this poem are not the easy and expected antitheses to vision and light. The climax of man's falling away from his source is, as we have seen, not the settling down of complete darkness, but of common day. In Stanza IX when the poet pays his debt of gratitude to the childhood vision he actually associates it with blindness and darkness:

> *But for those obstinate questionings*
> *Of sense and outward things,*
> *Fallings from us, vanishings;*
> *Blank misgivings. . . .*

> *But for those first affections,*
> *Those shadowy recollections,*
>   *Which, be they what they may,*
> *Are yet the fountain light of all our day,*
> *Are yet a master light of all our seeing. . . .*

The supernal light, the master-light of all our seeing, is here made to flow from the shadowy recollections. Even if we argue that "shadowy" means merely "fitful," "fugitive," we shall still find it difficult to discount some connection of the word with shades and darkness. And if we consider the changing points of view in the "Ode," we shall see that it is inevitable that light should shift into dark and dark into light. For the man who has become immersed in the hard, white light of common day, the recollections of childhood are shadowy; just as from the standpoint of the poet, such a man, preoccupied with his analysis and dissection, must appear merely blind.

As a matter of fact, I think we shall have to agree that there is method in Wordsworth's paradoxes: he is trying to state with some sensitiveness the relation between the two modes of perception, that of the analytic reason and that of the synthesizing imagination. They do have their relationships; they are both ways of seeing. The ambiguities which light and darkness take on in this poem are, therefore, not confusions, as it seems to me, but necessary paradoxes.

A further treatment of the relationship in which Wordsworth is certainly making a conscious use of paradox seems to clinch the interpretation given. I refer to the passage in which the child is addressed as

Thou best Philosopher, who yet dost keep
Thy heritage, thou Eye among the blind,
That, deaf and silent, read'st the eternal deep. . . .

Why with such earnest pains dost thou provoke
The years to bring the inevitable yoke,
Thus blindly with thy blessedness at strife?

The child who sees, does not know that he sees, and is not even aware that others are blind. Indeed, he is trying his best (or soon will try his best) to become blind like the others. Yet, in this most extravagant passage in the poem, Wordsworth keeps the balance. In the child we are dealing with the isolated fact of vision.* The eye, taken as an organ of sense, is naturally deaf and silent. The child cannot tell what he reads in the eternal deep, nor can he hear the poet's warning that he is actually trying to cast away his vision. If the passage seems the high point of extravagance, it is also the high point of ironic qualification. How blind is he who, possessed of rare sight, *blindly* strives to forfeit it and become blind!

In pursuing the implications of the light-darkness symbolism, however, I do not mean to lose sight of the "Ode" as a rhetorical structure. To this matter—the alternation of mood, the balance of stanza against stanza, the metrical devices by which the poet attempts to point up these contrasts—to this matter, I shall be able to give very little attention. But I do not mean to desert altogether the line of development of the poem. It is high time to turn back to Stanzas III and IV.

With Stanza III the emphasis is shifted from sight to sound. It is a very cunning touch. The poet has lamented the passing of a glory from the earth. But he can, he suggests, at least *hear* the mirth of the blessed creatures for whom the earth still wears that glory. Stanza III is dominated by sound: the birds' songs, the trumpets of the cataracts, echoes, the winds—presumably their sound—one can't *see* them. Even the gamboling of the lambs is associated with a strong auditory image—"As to the tabor's sound." Hearing these sounds, the poet tries to enter into the gaiety of the season. He asks the shepherd boy to shout, and he goes on to say in Stanza IV,

> *Ye blessed Creatures, I have heard the call*
> *Ye to each other make. . . .*

* Cf. I. A. Richards' discussion of this passage in *Coleridge on Imagination*, pp. 133 ff.

The effect is that of a blind man trying to enter the joyful dawn world. He can bear the blessed creatures as they rejoice in the world, but he himself is shut out from it. If one argues against this as oversubtle—and perhaps it is—and points out that after the poet says,

> . . . *I have heard the call*
> *Ye to each other make*

he goes on immediately to say

> *I see*
> *The heavens laugh with you in your jubilee,*

we are not left entirely without a rejoinder. One can point out that at this point another strong auditory image intervenes again to make sound the dominant sense, not sight. One sees a smile, but laughter is vocal. The heavens are laughing with the children. The poet does in a sense enter into the scene; certainly he is trying very hard to enter into it. But what I notice is that the poet seems to be straining to work up a gaiety that isn't there. If his heart is at the children's festival, it is their festival, after all, not his. I hasten to add that this sense of a somewhat frenetically whipped-up enthusiasm is dramatically quite appropriate. (The metrical situation of the stanza, by the way, would seem to support the view that the strained effect is intentional.*) The poet under the influence of the morning

---

* I concede that it is quite possible that Wordsworth meant to convey no sense of strain—that the rhythm of the first part of the stanza may have pleased him absolutely and been intended to seem pleasing to others. But the cluster of feminine rimes and the syncopation of the rhythm, apparently meant to connote gaiety, are actually awkward as Wordsworth uses them here.

> *My heárt is át your féstivál,*
> *Mý head háth its córonál. . . .*

Heart and *head* are the points of contrast. Yet the accents awkwardly distinguish between them.

scene, feeling the winds that blow "from the fields of sleep," tries to relive the dream. He fails.

But to return to the contrast between sight and sound, the poet should be saying at the climax of his ecstasy,

> *I see, I see, with joy I see!*

not,

> *I hear, I hear, with joy I hear!*

Consequently, we are not surprised that the sudden collapse of his afflatus occurs in the very next line, and occurs with the first particular object which is concretely visualized in this stanza:

> *—But there's a Tree, of many, one,*
> *A single Field which I have looked upon . . .*

The influences of the May morning will no longer work.

I have already discussed the manner in which the first two stanzas of the "Ode" charge the imagery of the famous fifth stanza. I should like to take a moment to glance at another aspect of this stanza. The poet, in "explaining" the loss of vision, says,

> *Our birth is but a sleep and a forgetting. . . .*

> *Oh évil dáy! if Í were súllen*
> *While Eárth hersélf is adórning,*
> *Thiś swéet Máy mórning,*
> *And the chíldren are cúlling . . .*

There may be other ways to scan the lines, but I believe that there is no way to read the lines so as to get a quick, gay rhythm. We are to read rapidly lines which are not so constructed as to allow such rapidity with grace. Whatever Wordsworth's intention, the sense of strain fits perfectly the effect which the poem as a whole demands. Unfortunately, some of the quickstep of Stanza VII—

> *A wedding or a festival,*
> *A mourning or a funeral,*

lacks this kind of justification.

The connection with

> *The glory and the freshness of a dream*

of Stanza I is obvious, but I think few have noticed that the expected relation between the two is neatly reversed. Our life's star is rising: it is dawn. We expect the poet to say that the child, in being born, is waking up, deserting sleep and the realm of dream. But instead, our birth, he says, is a sleep and a forgetting. Reality and unreality, learning and forgetting, ironically change places.

Parallel ambiguities are involved in the use of "earth." In general, earth is made to serve as a foil for the celestial light. For example, when the poet writes,

> . . . *when meadow, grove, and stream,*
> *The earth and every common sight,*

it is almost as if he had said "even the earth," and this is the implication of "While earth *herself* is adorning," in Stanza IV. Yet, logically and grammatically, we can look back and connect "earth" with "meadow, grove, and stream"—all of which are aspects of earth—just as properly as we can look forward to connect "earth" with "every common sight." The poet himself is willing at times in the poem to treat the earth as the aggregate of all the special aspects of nature, at least of terrestrial nature. This surely is the sense of such a line as

> . . . *there hath passed away a glory from the earth*

where the emphasis suggests some such statement as: the whole world has lost its glory.

But these somewhat contradictory aspects of the word "earth" overlay a far more fundamental paradox: in general, we think of this poem as a celebration of the influence of nature on the developing mind, and

surely, to a large degree, this is true. The poem is filled
with references to valleys, mountains, streams, cataracts,
meadows, the sea. Yet, though these aspects are so thor-
oughly interwoven with the spontaneous joy of the
child which the poet has himself lost, it is the earth
which is responsible for the loss. Stanza VI is concerned
with this paradox:

> *Earth fills her lap with pleasures of her own. . . .*

What are these pleasures? They would seem to be
suspiciously like the pleasures which engage the chil-
dren on this May morning and in which the speaker
of the poem regrets that he cannot fully indulge. It is
true that the next stanza of the "Ode" does emphasize
the fact that the world of human affairs, as the stanza
makes clear, is seized upon by the child with joy, and
that this is a process which is eminently "natural":

> *Fretted by sallies of his mother's kisses,*
> *With light upon him from his father's eyes!*

Earth, "even with something of a Mother's mind,"
"fills her lap with pleasures."

> *Yearnings she hath in her own natural kind.*

What are these yearnings but yearnings to involve the
child with herself? We can translate "in her own
natural kind" as "pertaining to her," "proper to the
earth"; yet there is more than a hint that "natural"
means "pertaining to nature," and are not the yearn-
ings proper to the earth, *natural* in this sense, anyway?

In trying to make the child forget the unearthly or
supernatural glory, the Earth is acting out of kindness.
The poet cannot find it in him to blame her. She wants
the child to be at home. Here we come close upon a
Wordsworthian pun, though doubtless an unpremedi-
tated pun. In calling the Earth "the homely Nurse"

there seems a flicker of this suggestion: that Earth wants the child to be at home. Yet "homely" must surely mean also "unattractive, plain." * She is the drudging common earth after all, homely, perhaps a little stupid, but sympathetic, and kind. Yet it is precisely this Earth which was once glorious to the poet, "Apparelled in celestial light."

This stanza, though not one of the celebrated stanzas of the poem, is one of the most finely ironical. Its structural significance too is of first importance, and has perhaps in the past been given too little weight. Two of its implications I should like to emphasize. First, the stanza definitely insists that the human soul is not merely natural. We do not of course, as Wordsworth himself suggested, have to take literally the doctrine about pre-existence; but the stanza makes it quite clear, I think, that man's soul brings an alien element into nature, a supernatural element. The child is of royal birth—"that imperial palace whence he came"— the Earth, for all her motherly affection, is only his foster-mother after all. The submerged metaphor at work here is really that of the foundling prince reared by the peasants, though the phrase, "her Inmate Man," suggests an even more sinister relation: "Inmate" can only mean inmate of the prison-house of the preceding stanza.

The second implication is this: since the Earth is really homely, the stanza underlies what has been hinted at earlier: namely, that it is the child himself who confers the radiance on the morning world upon which he looks with delight. The irony is that if the child looks long enough at that world, becomes deeply

---

* It has been objected that "homely" in British English does not have this sense. Perhaps it does not today, but see Milton's *Comus:*

> *It is for homely features to keep home,*
> *They had their name thence. . . .*

enough involved in its beauties, the celestial radiance itself disappears.

In some respects, it is a pity that Wordsworth was not content to rely upon this imagery to make his point and that he felt it necessary to include the weak Stanza VII. Presumably, he thought the reader required a more explicit account. Moreover, Wordsworth is obviously trying to establish his own attitude toward the child's insight. In the earlier stanzas, he has attempted to define the quality of the visionary gleam, and to account for its inevitable loss. Now he attempts to establish more definitely his attitude toward the whole experience. One finds him here, as a consequence, no longer trying to recapture the childhood joy or lamenting its loss, but withdrawing to a more objective and neutral position. The function of establishing this attitude is assigned to Stanza VII. The poet's treatment of the child here is tender, but with a hint of amused patronage in the tenderness. There is even a rather timid attempt at humor. But even if we grant Wordsworth's intention, the stanza must still be accounted very weak, and some of the lines are very flat indeed. Moreover, the amused tenderness is pretty thoroughly over-balanced by the great stanza that follows. I am not sure that the poem would not be improved if Stanza VII were omitted.

If Stanza VII patronizes the child, Stanza VIII apparently exalts him. What is the poet's attitude here? Our decision as to what it is—that is, our decision as to what the poem is actually saying here—is crucial for our interpretation of the poem as a whole. For this reason I believe that it is worth going back over some of the ground already traversed.

Coleridge, one remembers, found the paradoxes which Wordsworth uses in Stanza VIII too startling. Several years ago, in his *Coleridge on Imagination*, I. A.

Richards answered Coleridge's strictures. He replies to one of Coleridge's objections as follows:

The syntax is "faulty" only in that the reader may be required to reflect. He may have to notice that *eye* is metaphorical already for *philosopher*—that the two conjointly then have a meaning that neither would have apart. "An idea in the mind is to a Natural Law as the power of seeing is to light," said Coleridge himself. As an eye, the philosopher is free from the need to do anything but respond to the laws of his being. *Deaf* and *silent* extend the metaphor by perfectly consentaneous movements. . . . The child will not hear (cannot understand) our words; and he will tell us nothing. That which Wordsworth would derive from him he cannot give; his silence (as we take it through step after step of interpretation, up to the point at which it negates the whole *overt* implication of the rest of Wordsworth's treatment) can become the most important point in the poem. We might look to Lao Tzu to support this: "Who knows speaks not; who speaks knows not." But it is enough to quote, from Coleridge himself, "the words with which Plotinus supposes NATURE to answer a similar difficulty. 'Should anyone interrogate her, how she works, if graciously she vouchsafe to listen and speak, she will reply, it behoves thee not to disquiet me with interrogatories, but to understand in silence even as I am silent, and work without words.'"

Before going further with Richards, however, the reader may wonder how far Wordsworth would be prepared to accept this defense of the lines, particularly in view of Richards' statement that the child's silence "*can* become the most important point in the poem." *Did* it become the most important part for Wordsworth? And regardless of how we answer that question, *does* it become such for us? How is it that the child is an eye among the blind?

Because he "yet [doth] keep/ [His] heritage"; because he still dreams and remembers, for all that birth is a sleep and a forgetting; because he is still near to God, who is our home. This, I take it, is what Richards calls the *"overt* implication of . . . Wordsworth's treatment." But it is not so simple as this in Wordsworth's poem. We have seen the hints of another interpretation: the suggestion that the child is like the moon which "with delight/ Look[s] round her," and the association of the joyous vision of the child with the child's own joyous activity, and further, with the joyous activity of the birds and the lambs. Is the poem theistic or pantheistic? Coleridge was certainly alive to the difficulties here. He went on to question:

> . . . In what sense can the magnificent attributes, above quoted, be appropriated to a *child,* which would not make them equally suitable to a *bee,* or a *dog,* or a *field of corn;* or even to a ship, or to the wind and waves that propel it?

Richards' answer is forthright:

> . . . why should Wordsworth deny that, in a much less degree, these attributes are equally suitable to a bee, or a dog, or a field of corn? What else had he been saying with his
>
> > *And let the young lambs bound*
> > *As to the tabor's sound!*

And what else is Coleridge himself to say in Appendix B of his *Statesman's Manual?* "Never can I look and meditate on the vegetable creation without a feeling similar to that with which we gaze at a beautiful infant. . . ."

Whatever Coleridge was to say later, there can be little doubt as to what Wordsworth's poem says. The lambs and birds are undoubtedly included, along with the children, in the apostrophe, "Ye blessed Creatures." It will be difficult, furthermore, to argue that the poet means to exclude the moon, the stars, and the sun. (If Wordsworth would have excluded the bee and the dog, the exclusion, we may be sure, would have been made on other grounds—not philosophical but poetic.) The matter of importance for the development of the poem is, of course, that the child is father to the man, to the man Wordsworth, for example, as the birds, the lamb, and the moon are not. But it is also a point of first importance for the poem that the child, whatever he is to develop into later, possesses the harmony and apparent joy of all these blessed creatures. It may not be amiss here to remind ourselves of Coleridge's definition of joy with which Wordsworth himself must have been familiar: ". . . a consciousness of entire and therefore well being, when the emotional and intellectual faculties are in equipoise."

Consider, in this general connection, one further item from the poem itself, the last lines from the famous recovery stanza, Stanza IX:

> *Nor all that is at enmity with joy,*
> *Can utterly abolish or destroy!*
> *Hence in a season of calm weather*
> *Though inland far we be,*
> *Our Souls have sight of that immortal sea*
> *Which brought us hither,*
> *Can in a moment travel thither,*
> *And see the Children sport upon the shore,*
> *And hear the mighty waters rolling evermore.*

Wordsworth has said that the child as the best philosopher "read'st the eternal deep," and here for the first time in the poem we have the children brought into explicit juxtaposition with the deep. And how, according to the poem, are these best philosophers reading it? By sporting on the shore. They are playing with their little spades and sand-buckets along the beach on which the waves break. This is the only explicit exhibit of their "reading" which the poem gives. It seems to corroborate Richards' interpretation perfectly.

In writing this, I am not trying to provoke a smile at Wordsworth's expense. Far from it. The lines are great poetry. They are great poetry because, although the sea is the sea of eternity, and the mighty waters are rolling evermore, the children are not terrified—are at home—are filled with innocent joy. The children exemplify the attitude toward eternity which the other philosopher, the mature philosopher, wins to with difficulty, if he wins to it at all. For the children are those

> *On whom these truths do rest,*
> *Which we are toiling all our lives to find.*

The passage carries with it an ironic shock—the associations of innocence and joy contrasted with the associations of grandeur and terror—but it is the kind of shock which, one is tempted to say, is almost normal in the greatest poetry.

I asked a few moments ago how the child was an "Eye among the blind." The poem seems to imply two different, and perhaps hostile, answers: because the child is from God and still is close to the source of supernal light; *and,* because the child is still close to, and like, the harmonious aspects of nature, just as are the lamb or the bee or the dog. According to the first view, the child is an eye among the blind because his soul is filled with the divine; according to the second, because he is utterly natural. Can these two views be reconciled? And are they reconciled in the poem?

Obviously, the question of whether "divine" and "natural" can be reconciled in the child depends on the senses in which we apply them to the child. What the poem is saying, I take it, is that the child, because he is close to the divine, is utterly natural—natural in the sense that he has the harmony of being, the innocence, and the joy which we associate with the harmonious forms of nature. Undoubtedly Wordsworth found a symbol of divinity in such "beauteous forms" of nature; but the poem rests on something wider than the general context of Wordsworth's poetry: throughout the entire Christian tradition, the lamb, the lilies of the field, etc., have been used as such symbols.

But we may protest further and say that such a reading of "nature" represents a selection, and a loaded selection at that, one which has been made by Wordsworth himself—that there are other accounts of nature which will yield "naturalism" which is hostile to the claims to the divine. It is profitable to raise this question, because an attempt to answer it may provide the most fundamental explanation of all for the ambiguities and paradoxes which fill the "Ode."

Richards says that from "Imagination as a 'fact of mind'" there are "two doctrines which Coleridge (and Wordsworth) at times drew from it as to a life in or behind Nature." The two doctrines he states as follows:

1. The mind of the poet at moments, penetrating "the film of familiarity and selfish solicitude," gains an insight into reality, reads Nature as a symbol of something behind or within Nature not ordinarily perceived. [In the "Ode," the child, untarnished by "the film of familiarity and selfish solicitude," sees nature clad in a *celestial* light.]

2. The mind of the poet creates a Nature into which his own feelings, his aspirations and apprehensions, are projected. [In the "Ode," the child projects his own joy over nature as the moon projects its light over the bare heavens.]

In the first doctrine man, through Nature, is linked with something other than himself which he perceives through her. In the second, he makes of her, as with a mirror, a transformed image of his own being.

But Richards interrupts the process of determining which of these doctrines Coleridge held and which, Wordsworth, to raise two questions which he suggests have a prior status: the questions are, namely, "(1) Are these doctrines necessarily in opposition to one another? (2) What is the relation of any such doctrine to the fact of mind from which it derives?" And Richards goes on to argue:

The Imagination projects the life of the mind not upon Nature . . . [in the sense of the whole] field of the influences from without to which we are subject, but upon a Nature that is already a projection of our sensibility. The deadest Nature that we can conceive is already a Nature of our making. It is a Nature shaped by certain of our needs, and when we "lend to it a life drawn from the human spirit" it is reshaped in accordance with our other needs. [We may interrupt Richards to use Wordsworth's own phrasing from "Tintern Abbey": ". . . all this mighty world/ Of eye, and ear,—both what they half create,/ And what perceive . . ."] But our needs do not originate in us. They come from our relations to Nature . . . [as the whole field of influences from without]. We do not create the food that we eat, or the air that we breathe, or the other people we talk to; we do create, from our relations to them, every image we have "of" them. *Image* here is a betraying and unsatisfactory word; it suggests that these images, with which all that we can know is composed, are in some way insubstantial or unreal, mere copies of actualities other than themselves—figments. But *figment* and *real* and *substantial* are themselves words with no meaning that is not drawn from our experience. To say of anything that it is a figment seems to presuppose things more real than itself; but there is nothing within our knowledge more real than these images. To say that anything is an image suggests that there is something else to which it corresponds; but here all correspondence is between images. In short, the notion of reality derives from comparison between images, and to apply it as between images and things that are not images is an illegitimate extension which makes nonsense of it.

This deceiving practice is an example of that process of abstraction which makes it almost inevitable that the two doctrines . . .—the projective and the realist doctrines of the life in Nature—should be conceived as contradictory. "If projected, not real; if real, not projected," we shall say, unless we are careful to recall that the meanings of *real* and *projected* derive from the imaginative fact of mind, and that when they are thus put in opposition they are products of abstraction and are useful only for other purposes than the comprehension of the fact of mind.

This is all very well, I can hear someone say; but even if we grant that the realist and projective doctrines are not necessarily in opposition, what warrant have we for believing that *Wordsworth* believed they were not in opposition? In trying to answer this objection, I should agree that merely to point out that both realist and projective doctrines seem to *occur* in the "Ode" is not to give an answer. We can argue for the reconciliation of these doctrines only if we can find where these doctrines impinge upon each other. Where do they meet? That is to say, where is the real center of the poem? What is the poem essentially about?

The poem is about the human heart—its growth, its nature, its development. The poem finds its center in what Richards has called the "fact of imagination." Theology, ethics, education are touched upon. But the emphasis is not upon these: Wordsworth's rather awkward note in which he repudiates any notion of trying to inculcate a belief in pre-existence would support this view. The greatness of the "Ode" lies in the fact that Wordsworth is about the poet's business here, and is not trying to inculcate anything. Instead, he is trying to dramatize the changing interrelations which determine the major imagery. And it is with this theme that the poem closes. Thanks are given, not to God— at least in this poem, not to God—but to

> . . . *the human heart by which we live,*
> *Thanks to its tenderness, its joys, and fears* . . .

It is because of the nature of the human heart that the meanest flower can give, if not the joy of the celestial light, something which the poet says is not sorrow and which he implies is deeper than joy: "Thoughts that do often lie too deep for tears."

If the poem is about the synthesizing imagination, that faculty by which, as a later poet puts it,

Man makes a superhuman
Mirror-resembling dream

the reason for the major ambiguities is revealed. These basic ambiguities, by the way, assert themselves as the poem ends. Just before he renders thanks to the human heart, you will remember, the poet says that the clouds do not give *to,* but take *from,* the eye their sober coloring. But in the last two lines of the stanza, the flower does not take *from,* but gives *to,* the heart. We can have it either way. Indeed, the poem implies that we must have it *both* ways. And we are dealing with more than optics. What the clouds take from the eye is more than a sober coloring—the soberness is from the mind and heart. By the same token, the flower, though it gives a color—gives more, it gives thought and emotion.

It has not been my purpose to present this statement of the theme as a discovery; it is anything but that. Rather, I have tried to show how the imagery of the poem is functionally related to a theme—not vaguely and loosely related to it—and how it therefore renders that theme powerfully, and even exactly, defining and refining it. But I can make no such claim for such precision in Wordsworth's treatment of the "resolution," the recovery. In a general sense we know what Wordsworth is doing here: the childhood vision is only one aspect of the "primal sympathy"; this vision has been lost—is, as the earlier stanzas show, inevitably lost—but the primal sympathy remains. It is the faculty by which we live. The continuity between child and man is actually unbroken.

But I must confess that I feel the solution is asserted rather than dramatized. Undoubtedly, we can reconstruct from Wordsworth's other writings the relationship between the primal sympathy and the joy, the "High instincts" and the "soothing thoughts," but the

relationship is hardly digested into poetry in the
"Ode." And some of the difficulties with which we meet
in the last stanzas appear to be not enriching ambigui-
ties but distracting confusions: *e.g.*, the years bring
the philosophical mind, but the child over which the
years are to pass is already the best philosopher. There
is "something" that remains alive in our embers, but
it is difficult for the reader to define it in relation to
what has been lost. If we make a desperate effort to
extend the implied metaphor—if we say that the
celestial light is the flame which is beautiful but which
must inevitably burn itself out—the primal sympathy
is the still-glowing coal—we are forced to realize that
such extension is overingenious. The metaphor was
not meant to bear so much weight. With regard to
this matter of imagery, it would be interesting to com-
pare with the "Ode" several poems by Vaughan which
embody a theme very closely related to that of the
"Ode." And lest this remark seem to hint at an inveter-
ate prejudice in favor of the metaphysicals, I propose
another comparison: a comparison with several of
Yeats's poem which deal with still another related
theme: unity of being and the unifying power of the
imagination.* Such comparisons, I believe, would
illuminate Wordsworth's difficulties and account for
some of the "Ode's" defects. Yet, in closing this account
of the "Ode," I want to repudiate a possible misappre-
hension. I do not mean to say that the general drift of
the poem does not come through. It does. I do not
mean that there is not much greatness in the poem.
There is. But there is some vagueness—which is not the
same thing as the rich multiplicity of the greatest
poetry; and there are some loose ends, and there is at
least one rather woeful anticlimax.

But if the type of analysis to which we have sub-

* See Chapter Ten.

jected the "Ode" is calculated to indicate such defi-
ciencies by demanding a great deal of the imagery, it
is only fair to remind the reader that it focuses atten-
tion on the brilliance and power of the imagery, a
power which is sustained almost throughout the poem,
and with which Wordsworth has hardly been suffi-
ciently credited in the past. Even the insistence on
paradox does not create the defects in the "Ode"—the
defects have been pointed out before—but it may help
account for them. Indeed, one can argue that we can
perhaps best understand the virtues and the weak-
nesses of the "Ode" if we see that what Wordsworth
wanted to say demanded his use of paradox, that it
could only be said powerfully through paradox, and
if we remember in what suspicion Wordsworth held
this kind of poetic strategy.

CHAPTER EIGHT
KEATS'S SYLVAN HISTORIAN:
HISTORY WITHOUT FOOTNOTES*

There is much in the poetry of Keats which suggests that he would have approved of Archibald MacLeish's dictum, "A poem should not mean/ But be." There is even some warrant for thinking that the Grecian urn (real or imagined) which inspired the famous ode was, for Keats, just such a poem, "palpable and mute," a poem in stone. Hence it is the more remarkable that the "Ode" itself differs from Keats's other odes by culminating in a statement—a statement even of some sententiousness in which the urn itself is made to say that beauty is truth, and—more sententious still—that this bit of wisdom sums up the whole of mortal knowledge.

This is "to mean" with a vengeance—to violate the

* This essay had been finished some months before I came upon Kenneth Burke's brilliant essay on Keats's "Ode" ("Symbolic Action in a Poem by Keats," *Accent*, Autumn, 1943). I have decided not to make any alterations, though I have been tempted to adopt some of Burke's insights, and, in at least one case, his essay has convinced me of a point which I had considered but rejected—the pun on "breed" and "Brede."

I am happy to find that two critics with methods and purposes so different should agree so thoroughly as we do on the poem. I am pleased, for my part, therefore, to acknowledge the amount of duplication which exists between the two essays, counting it as rather important corroboration of a view of the poem which will probably seem to some critics overingenious. In spite of the common elements, however, I feel that the emphasis of my essay is sufficiently different from Burke's to justify my going on with its publication.

doctrine of the objective correlative, not only by stating truths, but by defining the limits of truth. Small wonder that some critics have felt that the unravished bride of quietness protests too much.

T. S. Eliot, for example, says that "this line ["Beauty is truth," etc.] strikes me as a serious blemish on a beautiful poem; and the reason must be either that I fail to understand it, or that it is a statement which is untrue." But even for persons who feel that they do understand it, the line may still constitute a blemish. Middleton Murry, who, after a discussion of Keats's other poems and his letters, feels that he knows what Keats meant by "beauty" and what he meant by "truth," and that Keats used them in senses which allowed them to be properly bracketed together, still, is forced to conclude: "My own opinion concerning the value of these two lines *in the context of the poem itself* is not very different from Mr. T. S. Eliot's." The troubling assertion is apparently an intrusion upon the poem—does not grow out of it—is not dramatically accommodated to it.

This is essentially Garrod's objection, and the fact that Garrod does object indicates that a distaste for the ending of the "Ode" is by no means limited to critics of notoriously "modern" sympathies.

But the question of real importance is not whether Eliot, Murry, and Garrod are right in thinking that "Beauty is truth, truth beauty" injures the poem. The question of real importance concerns beauty and truth in a much more general way: what is the relation of the beauty (the goodness, the perfection) of a poem to the truth or falsity of what it seems to assert? It is a question which has particularly vexed our own generation—to give it I. A. Richards' phrasing, it is the problem of belief.

The "Ode," by its bold equation of beauty and truth,

raises this question in its sharpest form—the more so when it becomes apparent that the poem itself is obviously intended to be a parable on the nature of poetry, and of art in general. The "Ode" has apparently been an enigmatic parable, to be sure: one can emphasize *beauty* is truth and throw Keats into the pure-art camp, the usual procedure. But it is only fair to point out that one could stress *truth* is beauty, and argue with the Marxist critics of the 'thirties for a propaganda art. The very ambiguity of the statement, "Beauty is truth, truth beauty" ought to warn us against insisting very much on the statement in isolation, and to drive us back to a consideration of the context in which the statement is set.

It will not be sufficient, however, if it merely drives us back to a study of Keats's reading, his conversation, his letters. We shall not find our answer there even if scholarship does prefer on principle investigations of Browning's ironic question, "What porridge had John Keats?" For even if we knew just what porridge he had, physical and mental, we should still not be able to settle the problem of the "Ode." The reason should be clear: our specific question is not what did Keats the man perhaps want to assert here about the relation of beauty and truth; it is rather: was Keats the poet able to exemplify that relation in this particular poem? Middleton Murry is right: the relation of the final statement in the poem to the total context is all-important.

Indeed, Eliot, in the very passage in which he attacks the "Ode" has indicated the general line which we are to take in its defense. In that passage, Eliot goes on to contrast the closing lines of the "Ode" with a line from *King Lear,* "Ripeness is all." Keats's lines strike him as false; Shakespeare's, on the other hand, as not clearly false, and as possibly quite true. Shakespeare's generalization, in other words, avoids raising the question of truth. But is it really a question of truth and falsity? One is tempted to account for the difference of effect which Eliot feels in this way: "Ripeness is all" is a statement put in the mouth of a dramatic character and a statement which is governed and qualified by the whole context of the play. It does not directly challenge an examination into its truth because its relevance is pointed up and modified by the dramatic context.

Now, suppose that one could show that Keats's lines, *in quite the same way,* constitute a speech, a consciously riddling paradox, put in the mouth of a particular character, and modified by the total context of the poem. If we could demonstrate that the speech was "in character," was dramatically appropriate, was properly prepared for—then would not the lines have all the justification of "Ripeness is all"? In such case, should we not have waived the question of the scientific or philosophic truth of the lines in favor of the application of a principle curiously like that of dramatic propriety? I suggest that some such principle is the only one legitimately to be invoked in any case. Be this as it may, the "Ode on a Grecian Urn" provides us with as neat an instance as one could wish in order to test the implications of such a maneuver.

It has seemed best to be perfectly frank about procedure: the poem is to be read in order to see whether the last lines of the poem are not, after all, dramatically prepared for. Yet there are some claims to be made upon the reader too, claims which he, for his part, will have to be prepared to honor. He must not be allowed to dismiss the early characterizations of the urn as merely so much vaguely beautiful description. He must not be too much surprised if "mere decoration" turns out to be meaningful symbolism—or if ironies develop where he has been taught to expect only sensuous pictures. Most of all, if the teasing riddle spoken finally by the urn is not to strike him as a bewildering break in tone, he must not be too much disturbed to have the element of paradox latent in the poem emphasized, even in those parts of the poem which have none of the energetic crackle of wit with which he usually associates paradox. This is surely not too much to ask of the reader—namely, to assume that Keats meant what he said and that he chose his words with care. After all, the poem begins on a note of paradox, though a mild one: for we ordinarily do not expect an urn to speak at all; and yet, Keats does more than this: he begins his poem by emphasizing the apparent contradiction.

The silence of the urn is stressed—it is a "bride of quietness"; it is a "foster-child of silence," but the urn is a "historian" too. Historians tell the truth, or are at least expected to tell the truth. What is a "Sylvan historian"? A historian who is like the forest rustic, a woodlander? Or, a historian who writes histories of the forest? Presumably, the urn is sylvan in both senses. True, the latter meaning is uppermost: the urn can "express / A flowery tale more sweetly than our rhyme," and what the urn goes on to express is a "leaf-fring'd legend" of "Tempe or the dales of Arcady." But the urn, like the "leaf-fring'd legend" which it tells, is covered with emblems of the fields and forests: "Overwrought, / With forest branches and the trodden weed." When we consider the way in which the urn utters its history, the fact that it must be sylvan in both senses is seen as inevitable. Perhaps too the fact that it is a rural historian, a rustic, a peasant historian, qualifies in our minds the dignity and the "truth" of the histories which it recites. Its histories, Keats has already conceded, may be characterized as "tales"—not formal history at all.

The sylvan historian certainly supplies no names and dates—"What men or gods are these?" the poet asks. What it does give is action—of men *or* gods, of godlike men or of superhuman (though not daemonic) gods—action, which is not the less intense for all that the urn is cool marble. The words "mad" and "ecstasy" occur, but it is the quiet, rigid urn which gives the dynamic picture. And the paradox goes further: the scene is one of violent love-making, a Bacchanalian scene, but the urn itself is like a "still unravish'd bride," or like a child, a child "of silence and slow time." It is not merely like a child, but like a "foster-child." The exactness of the term can be defended. "Silence and slow time," it is suggested, are not the true parents, but foster-parents. They are too old, one feels, to have borne the child themselves. Moreover, they dote upon the "child" as grandparents do. The urn is fresh and unblemished; it is still young, for all its antiquity, and time which destroys so much has "fostered" it.

With Stanza II we move into the world presented by the urn, into an examination, not of the urn as a whole —as an entity with its own form—but of the details which overlay it. But as we enter that world, the paradox of silent speech is carried on, this time in terms of the objects portrayed on the vase.

The first lines of the stanza state a rather bold paradox—even the dulling effect of many readings has hardly blunted it. At least we can easily revive its sharpness. Attended to with care, it is a statement which is preposterous, and yet true—true on the same level on which the original metaphor of the speaking urn is true. The unheard music is sweeter than any audible music. The poet has rather cunningly enforced his conceit by using the phrase, "ye soft pipes." Actually, we might accept the poet's metaphor without being forced to accept the adjective "soft." The pipes might, although "unheard," be shrill, just as the action which is frozen in the figures on the urn can be violent and ecstatic as in Stanza I and slow and dignified as in Stanza IV (the procession to the sacrifice). Yet, by characterizing the pipes as "soft," the poet has provided a sort of realistic basis for his metaphor: the pipes, it is suggested, are playing very softly; if we listen carefully, we can hear them; their music is just below the threshold of normal sound.

This general paradox runs through the stanza: action goes on though the actors are motionless; the song will not cease; the lover cannot leave his song; the maiden, always to be kissed, never actually kissed, will remain changelessly beautiful. The maiden is, indeed, like the urn itself, a "still unravished bride of quietness"—not even ravished by a kiss; and it is implied, perhaps, that her changeless beauty, like that of the urn, springs from this fact.

The poet is obviously stressing the fresh, unwearied charm of the scene itself which can defy time and is deathless. But, at the same time, the poet is being perfectly fair to the terms of his metaphor. The beauty portrayed is deathless because it is lifeless. And it would be possible to shift the tone easily and ever so slightly by insisting more heavily on some of the phrasings so as to give them a darker implication. Thus, in the case of "thou canst not leave/ Thy song," one could interpret: the musician cannot leave the song even if he would: he is fettered to it, a prisoner. In the same way, one could enlarge on the hint that the lover is not wholly satisfied and content: "never canst thou kiss,/ . . . *yet, do not grieve.*" These items are mentioned here, not because one wishes to maintain that the poet is bitterly ironical, but because it is important for us to see that even here the paradox is being used fairly, particularly in view of the shift in tone which comes in the next stanza.

This third stanza represents, as various critics have pointed out, a recapitulation of earlier motifs. The boughs which cannot shed their leaves, the unwearied melodist, and the ever-ardent lover reappear. Indeed, I am not sure that this stanza can altogether be defended against the charge that it represents a falling-off from the delicate but firm precision of the earlier stanzas. There is a tendency to linger over the scene sentimentally: the repetition of the word "happy" is perhaps symptomatic of what is occurring. Here, if anywhere, in my opinion, is to be found the blemish on the ode—not in the last two lines. Yet, if we are to attempt a defense of the third stanza, we shall come nearest success by emphasizing the paradoxical implications of the repeated items; for whatever development there is in the stanza inheres in the increased stress on the paradoxical element. For example, the boughs cannot "bid the Spring adieu," a phrase which repeats "nor ever can those trees be bare," but the new line strengthens the implications of speaking: the falling leaves are a gesture, a word of farewell to the joy of spring. The melodist of Stanza II played sweeter music because unheard, but here, in the third stanza, it is implied that he does not tire of his song for the same reason that the lover does not tire of his love—neither song nor love is consummated. The songs are "for ever new" because they cannot be completed.

The paradox is carried further in the case of the lover whose love is "For ever warm and still to be enjoy'd." We are really dealing with an ambiguity here, for we can take "still to be enjoy'd" as an adjectival phrase on the same level as "warm"—that is, "still virginal and warm." But the tenor of the whole poem suggests that the warmth of the love depends upon the fact that it has not been enjoyed—that is, "warm and still to be enjoy'd" may mean also "warm *because* still to be enjoy'd."

But though the poet has developed and extended his metaphors furthest here in this third stanza, the ironic counterpoise is developed furthest too. The love which a line earlier was "warm" and "panting" becomes suddenly in the next line, "All breathing human passion far above." But if it is *above* all breathing passion, it is, after all, outside the realm of breathing passion, and therefore, not human passion at all.

(If one argues that we are to take "All breathing human passion" as qualified by "That leaves a heart high-sorrowful and cloy'd"—that is, if one argues that Keats is saying that the love depicted on the urn is above only that human passion which leaves one cloyed and not above human passion in general, he misses the point. For Keats in the "Ode" is stressing the ironic fact that all human passion *does* leave one cloyed; hence the superiority of art.)

The purpose in emphasizing the ironic undercurrent in the foregoing lines is not at all to disparage Keats— to point up implications of his poem of which he was himself unaware. Far from it: the poet knows precisely what he is doing. The point is to be made simply in order to make sure that we are completely aware of what he *is* doing. Garrod, sensing this ironic undercurrent, seems to interpret it as an element over which Keats was not able to exercise full control. He says: "Truth to his main theme [the fixity given by art to forms which in life are impermanent] has taken Keats farther than he meant to go. The pure and ideal art of this 'cold Pastoral,' this 'silent form,' *has* a cold silentness which in some degree saddens him. In the last lines of the fourth stanza, especially the last three lines . . . every reader is conscious, I should suppose, of an undertone of sadness, of disappointment." The undertone is there, but Keats has not been taken "farther than he meant to go." Keats's attitude, even in the early stanzas, is more complex than Garrod would allow: it is more complex and more ironic, and a recognition of this is important if we are to be able to relate the last stanza to the rest of the "Ode." Keats is perfectly aware that the frozen moment of loveliness is more dynamic than is the fluid world of reality *only* because it is frozen. The love depicted on the urn remains warm and young because it is not human flesh at all but cold, ancient marble.

With Stanza IV, we are still within the world depicted by the urn, but the scene presented in this stanza forms a contrast to the earlier scenes. It emphasizes, not individual aspiration and desire, but communal life. It constitutes another chapter in the history that the "Sylvan historian" has to tell. And again, names and dates have been omitted. We are not told to what god's altar the procession moves, nor the occasion of the sacrifice.

Moreover, the little town from which the celebrants come is unknown; and the poet rather goes out of his way to leave us the widest possible option in locating it. It may be a mountain town, or a river town, or a tiny seaport. Yet, of course, there is a sense in which the nature of the town—the essential character of the town—is actually suggested by the figured urn. But it is not given explicitly. The poet is willing to leave much to our imaginations; and yet the stanza in its organization of imagery and rhythm does describe the town clearly enough; it is small, it is quiet, its people are knit together as an organic whole, and on a "pious morn" such as this, its whole population has turned out to take part in the ritual.

The stanza has been justly admired. Its magic of effect defies reduction to any formula. Yet, without pretending to "account" for the effect in any mechanical fashion, one can point to some of the elements active in securing the effect: there is the suggestiveness of the word "green" in "green altar"—something natural, spontaneous, living; there is the suggestion that the little town is caught in a curve of the seashore, or nestled in a fold of the mountains—at any rate, is something secluded and something naturally related to its terrain; there is the effect of the phrase "peaceful citadel," a phrase which involves a clash between the ideas of war and peace and resolves it in the sense of stability and independence without imperialistic ambition—the sense of stable repose.

But to return to the larger pattern of the poem: Keats does something in this fourth stanza which is highly interesting in itself and thoroughly relevant to the sense in which the urn is a historian. One of the most moving passages in the poem is that in which the poet speculates on the strange emptiness of the little town which, of course, has not been pictured on the urn at all.

The little town which has been merely implied by the procession portrayed on the urn is endowed with a poignance beyond anything else in the poem. Its streets "for evermore/ Will silent be," its desolation forever shrouded in a mystery. No one in the figured procession will ever be able to go back to the town to break the silence there, not even one to tell the stranger there why the town remains desolate.

If one attends closely to what Keats is doing here, he may easily come to feel that the poet is indulging himself in an ingenious fancy, an indulgence, however, which is gratuitous and finally silly; that is, the poet has created in his own imagination the town implied by the procession of worshipers, has given it a special character of desolation and loneliness, and then has gone on to treat it as if it were a real town to which a stranger might actually come and be puzzled by its emptiness. (I can see no other interpretation of the lines, "and not a soul to tell/ Why thou art desolate can e'er return.") But, actually, of course, no one will ever discover the town except by the very same process by which Keats has discovered it: namely, through the figured urn, and then, of course, he will not need to ask why it is empty. One can well imagine what a typical eighteenth-century critic would have made of this flaw in logic.

It will not be too difficult, however, to show that Keats's extension of the fancy is not irrelevant to the poem as a whole. The "reality" of the little town has a very close relation to the urn's character as a historian. If the earlier stanzas have been concerned with such paradoxes as the ability of static carving to convey dynamic action, of the soundless pipes to play music sweeter than that of the heard melody, of the figured lover to have a love more warm and panting than that of breathing flesh and blood, so in the same way the town implied by the urn comes to have a richer and more important history than that of actual cities. Indeed, the imagined town is to the figured procession as the unheard melody is to the carved pipes of the unwearied melodist. And the poet, by pretending to take the town as real—so real that he can imagine the effect of its silent streets upon the stranger who chances to come into it—has suggested in the most powerful way possible its essential reality for him—and for us. It is a case of the doctor's taking his own medicine: the poet is prepared to stand by the illusion of his own making.

With Stanza V we move back out of the enchanted world portrayed by the urn to consider the urn itself once more as a whole, as an object. The shift in point of view is marked with the first line of the stanza by the apostrophe, "O Attic shape . . ." It is the urn itself as a formed thing, as an autonomous world, to which the poet addresses these last words. And the rich, almost breathing world which the poet has conjured up for us contracts and hardens into the decorated motifs on the urn itself: "with brede/ Of marble men and maidens overwrought." The beings who have a life above life—"All breathing human passion far above" —are marble, after all.

This last is a matter which, of course, the poet has never denied. The recognition that the men and maidens are frozen, fixed, arrested, has, as we have already seen, run through the second, third, and fourth stanzas as an ironic undercurrent. The central paradox of the poem, thus, comes to conclusion in the phrase, "Cold Pastoral." The word "pastoral" suggests warmth, spontaneity, the natural and the informal as well as the idyllic, the simple, and the informally charming. What the urn tells is a "flowery tale," a "leaf-fring'd legend," but the "sylvan historian" works in terms of marble. The urn itself is cold, and the life beyond life which it expresses is life which has been formed, arranged. The urn itself is a "silent form," and it speaks, not by means of statement, but by "teasing us out of thought." It is as enigmatic as eternity is, for, like eternity, its history is beyond time, outside time, and for this very reason bewilders our time-ridden minds: it teases us.

The marble men and maidens of the urn will not age as flesh-and-blood men and women will: "When old age shall this generation waste." (The word "generation," by the way, is very rich. It means on one level "that which is generated"—that which springs from human loins—Adam's breed; and yet, so intimately is death wedded to men, the word "generation" itself has become, as here, a measure of time.) The marble men and women lie outside time. The urn which they adorn will remain. The "Sylvan historian" will recite its history to other generations.

What will it say to them? Presumably, what it says to the poet now: that "formed experience," imaginative insight, embodies the basic and fundamental perception of man and nature. The urn is beautiful, and yet its beauty is based—what else is the poem concerned with?—on an imaginative perception of essentials. Such a vision is beautiful but it is also true. The sylvan historian presents us with beautiful histories, but they are true histories, and it is a good historian.

Moreover, the "truth" which the sylvan historian gives is the only kind of truth which we are likely to get on this earth, and, furthermore, it is the only kind that we *have* to have. The names, dates, and special circumstances, the wealth of data—these the sylvan historian quietly ignores. But we shall never get all the facts anyway—there is no end to the accumulation of facts. Moreover, mere accumulations of facts—a point our own generation is only beginning to realize—are meaningless. The sylvan historian does better than that: it takes a few details and so orders them that we have not only beauty but insight into essential truth. Its "history," in short, is a history without footnotes. It has the validity of myth—not myth as a pretty but irrelevant make-belief, an idle fancy, but myth as a valid perception into reality.

So much for the "meaning" of the last lines of the "Ode." It is an interpretation which differs little from past interpretations. It is put forward here with no pretension to novelty. What is important is the fact that it can be derived from the context of the "Ode" itself.

And now, what of the objection that the final lines break the tone of the poem with a display of misplaced sententiousness? One can summarize the answer already implied thus: throughout the poem the poet has stressed the paradox of the speaking urn. First, the urn itself can tell a story, can give a history. Then, the various figures depicted upon the urn play music or speak or sing. If we have been alive to these items, we shall not, perhaps, be too much surprised to have the urn speak once more, not in the sense in which it tells a story—a metaphor which is rather easy to accept—but, to have it speak on a higher level, to have it make a commentary on its own nature. If the urn has been properly dramatized, if we have followed the development of the metaphors, if we have been alive to the paradoxes which work throughout the poem, perhaps then, we shall be prepared for the enigmatic, final paradox which the "silent form" utters. But in that case, we shall not feel that the generalization, unqualified and to be taken literally, is meant to march out of its context to compete with the scientific and philosophical generalizations which dominate our world.

"Beauty is truth, truth beauty" has precisely the same status, and the same justification as Shakespeare's "Ripeness is all." It is a speech "in character" and supported by a dramatic context.

To conclude thus may seem to weight the principle of dramatic propriety with more than it can bear. This would not be fair to the complexity of the problem of truth in art nor fair to Keats's little parable. Granted; and yet the principle of dramatic propriety may take us further than would first appear. Respect for it may at least insure our dealing with the problem of truth at the level on which it is really relevant to literature. If we can see that the assertions made in a poem are to be taken as part of an organic context, if we can resist the temptation to deal with them in isolation, then we may be willing to go on to deal with the world-view, or "philosophy," or "truth" of the *poem as a whole* in terms of its dramatic wholeness: that is, we shall not neglect the maturity of attitude, the dramatic tension, the emotional *and* intellectual coherence in favor of some statement of theme abstracted from it by paraphrase. Perhaps, best of all, we might learn to distrust our ability to represent any poem adequately by paraphrase. Such a distrust is healthy. Keats's sylvan historian, who is not above "teasing" us, exhibits such a distrust, and perhaps the point of what the sylvan historian "says" is to confirm us in our distrust.

CHAPTER NINE
THE MOTIVATION OF
TENNYSON'S WEEPER

Tennyson is perhaps the last English poet one would think of associating with the subtleties of paradox and ambiguity. He is not the thoughtless poet, to be sure: he grapples—particularly in his later period—with the "big" questions which were up for his day; and he struggles manfully with them. But the struggle, as Tennyson conducted it, was usually kept out of the grammar and symbolism of the poetry itself. Like his own protagonist in "In Memoriam," Tennyson "fought his doubts"—he does not typically build them into the structure of the poetry itself as enriching ambiguities.

Yet substantially true as this generalization is, Tennyson was not always successful in avoiding the ambiguous and the paradoxical; and indeed, in some of his poems his failure to avoid them becomes a saving grace. The lyric "Tears, Idle Tears" is a very good instance. It is a poem which, from a strictly logical point of view, Tennyson may be thought to have blundered into. But, whether he blundered into it or not, the poem gains from the fact that it finds its unity in a principle of organization higher than that which seems to be operative in many of Tennyson's more "thoughtful" poems.

Any account of the poem may very well begin with a consideration of the nature of the tears. Are they *idle* tears? Or are they not rather the most meaningful of tears? Does not the very fact that they are "idle" (that is, tears occasioned by no immediate grief) become in itself a guarantee of the fact that they spring from a deeper, more universal cause?

It would seem so, and that the poet is thus beginning his poem with a paradox. For the third line of the poem indicates that there is no doubt in the speaker's mind about the origin of the tears in some divine despair. They "rise in the heart"—for all that they have been first announced as "idle."

But the question of whether Tennyson is guilty of (or to be complimented upon) a use of paradox may well wait upon further discussion. At this point in our commentary, it is enough to observe that Tennyson has chosen to open his poem with some dramatic boldness—if not with the bold step of equating "idle" with "from the depth of some divine despair," then at least with a bold and violent reversal of the speaker's first characterization of his tears.

The tears "rise in the heart" as the speaker looks upon a scene of beauty and tranquillity. Does looking on the "happy Autumn-fields" bring to mind the days that are no more? The poet does not say so. The tears rise to the eyes in looking on the "happy Autumn-fields" *and* thinking of the days that are no more. The poet himself does not stand responsible for any closer linkage between these actions, though, as a matter of fact, most of us will want to make a closer linkage here. For, if we change "happy Autumn-fields," say, to "happy April-fields," the two terms tend to draw apart. The fact that the fields are autumn-fields which, though happy, point back to something which is over—which is finished—*does* connect them with the past and therefore properly suggests to the observer thoughts about that past.

To sum up: The first stanza has a unity, but it is not a unity which finds its sanctions in the ordinary logic of language. Its sanctions are to be found in the dramatic context, and, to my mind, there alone. Indeed, the stanza suggests the play of the speaker's mind as the tears unexpectedly start, tears for which there is no apparent occasion, and as he searches for an explanation of them. He calls them "idle," but, even as he says "I know not what they mean," he realizes that they must spring from the depths of his being—is willing, with his very next words, to associate them with "some divine despair." Moreover, the real occasion of the tears, though the speaker himself comes to realize it only as he approaches the end of the stanza, is the thought about the past. It is psychologically and dramatically right, therefore, that the real occasion should be stated explicitly only with the last line of the stanza.

This first stanza, then, recapitulates the surprise and bewilderment in the speaker's own mind, and sets the problem which the succeeding stanzas are to analyze. The dramatic effect may be described as follows: the stanza seems, not a meditated observation, but a speech begun impulsively—a statement which the speaker has begun before he knows how he will end it.

In the second stanza we are not surprised to have the poet characterize the days that are no more as "sad," but there is some shock in hearing him apply to them the adjective "fresh." Again, the speaker does not pause to explain: the word "fresh" actually begins the stanza. Yet the adjective justifies itself.

The past is fresh as with a dawn freshness—as fresh as the first beam glittering on the sail of an incoming ship. The ship is evidently expected; it brings friends, friends "up from the underworld." On the surface, the comparison is innocent: the "underworld" is merely the antipodes, the world which lies below the horizon—an underworld in the sense displayed in old-fashioned geographies with their sketches illustrating the effects of the curvature of the earth. The sails, which catch the light and glitter, will necessarily be the part first seen of any ship which is coming "up" over the curve of the earth.

But the word "underworld" will necessarily suggest the underworld of Greek mythology, the realm of the shades, the abode of the dead. The attempt to characterize the freshness of the days that are no more has, thus, developed, almost imperceptibly, into a further characterization of the days themselves as belonging, not to our daylight world, but to an "underworld." This suggestion is, of course, strengthened in the lines that follow in which the ship metaphor is reversed so as to give us a picture of sadness: evening, the last glint of sunset light on the sail of a ship

That sinks with all we love below the verge . . .

The conjunction of the qualities of sadness and freshness is reinforced by the fact that the same basic symbol—the light on the sails of a ship hull down—has been employed to suggest both qualities. With the third stanza, the process is carried one stage further: the two qualities (with the variant of "strange" for "fresh") are explicitly linked together:

Ah, sad and strange as in dark summer dawns . . .

And here the poet is not content to suggest the qualities of sadness and strangeness by means of two different, even if closely related, figures. In this third stanza the special kind of sadness and strangeness is suggested by one and the same figure.

It is a figure developed in some detail. It, too, involves a dawn scene, though ironically so, for the beginning of the new day is to be the beginning of the long night for the dying man. The dying eyes, the poem suggests, have been for some time awake—long enough to have had time to watch the

. . . *casement slowly [grow] a glimmering square.* . . .

The dying man, soon to sleep the lasting sleep, is more fully awake than the "half-awaken'd birds" whose earliest pipings come to his dying ears. We know why these pipings are sad; but why are they *strange?* Because to the person hearing a bird's song for the last time, it will seem that he has never before really heard one. The familiar sound will take on a quality of unreality—of strangeness.

If this poem were merely a gently melancholy reverie on the sweet sadness of the past, Stanzas II and III would have no place in the poem. But the poem is no such reverie: the images from the past rise up with a strange clarity and sharpness that shock the speaker. Their sharpness and freshness account for the sudden tears and for the psychological problem with which the speaker wrestles in the poem. If the past would only remain melancholy but dimmed, sad but worn and familiar, we should have no problem and no poem. At least, we should not have *this* poem; we should certainly not have the intensity of the last stanza.

That intensity, if justified, must grow out of a sense of the apparent nearness and intimate presence of what is irrevocably beyond reach: the days that are no more must be more than the conventional "dear, dead days beyond recall." They must be beyond recall, yet alive—tantalizingly vivid and near. It is only thus that we can feel the speaker justified in calling them

> *Dear as remember'd kisses after death,*
> *And sweet as those by hopeless fancy feign'd*
> *On lips that are for others. . . .*

It is only thus that we can accept the culminating paradox of

> *O Death in Life, the days that are no more.*

We have already observed, in the third stanza, how the speaker compares the strangeness and sadness of the past to the sadness of the birds' piping as it sounds to dying ears. There is a rather brilliant ironic contrast involved in the comparison. The speaker, a living man, in attempting to indicate how sad and strange to him are the days of the past, says that they are as sad and strange as is the natural activity of the awakening world to the man who is dying: the dead past seems to the living man as unfamiliar and fresh in its sadness as the living present seems to the dying man. There is more here, however, than a mere, ironic reversal of roles; in each case there is the sense of being irrevocably barred out from the known world.

This ironic contrast, too, accounts for the sense of desperation which runs through the concluding lines of the poem. The kisses feigned by "hopeless fancy" are made the more precious because of the very hopelessness; but memory takes on the quality of fancy. It is equally hopeless—the kisses can as little be renewed as those "feign'd/ On lips that are for others" can be obtained. The realized past has become as fabulous as the unrealizable future. The days that are no more are as dear as the one, as sweet as the other, the speaker says; and it does not matter whether we compare them to the one or to the other or to both: it comes to the same thing.

But the days that are no more are not merely "dear"

and "sweet"; they are "deep" and "wild." Something has happened to the grammar here. How can the *days* be "deep as love" or "wild with all regret"? And what is the status of the exclamation "O Death in Life"? Is it merely a tortured cry like "O God! the days that are no more"? Or is it a loose appositive: "the days that are no more are a kind of death in life"?

The questions are not asked in a censorious spirit, as if there were no justification for Tennyson's license here. But it is important to see how much license the poem requires, and the terms on which the reader decides to accord it justification. What one finds on closer examination is not muddlement but richness. But it is a richness achieved through principles of organization which many an admirer of the poet has difficulty in allowing to the "obscure" modern poet.

For example, how can the days of the past be *deep?* Here, of course, the problem is not very difficult. The past is buried within one: the days that are no more constitute the deepest level of one's being, and the tears that arise from thinking on them may be said to come from the "depth of some divine despair." But how can the days be "wild with all regret"? The extension demanded here is more ambitious. In matter of fact, it is the speaker, the man, who is made wild with regret by thinking on the days.

One can, of course, justify the adjective as a transferred epithet on the model of Vergil's *maestum timorem;* and perhaps this was Tennyson's own conscious justification (if, indeed, the need to justify it ever occurred to him). But one can make a better case than a mere appeal to the authority of an established literary convention. There is a sense in which the man and the remembered days are one and the same. A man is the sum of his memories. The adjective which applies to the man made wild with regret can apply to those

memories which make him wild with regret. For, does
the man charge the memories with his own passion, or
is it the memories that give the emotion to him? If
we pursue the matter far enough, we come to a point
where the distinction lapses. Perhaps I should say, more
accurately, adopting the metaphor of the poem itself,
we *descend* to a depth where the distinction lapses. The
days that are no more are *deep* and *wild,* buried but
not dead—below the surface and unthought of, yet at
the deepest core of being, secretly alive.

The past *should* be tame, fettered, brought to heel;
it is not. It is capable of breaking forth and coming
to the surface. The word "wild" is bold, therefore, but
justified. It reasserts the line of development which
has been maintained throughout the earlier stanzas:
"fresh," "strange," and now "wild"—all adjectives
which suggest passionate, irrational life. The word
"wild," thus, not only pulls into focus the earlier
paradoxes, but is the final stage in the preparation for
the culminating paradox, "O Death in Life."

The last stanza evokes an intense emotional response
from the reader. The claim could hardly be made good
by the stanza taken in isolation. The stanza leans heav-
ily upon the foregoing stanzas, and the final paradox
draws heavily upon the great metaphors in Stanzas II
and III. This is as it should be. The justification for
emphasizing the fact here is this: the poem, for all its
illusion of impassioned speech—with the looseness and
apparent confusion of unpremeditated speech—is very
tightly organized. It represents an organic structure;
and the intensity of the total effect is a reflection of the
total structure.

The reader, I take it, will hardly be disposed to
quarrel with the general statement of the theme of the
poem as it is given in the foregoing account; and he
will probably find himself in accord with this general

estimate of the poem's value. But the reader may well feel that the amount of attention given to the structure of the poem is irrelevant, if not positively bad. In particular, he may find the emphasis on paradox, ambiguity, and ironic contrast displeasing. He has not been taught to expect these in Tennyson, and he has had the general impression that the presence of these qualities represents the intrusion of alien, "unpoetic" matter.

I have no wish to intellectualize the poem—to make conscious and artful what was actually spontaneous and simple. Nevertheless, the qualities of ironic contrast and paradox *do* exist in the poem; and they *do* have a relation to the poem's dramatic power.

Those who still feel that "simple eloquence" is enough might compare "Tears, Idle Tears" with another of Tennyson's poems which has somewhat the same subject matter and hints of the same imagery, the lyric "Break, Break, Break."

> *Break, break, break,*
> > *On thy cold grey stones, O sea!*
> *And I would that my tongue could utter*
> > *The thoughts that arise in me.*
>
> *O, well for the fisherman's boy,*
> > *That he shouts with his sister at play!*
> *O well for the sailor lad,*
> > *That he sings in his boat on the bay!*
>
> *And the stately ships go on*
> > *To their haven under the hill;*
> *But O for the touch of a vanished hand,*
> > *And the sound of a voice that is still!*
>
> *Break, break, break,*
> > *At the foot of thy crags, O sea!*
> *But the tender grace of a day that is dead*
> > *Will never come back to me.*

It is an easier poem than "Tears," and, in one sense, a less confusing poem. But it is also a much thinner poem, and unless we yield comfortably and easily to the strain of gentle melancholy, actually a coarser and a more confused poem. For example, the ships are said to be "stately," but this observation is idle and finally irrelevant. What relation has their stateliness to the experience of grief? (Perhaps one may argue that the term suggests that they go on to fulfill their missions, unperturbed and with no regard for the speaker's mood. But this interpretation is forced, and even under forcing, the yield of relevance is small.)

Again, consider the status of the past as it appears in this poem: the hand is vanished, the voice is still. It is true, as the poem itself indicates, that there is a sense in which the hand has not vanished and the voice is yet heard; otherwise we should not have the poem at all. But the poet makes no effort to connect this activity, still alive in memory, with its former "actual" life. He is content to keep close to the conventional prose account of such matters. Memory in this poem does not become a kind of life: it is just "memory"—whatever that is—and, in reading the poem, we are not forced beyond the bounds of our conventional thinking on the subject.

In the same way, the elements of the line, "the tender grace of a day that is dead," remain frozen at the conventional prose level. The day is "dead"; the "tender grace" of it will never "come back" to him. We are not encouraged to take the poignance of his present memory of it as a ghost from the tomb. The poet does not recognize that his experience represents such an ironical resurrection; nor does he allow the metaphors buried in "dead" and "come back" to suffer a resurrection into vigorous poetic life. With such phenomena the poet is not concerned.

Of course, the poet *need* not be concerned with them; I should agree that we have no right to demand that this poem should explore the nature of memory as "Tears, Idle Tears" explores it. At moments, men are unaccountably saddened by scenes which are in themselves placid and even happy. The poet is certainly entitled, if he chooses, to let it go at that. Yet, it should be observed that in avoiding the psychological exploration of the experience, the poet risks losing dramatic force.

Mere psychological analysis is, of course, not enough to insure dramatic force; and such analysis, moreover, carries its own risks: the poem may become unnatural and coldly rhetorical. But when the poet is able, as in "Tears, Idle Tears," to analyze his experience, and in the full light of the disparity and even apparent contradiction of the various elements, bring them into a new unity, he secures not only richness and depth but dramatic power as well. Our conventional accounts of poetry which oppose emotion to intellect, "lyric simplicity" to "thoughtful meditation," have done no service to the cause of poetry. The opposition is not only merely superficial: it falsifies the real relationships. For the lyric quality, if it be genuine, is not the result of some transparent and "simple" redaction of a theme or a situation which is somehow poetic in itself; it is, rather, the result of an imaginative grasp of diverse materials—but an imaginative grasp so sure that it may show itself to the reader as unstudied and unpredictable without for a moment relaxing its hold on the intricate and complex stuff which it carries.

"Among School Children" has more than one point of resemblance with Wordsworth's "Intimations" ode. In both poems the mature man confronts the child and meditates on what has been gained and what lost in the process of growing up. In Yeats's poem, to be sure, the children are met inside the schoolroom; they are not outside gamboling with the lambs on a spring morning when "every beast keeps holiday"; and in Yeats's poem the children are not oblivious of his presence but gaze "in momentary wonder." "Among School Children" is more realistic than Wordsworth's poem in its opening, more casual in its tone, more indirect in its progression. Yet the resemblance between the poems extends even so far as a common reference to the Platonic doctrine of prenatal recollection. If the babe's soul does not come into the world of Yeats's poem "trailing clouds of glory," still the soul is conceived to be capable of trying to escape the penalty of birth—

> *What youthful mother, a shape upon her lap*
> *Honey of generation had betrayed,*
> *And that must sleep, shriek, struggle to escape*
> *As recollection or the drug decide . . .*

Yeats has supplied a note on the lines: "I have taken 'the honey of generation' from Porphyry's essay on 'The Cave of the Nymphs,' but find no warrant in Porphyry

for considering it the 'drug' that destroys the 'recollec-
tion' of prenatal freedom. He blamed a cup of oblivion,
given in the zodiacal sign of Cancer."

This is fantastic, and would have been considered so
by Wordsworth no less than by ourselves. Wordsworth,
in his poem, was careful to append a note explicitly
repudiating any "real" belief in the notion of pre-
natal recollection which some of the lines of the "Ode"
seem to reflect. Yeats, presumably, assumed that the
casualness and realism of his poem—"one child or
t'other there"—"Upon the bottom of a king of kings"
—"a comfortable kind of old scarecrow"—would, of
itself, maintain the balance. At any rate, that is what
he does: the texture of the poem itself supplies what-
ever qualification the doctrine ought to receive, for the
note puts the doctrine forward quite without apologies.

But the common reference to the prenatal recollec-
tion is perhaps an accidental oddity; in the case of
neither poem is it a point of first importance. What
the "Ode" and "Among School Children" have in com-
mon that is of primary significance is a reliance on
what is essentially the same dramatic situation, and
a common dependence on a complex symbolism. If
Wordsworth's poem is at once more general with regard
to the initial situation and more direct in its attack
upon its theme, still, even here, as we have seen, the
life of the poem resides in the vitality of the imagery
which—almost in spite of Wordsworth himself—comes
to develop and carry the theme.

Yeats, on the other hand, is willing from the start
to commit the development of his theme to the imagery
—even to the special imagery of the particular scene in
the schoolroom with which the poem opens. The dra-
matic method is that of an apparently rambling and
whimsical meditation which meanders toward no goal
in particular. One item of reflection suggests another

until, at the end of the poem, the stream of consciousness has flowed with all the seeming purposelessness of a real stream to a point far from its source, casually floating on its surface references to Leda, Plato, the ugly duckling, and a host of personal reminiscences.

Certainly, as compared with Wordsworth's pattern of statement of the problem, development of the problem, solution of the problem, the progression of "Among School Children" seems aimless. Yet Yeats's poem has an inner logic more strict than Wordsworth's. There is an absolute economy of symbol. There is no waste motion. The poem moves, by what turns out on inspection to be the shortest route, to its determined goal.

That goal, one should not need to say, is not some abstract proposition about old age or education or life in general. If the goal were an abstract proposition, the statement that the poem takes the shortest route to it would be nonsense. The six stanzas which intervene between the opening scene and the statement that "Labour is blossoming or dancing, etc." are not so many pleasant distractions from the culminating observaion. Not only do they justify that observation dramatically but they so qualify it that it "means" something very different from what it would mean if we took it in isolation. One can, and must, go further: the very inconsequence of some of the reflection—the apparent aimlessness itself of the progression—are brought to bear upon the final statement. If they account for it, in a sense they also guarantee its validity. For they suggest that it is not a "loaded" statement prepared beforehand, and forced upon the occasion; but rather a statement which the impact of the opening scene has precipitated out of the experience of a lifetime.

The movement of the verse which describes the occasion for the meditation is pleasantly sing-song:

> *The children learn to cipher and to sing,*
> *To study reading-books and history,*
> *To cut and sew, be neat in everything . . .*

Dramatically, the effect is just right, for all that is said is thoroughly predictable. We are not really listening to the kind old nun's explanations. We need not be —we shall miss nothing. We, like the speaker, are watching the children, who, staring at the new arrival in "momentary wonder," are not listening either.

The abrupt transition to the next stanza is thus partially prepared for, though the contrast between the humdrum world of the modern schoolroom and the world announced by "I dream of a Ledaean body" is decisively sharp. What right has a "sixty-year-old smiling public man" to dream of Ledaean bodies? And on this, of all occasions? The schoolroom, filled with little girls, presided over by the kind old nun, and dedicated to education "In the best modern way" has, apparently, nothing to do with the heroic and sensuous world of the mother of Helen of Troy.

Yet the two worlds are connected. One of the little girls has reminded him of a "Ledaean body, bent/ Above a sinking fire," reciting to him some sorrow out of her childhood. He cannot remember what the sorrow was which she

> *Told of a harsh reproof, or trivial event . . .*

But the sense of sympathetic union was intense, and remains memorable: their two natures were

> *. . . blent*
> *Into a sphere from youthful sympathy.*

In Yeats's system of symbols, man and woman are related as the two cones in his figure of the double cone—one waxing as the other wanes, waning as the

other waxes—in dynamic antithesis. The sphere, by
contrast, is a type of harmony and repose. The blend-
ing of nature which they experienced went beyond
sexual attraction and repulsion: it was a childlike unity
of being.

In attempting to describe it, the speaker ventures
one more comparison. He turns from his own parable
to Plato's. In the "Symposium" Plato has Aristophanes
account for the origin of love in the following myth:
men were originally double; in punishment for their
attack on the gods, Zeus split them in two "as you
might divide an egg with a hair"; and ever since, the
half-men have tried to unite with each other. But the
speaker "alters" the parable: the speaker's union with
his loved one was more intimate still: it was more than
the halves of the egg coming together: their natures
blent "Into the yolk and white of the one shell."

The reference to the egg owes most of course to
Plato's parable. But the egg image ties in with other
elements already suggested in the poem—with the swan
image, of course; but also with the theme of becoming,
a theme which is later to be developed powerfully in
the poem. The suggestion is that "youthful sympathy,"
sympathy as of children, is the strongest tie of all: the
man and woman become one in going back into the
past—into the egg itself, as it were. From the egg, they
have diverged more and more through the process of
time—have become birds of a very different feather;
she, a "daughter of the swan"; he, a "scarecrow."

But as a child, she must have looked just like this
little girl or that one in the schoolroom, for every
daughter of the swan was an "ugly duckling" once.
Both the fairy story with its associations with child-
hood and the heroic legend out of Greek mythology are
levied upon. Yet the collocation of these items is not
an idle, "witty" association: the very jarring of the

collocation reflects the theme itself: the development of the gangly legged little girl into the beautiful woman, or—for the matter may be reversed—the development of the child which was himself, the child with its once "pretty plumage," into the old clothes draped on old sticks "to scare a bird."

On the flood of recollection, her present image *floats* into his mind, as the swan itself might float into view. It is as ideal as if a painter like Botticelli, say, had fashioned it

> *Hollow of cheek as though it drank the wind*
> *And took a mess of shadows for its meat . . .*

Several critics with whom I never disagree without a certain hesitance have taken these lines to mean that the beloved woman is now old with her beauty in decay. But I believe that, in making this interpretation, they have allowed themselves to be too much influenced by the assumption that the woman in Yeats's thought must be Maude Gonne; and have therefore concluded, from the dates of the poem—the perils of biographical bias!—that the Ledaean body is that of an old woman. But the lines in question do not require such an interpretation. And, in any case, what the lines insist on is the contrast between the ugly duckling and the swan, upon the transcendence of the "paddler's heritage" and its common earthiness by the developed beauty that seems so spiritual that one cannot believe that it has been nourished on common food.

With Stanza V, the theme is generalized: what youthful mother would think her birthpangs compensated if she could see at that moment her son as he is to look sixty years later. The present formless anonymity of the babe is hinted at by twice referring to the babe as a "shape." As shape, it is pure potentiality—plastic enough to be molded even to a mother's dream. But the reality, whatever it will come to be, will deny the mother's dream.

How is the formless given form? Where do the forms come from? It is the prime problem of Greek philosophy. The Greek philosophers come into his mind, three famous examples of *bipes implumis*, who for all their fame, ended as scarecrows too—

Old clothes upon old sticks to scare a bird.

But even here with the explicit reference to the philosophers, the tone of half-amused whimsy is not relaxed. We are not confronted with summaries of philosophies so much as with personalities, and personalities in characteristic activity. Plato's thought is given again in "parable" form—though the parable is brilliantly apt: nature is a mist playing over the divine forms, half revealing, half concealing them. But with the mention of Aristotle we get, not speculation but application: Aristotle is imposing the form on the more or less tractable material, forming the mind of the schoolboy Alexander by playing the cat-o-nine-tails on his bottom. (The lines are a reminder that the meditation has not actually taken us very far away from the schoolroom setting after all.)

The third representative of philosophy, Pythagoras, presided over by careless muses, fiddles his intuitions "on a fiddle-stick or strings." But if we are inclined to take Pythagoras to be the hero of the scene, we are reminded that even the golden thighs with which his disciples credited him as a proof of his divinity become eventually "old sticks" supporting "old clothes" . . . "to scare a bird." The minds of the philosophers, with all their diverse speculations, may disagree; but the testimony of their bodies comes to complete agreement. The pretty plumage disappears, and the man, now a mere effigy of a man, is calculated to repel the Ledaean body.

But the poet insists on a wider reference still. It is not merely the Platonic Ideas which may be said to mock, in their divine ideality, the material objects in which they are imperfectly realized. This is true of all ideals, and true not only for the philosopher but even for those human beings who take life most "concretely." For among the "Presences," as he calls them, he includes those images which "animate a mother's reveries" and those which the "nuns . . . worship." If the latter seem unchanging (as compared to the mother's dreams for her child) and "keep a marble or a bronze repose," yet they too break hearts. It is to the "Presences" that he addresses the vision of totality of being and unity of being which occupies the last stanza. What is drudgery becomes "blossoming or dancing where/ The body is not bruised to pleasure soul."

In the total activity, one can separate the actor from the action only by an act of abstraction. What is the tree—leaf, blossom, or bole? When the dance is completed, has not the dancer ceased to be a dancer? Yet, is the last line a powerful insight or an obvious quibble? Does this whole last stanza, with all of its power and beauty, constitute the poet's refutation to Plato and all cruel idealisms? Or, does it mark a desertion of —or a transcendence of—the common-sense world in which we feel we have so little difficulty in distinguishing dancers from the dances in which they engage?

Even a careful paraphrase of the stanza may distort what is being said. Certainly, we ought to do no less here than to apply Yeats's doctrine to his own poem. The poem, like the "great rooted blossomer" that it celebrates is not to be isolated in the "statement" made by Stanza V or by Stanza VII or by Stanza VIII. Nor is it—doctrine of desperation—to be isolated in the

flowering of a few delightful images. We must examine
the bole and the roots, and most of all, their organic
interrelations.

In the first place, one notes that the generalizations
with which the last stanza opens have been thoroughly
dramatized. Those generalizations are really extensions
of the metaphorical fabric of the poem. Throughout
the poem, birth and growth and decay have run as
motifs: more specifically, the egg, the fledgling, the full-
grown bird, the molting bird, the scarecrow; or, the
babe at birth, the child, youth and maturity, Leda and
golden-thighed Pythagoras, the man with sixty winters
on his head.

And it is these metaphors which are continued into
the concluding stanza. The very first word of that
stanza, "labour," carries an element of the birth meta-
phor as an undertone. Labor is not merely *work* but
the labor of childbirth as well. For the chestnut-tree
there are no birthpangs: "labour is blossoming." For
the great rooted blossomer it is just that—literally!

On the other hand, the worst indictment that the
poet can utter against the "mockers of man's enter-
prise" is that they are "self-born." They are *a priori;*
they know no development; they have no parentage;
they experience no old age. Like the artifacts of Yeats's
Byzantium (or like the figures on Keats's urn), they are
timeless. And the world of becoming must always suf-
fer when measured against the world of pure being.

"Among School Children," as Kenneth Burke has
suggested in his article on "Symbolic Action," balances
"Sailing to Byzantium." (The two poems, by the way,
according to Yeats's biographer, were written in the
same year.) One seems to celebrate "natural" beauty,
the world of becoming; the other, intellectual beauty,
the world of pure being. To which world is Yeats com-
mitted? Which does he choose?

The question is idle—as idle as the question which the earnest schoolmarm puts to the little girl reading for the first time "L'Allegro-Il Penseroso": which does Milton *really* prefer, mirth or melancholy? Does Yeats choose idealism or materialism—the flowering chestnut or the golden bird whose metal plumage will not molt?

Yeats chooses both and neither. One cannot know the world of being save through the world of becoming (though one must remember that the world of becoming is a meaningless flux apart from the world of being which it implies).

If the last sentence seems to make Yeats more of a metaphysician than we feel he really was, one can only appeal to the poems themselves. Both of them are shot through and through with a recognition of the problem which the reflective human being can never escape— the dilemma which is the ground of the philosophic problem; and the "solution" which is reached in neither case *solves* the problem. The poet in both cases comes to terms with the situation—develops an attitude toward the situation which everywhere witnesses to the insolubility of the problem. As I. A. Richards has suggested of Wordsworth's "Ode," so here: "Among School Children" (or, for that matter, "Sailing to Byzantium") is finally a poem "about" the nature of the human imagination itself.

It is true that the reader is tempted to say that "Among School Children" makes a protest against the imposition of all disciplines from the outside—a protest against all that "bruises" the body "to pleasure soul." Yet since all idealisms are categorized as

> . . . *self-born mockers of man's enterprise*

it is evident that the poet does not think that one could or should do away with them. If they break hearts, still they are the "Presences/ That passion, piety or affection knows." The human world of passion, piety, and affection will necessarily be a world in which those Presences exist. They are not merely a concoction of the philosophers. If the philosophers and even the nuns constitute a special case, the mothers are not special. Their worship of images is taken for granted.

The last stanza does not refute Plato—is not intended to refute him. For if we try to read into the vision of the chestnut-tree an affirmation of the beautiful, careless play of nature, and thus a rebuke to Plato's holding nature a mere play "of spume" upon a "ghostly paradigm of things"; or a taunt at Aristotle's "playing" the taws on the behind of the youthful Alexander, we remember that Pythagoras' activity is play too—fingering "upon a fiddle-stick or strings." (Perhaps one weights the word *play* too heavily. Yet the word is used specifically with regard to Plato's thought and Aristotle's action, and Pythagoras is definitely represented as playing upon an instrument. The word *play* has senses which can encompass the activity of all three and that of the dancer of the last stanza as well.)

Or, one may approach the matter in this way: is Yeats less respectful to the Greek sages of "Among School Children" than he is to the sages whom he invokes in "Sailing to Byzantium"? It is true that he visualizes these last as "standing in God's holy fire" and concerned with no activity so mundane as that of administering a spanking. Yet his last petition to them is to

> . . . *gather me*
> *Into the artifice of eternity.*

The word "artifice" fits the prayer at one level after another: the fact that he is to be taken *out of nature;* that his body is to be an artifice hammered out of gold; that it will not age but will have the finality of a work of art. But "artifice" unquestionably carries an ironic qualification too. The prayer, for all its passion, is a modest one. He does not ask that he be gathered into eternity—it will be enough if he is gathered into the "artifice of eternity." The qualification does not turn the prayer into mockery, but it is all-important: it limits as well as defines the power of the sages to whom the poet appeals.

The golden bird of "Sailing to Byzantium" and the flowering chestnut-tree of our poem are not, it should be apparent, on precisely the same level. Indeed, we need to add another term: the scarecrow. For the golden bird and the scarecrow are, as it were, limiting terms—or, if the scarecrow is not strictly a limiting term, it points to the other limit: the utter wreck and dissolution of the body in the grave. Between the limits of "unageing intellect" and the wreck of the body, are the blossoming chestnut-tree or the dancer moving through the mazes of the dance or golden-thighed Pythagoras fiddling away at his intuition of the music of the spheres. All of them represent something divine or supernatural, but as man can know it, always intermixed with the "natural." The divinely beautiful woman has not really subsisted on shadows and the wind, even if it seems that her flesh could not have been nourished on common food; the golden thighs of Pythagoras do turn to the spindly shanks of the scarecrow. Yet the tone of the poem indicates that the speaker is not mocking these intimations of the supernatural as mere easy illusions. The beloved is really worthy of the name "Ledaean"; the music of Pythagoras does give one an intimation of the song of the golden bird.

The irony of both poems is directed, it seems to me, not at our yearning to transcend the world of nature, but at the human situation itself in which supernatural

and natural are intermixed—the human situation
which is inevitably caught between the claims of both
natural and supernatural. The golden bird whose
bodily form the speaker will take in Byzantium will be
withdrawn from the flux of the world of becoming. But
so withdrawn, it will sing of the world of becoming—
"Of what is past, or passing, or to come." Removed
from that world, it will *know* as the chestnut-tree im-
mersed in life, drenched in the world of becoming can-
not know. Full life is instinctive like the life of Words-
worth's child. It is a harmony which is too blind to be
aware of its own harmony. Here we have the dilemma
of Wordsworth's "Intimations" ode all over again. The
mature man can see the harmony, the unity of being,
possessed by the tree or the lamb or the child; but the
price of being able to see it is not to possess it in one's
self, just at the price of possessing it in one's self is an
unawareness that one does possess it. Or to state the
matter in Yeats's own terms:

> *For wisdom is the property of the dead,*
> *A something incompatible with life . . .*

Or, again, as Yeats liked to put it in the letters of his
last years: "man can embody truth but he cannot know
truth."

But, in attempting to reconcile the "meanings" of
the two poems, one should not tempt the reader to
substitute another abstract proposition for the "mean-
ing." What is important is that, in the case of either
poem, any statement which we attempt to abstract from
the whole context as the "meaning" of the poem is
seen to be qualified and modified by the context of
the poem taken as a whole.

The poem is a dramatization, not a formula; a con-
trolled experience which has to be *experienced,* not a
logical process, the conclusion of which is reached by

logical methods and the validity of which can be checked by logical tests. In each case, the unifying principle of the organization which *is* the poem is an attitude or complex of attitudes. We can discover, to be sure, propositions which seem to characterize, more or less accurately, the unifying attitude. But if we take such propositions to be the core of the poem we are contenting ourselves with reductions and substitutions. To do this, is to take the root or the blossoms of the tree for the tree itself.

The point is not a very abstruse one. It seems worth repeating here only because many of our professors and popular reviewers continue to act as if it were an esoteric principle. Our staple study of literature consists in investigations of the root system (the study of literary sources) or in sniffing the blossoms (impressionism), or—not to neglect Yeats's alternative symbol—in questioning the quondam dancer, no longer a dancer, about her life history (the study of the poet's biography).

I want to use the metaphor fairly: it is entirely legitimate to inquire into the dancer's history, and such an inquiry is certainly interesting for its own sake, and may be of value for our understanding of the dance. But we cannot question her as dancer without stopping the dance or waiting until the dance has been completed. And in so far as our interest is in poetry, the dance must be primary for us. We cannot afford to neglect it; no amount of notes on the personal history of the dancer will prove to be a substitute for it; and even our knowledge of the dancer *qua* dancer will depend in some measure upon it: How else can we know her? "How can we know the dancer from the dance?"

CHAPTER ELEVEN
THE HERESY OF PARAPHRASE

The ten poems that have been discussed were not se-
lected because they happened to express a common
theme or to display some particular style or to share
a special set of symbols. It has proved, as a matter of
fact, somewhat surprising to see how many items they
do have in common: the light symbolism as used in
"L'Allegro-Il Penseroso" and in the "Intimations" ode,
for example; or, death as a sexual metaphor in "The
Canonization" and in *The Rape of the Lock;* or the
similarity of problem and theme in the "Intimations"
ode and "Among School Children."

On reflection, however, it would probably warrant
more surprise if these ten poems did not have much in
common. For they are all poems which most of us will
feel are close to the central stream of the tradition.
Indeed, if there is any doubt on this point, it will have
to do with only the first and last members of the series
—poems whose relation to the tradition I shall, for
reasons to be given a little later, be glad to waive. The
others, it will be granted, are surely in the main stream
of the tradition.

As a matter of fact, a number of the poems dis-
cussed in this book were not chosen by me but were
chosen for me. But having written on these, I found
that by adding a few poems I could construct a chrono-
logical series which (though it makes no pretension

to being exhaustive of periods or types) would not leave seriously unrepresented any important period since Shakespeare. In filling the gaps I tried to select poems which had been held in favor in their own day and which most critics still admire. There were, for example, to be no "metaphysical" poems beyond the first exhibit and no "modern" ones other than the last. But the intervening poems were to be read as one has learned to read Donne and the moderns. One was to attempt to see, in terms of this approach, what the masterpieces had in common rather than to see how the poems of different historical periods differed—and in particular to see whether they had anything in common with the "metaphysicals" and with the moderns.

The reader will by this time have made up his mind as to whether the readings are adequate. (I use the word advisedly, for the readings do not pretend to be exhaustive, and certainly it is highly unlikely that they are not in error in one detail or another.) If the reader feels that they are seriously inadequate, then the case has been judged; for the generalizations that follow will be thoroughly vitiated by the inept handling of the particular cases on which they depend.

If, however, the reader does feel them to be adequate, it ought to be readily apparent that the common goodness which the poems share will have to be stated, not in terms of "content" or "subject matter" in the usual sense in which we use these terms, but rather in terms of structure. The "content" of the poems is various, and if we attempt to find one *quality* of content which is shared by all the poems—a "poetic" subject matter or diction or imagery—we shall find that we have merely confused the issues. For what is it to be poetic? Is the schoolroom of Yeats's poem poetic or unpoetic? Is Shakespeare's "new-borne babe/ Striding the blast" poetic whereas the idiot of his "Life is a tale tolde by an idiot" is unpoetic? If Herrick's "budding boy or girl" is poetic, then why is not that monstrosity of the newspaper's society page, the "society bud," poetic too?

To say this is not, of course, to say that all materials have precisely the same potentialities (as if the various pigments on the palette had the same potentialities, any one of them suiting the given picture as well as another). But what has been said, on the other hand, requires to be said: for, if we are to proceed at all, we must draw a sharp distinction between the attractiveness or beauty of any particular item taken as such and the "beauty" of the poem considered as a whole. The latter is the effect of a total pattern, and of a kind of pattern which can incorporate within itself items intrinsically beautiful or ugly, attractive or repulsive. Unless one asserts the primacy of the pattern, a poem becomes merely a bouquet of intrinsically beautiful items.

But though it is in terms of structure that we must describe poetry, the term "structure" is certainly not altogether satisfactory as a term. One means by it something far more internal than the metrical pattern, say, or than the sequence of images. The structure meant is certainly not "form" in the conventional sense in which we think of form as a kind of envelope which "contains" the "content." The structure obviously is everywhere conditioned by the nature of the material which goes into the poem. The nature of the material sets the problem to be solved, and the solution is the ordering of the material.

Pope's *Rape of the Lock* will illustrate: the structure is not the heroic couplet as such, or the canto arrangement; for, important as is Pope's use of the couplet as one means by which he secures the total effect, the heroic couplet can be used—has been used many times

—as an instrument in securing very different effects. The structure of the poem, furthermore, is not that of the mock-epic convention, though here, since the term "mock-epic" has implications of attitude, we approach a little nearer to the kind of structure of which we speak.

The structure meant is a structure of meanings, evaluations, and interpretations; and the principle of unity which informs it seems to be one of balancing and harmonizing connotations, attitudes, and meanings. But even here one needs to make important qualifications: the principle is not one which involves the arrangement of the various elements into homogeneous groupings, pairing like with like. It unites the like with the unlike. It does not unite them, however, by the simple process of allowing one connotation to cancel out another nor does it reduce the contradictory attitudes to harmony by a process of subtraction. The unity is not a unity of the sort to be achieved by the reduction and simplification appropriate to an algebraic formula. It is a positive unity, not a negative; it represents not a residue but an achieved harmony.

The attempt to deal with a structure such as this may account for the frequent occurrence in the preceding chapters of such terms as "ambiguity," "paradox," "complex of attitudes," and—most frequent of all, and perhaps most annoying to the reader—"irony." I hasten to add that I hold no brief for these terms as such. Perhaps they are inadequate. Perhaps they are misleading. It is to be hoped in that case that we can eventually improve upon them. But adequate terms—whatever those terms may turn out to be—will certainly have to be terms which do justice to the special kind of structure which seems to emerge as the common structure of poems so diverse on other counts as are *The Rape of the Lock* and "Tears, Idle Tears."

The conventional terms are much worse than in-adequate: they are positively misleading in their im-plication that the poem constitutes a "statement" of some sort, the statement being true or false, and ex-pressed more or less clearly or eloquently or beautifully; for it is from this formula that most of the common heresies about poetry derive. The formula begins by introducing a dualism which thenceforward is rarely overcome, and which at best can be overcome only by the most elaborate and clumsy qualifications. Where it is not overcome, it leaves the critic lodged upon one or the other of the horns of a dilemma: the critic is forced to judge the poem by its political or scientific or philosophical truth; or, he is forced to judge the poem by its form as conceived externally and detached from human experience. Mr. Alfred Kazin, for example, to take an instance from a recent and popular book, accuses the "new formalists"—his choice of that epithet is revealing—of accepting the latter horn of the dilem-ma because he notices that they have refused the former. In other words, since they refuse to rank poems by their messages, he assumes that they are compelled to rank them by their formal embellishments.

The omnipresence of this dilemma, a false dilemma, I believe, will also account for the fact that so much has been made in the preceding chapters of the resist-ance which any good poem sets up against all attempts to paraphrase it. The point is surely not that we cannot describe adequately enough for many purposes what the poem in general is "about" and what the general effect of the poem is: *The Rape of the Lock* is *about* the foibles of an eighteenth-century belle. The effect of "Corinna's going a-Maying" is one of gaiety tempered by the poignance of the fleetingness of youth. We can very properly use paraphrases as pointers and as short-hand references provided that we know what we are doing. But it is highly important that we know what we are doing and that we see plainly that the paraphrase is not the real core of meaning which constitutes the essence of the poem.

For the imagery and the rhythm are not merely the instruments by which this fancied core-of-meaning-which-can-be-expressed-in-a-paraphrase is directly rendered. Even in the simplest poem their mediation is not positive and direct. Indeed, whatever statement we may seize upon as incorporating the "meaning" of the poem, immediately the imagery and the rhythm seem to set up tensions with it, warping and twisting it, qualifying and revising it. This is true of Wordsworth's "Ode" no less than of Donne's "Canonization." To illustrate: if we say that the "Ode" celebrates the spontaneous "naturalness" of the child, there is the poem itself to indicate that Nature has a more sinister aspect—that the process by which the poetic lamb becomes the dirty old sheep or the child racing over the meadows becomes the balding philosopher is a process that is thoroughly "natural." Or, if we say that the thesis of the "Ode" is that the child brings into the natural world a supernatural glory which acquaintance with the world eventually and inevitably quenches in the light of common day, there is the last stanza and the drastic qualifications which it asserts: it is significant that the thoughts that lie too deep for tears are mentioned in this sunset stanza of the "Ode" and that they are thoughts, not of the child, but of the man.

We have precisely the same problem if we make our example *The Rape of the Lock*. Does the poet assert that Belinda is a goddess? Or does he say that she is a brainless chit? Whichever alternative we take, there are elaborate qualifications to be made. Moreover, if the simple propositions offered seem in their forthright simplicity to make too easy the victory of the poem over any possible statement of its meaning, then let the reader try to formulate a proposition that will say what the poem "says." As his proposition approaches adequacy, he will find, not only that it has increased greatly in length, but that it has begun to fill itself up with reservations and qualifications—and most significant of all—the formulator will find that he has himself begun to fall back upon metaphors of his own in his attempt to indicate what the poem "says." In sum, his proposition, as it approaches adequacy, ceases to be a proposition.

Consider one more case, "Corinna's going a-Maying." Is the doctrine preached to Corinna throughout the first four stanzas true? Or is it damnably false? Or is it a "harmlesse follie"? Here perhaps we shall be tempted to take the last option as the saving mean—what the poem really *says*—and my account of the poem at the end of the third chapter is perhaps susceptible of this interpretation—or misinterpretation. If so, it is high time to clear the matter up. For we mistake matters grossly if we take the poem to be playing with opposed extremes, only to point the golden mean in a doctrine which, at the end, will correct the falsehood of extremes. The reconcilement of opposites which the poet characteristically makes is not that of a prudent splitting of the difference between antithetical overemphases.

It is not so in Wordsworth's poem nor in Keats's nor in Pope's. It is not so even in this poem of Herrick's. For though the poem reflects, if we read it carefully, the primacy of the Christian mores, the pressure exerted throughout the poem is upon the pagan appeal; and the poem ends, significantly, with a reiteration of the appeal to Corinna to go a-Maying, an appeal which, if qualified by the Christian view, still, in a sense, has been deepened and made more urgent by that very qualification. The imagery of loss and decay, it must be remembered, comes in this last stanza after the admission that the May-day rites are not a real religion but a "harmless follie."

If we are to get all these qualifications into our formulation of what the poem says—and they are relevant —then, our formulation of the "statement" made by Herrick's poem will turn out to be quite as difficult as that of Pope's mock-epic. The truth of the matter is that all such formulations lead away from the center of the poem—not toward it; that the "prose-sense" of the poem is not a rack on which the stuff of the poem is hung; that it does not represent the "inner" structure or the "essential" structure or the "real" structure of the poem. We may use—and in many connections must use—such formulations as more or less convenient ways of referring to parts of the poem. But such formulations are scaffoldings which we may properly for certain purposes throw about the building: we must not mistake them for the internal and essential structure of the building itself.

Indeed, one may sum up by saying that most of the distempers of criticism come about from yielding to the temptation to take certain remarks which we make *about* the poem—statements about what it says or about what truth it gives or about what formulations it illustrates—for the essential core of the poem itself. As W. M. Urban puts it in his *Language and Reality:* "The general principle of the inseparability of intuition and expression holds with special force for the aesthetic intuition. Here it means that form and content, or content and medium, are inseparable. The artist does not first intuit his object and then find the appropriate medium. It is rather in and through his medium that he intuits the object." So much for the process of composition. As for the critical process: "To pass from the intuitible to the nonintuitible is to negate the function and meaning of the symbol." For it "is precisely because the more universal and ideal relations cannot be adequately expressed directly that they are indirectly expressed by means of the more intuitible." The most obvious examples of such error (and for that reason those which are really least dangerous) are those theories which frankly treat the poem as propaganda. The most subtle (and the most stubbornly rooted in the ambiguities of language) are those which, beginning with the "paraphrasable" elements of the poem, refer the other elements of the poem finally to some role subordinate to the paraphrasable elements. (The relation between all the elements must surely be an organic one—there can be no question about that. There is, however, a very serious question as to whether the paraphrasable elements have primacy.)

Mr. Winters' position will furnish perhaps the most respectable example of the paraphrastic heresy. He assigns primacy to the "rational meaning" of the poem. "The relationship, in the poem, between rational statement and feeling," he remarks in his latest book, "is thus seen to be that of motive to emotion." He goes on to illustrate his point by a brief and excellent analysis of the following lines from Browning:

> So wore night; the East was gray,
>   White the broad-faced hemlock flowers. . . .

"The verb wore," he continues, "means literally that the night passed, but it carries with it connotations of exhaustion and attrition which belong to the condition of the protagonist; and grayness is a color which we associate with such a condition. If we change the phrase to read: 'Thus night passed,' we shall have the same rational meaning, and a meter quite as respectable, but no trace of the power of the line: the connotation of *wore* will be lost, and the connotation of *gray* will remain in a state of ineffective potentiality."

But the word *wore* does not mean *literally* "that the night passed," it means literally "that the night *wore*" —whatever *wore* may mean, and as Winters' own admirable analysis indicates, *wore* "means," whether *rationally* or *irrationally,* a great deal. Furthermore, "So wore night" and "Thus night passed" can be said to have "the same rational meaning" only if we equate "rational meaning" with the meaning of a loose paraphrase. And can a loose paraphrase be said to be the "motive to emotion"? Can it be said to "generate" the feelings in question? (Or, would Mr. Winters not have us equate "rational statement" and "rational meaning"?)

Much more is at stake here than any quibble. In view of the store which Winters sets by rationality and of his penchant for poems which make their evaluations overtly, and in view of his frequent blindness to those poems which do not—in view of these considerations, it is important to see that what "So wore night" and "Thus night passed" have in common as their "rational meaning" is not the "rational meaning" of each but the lowest common denominator of both. To refer the structure of the poem to what is finally a paraphrase of the poem is to refer it to something outside the poem.

To repeat, most of our difficulties in criticism are rooted in the heresy of paraphrase. If we allow ourselves to be misled by it, we distort the relation of the poem to its "truth," we raise the problem of belief in a vicious and crippling form, we split the poem between its "form" and its "content"—we bring the statement to be conveyed into an unreal competition with science or philosophy or theology. In short, we put our ques-

tions about the poem in a form calculated to produce
the battles of the last twenty-five years over the "use of
poetry." *

If we allow ourselves to be misled by the heresy of
paraphrase, we run the risk of doing even more violence
to the internal order of the poem itself. By taking the
paraphrase as our point of stance, we misconceive the
function of metaphor and meter. We demand logical
coherences where they are sometimes irrelevant, and
we fail frequently to see imaginative coherences on
levels where they are highly relevant. Some of the im-
plications of the paraphrastic heresy are so stubborn
and so involved that I have thought best to relegate
them to an appendix. There the reader who is in-
terested may find further discussion of the problem and,
I could hope, answers to certain misapprehensions of
the positive theory to be adumbrated here.

But what would be a positive theory? We tend to em-
brace the doctrine of a logical structure the more
readily because, to many of us, the failure to do so
seems to leave the meaning of the poem hopelessly up
in the air. The alternative position will appear to us to
lack even the relative stability of an Ivory Tower: it
is rather commitment to a free balloon. For, to deny the
possibility of pinning down what the poem "says" to
some "statement" will seem to assert that the poem
really says nothing. And to point out what has been
suggested in earlier chapters and brought to a head in
this one, namely, that one can never measure a poem
against the scientific or philosophical yardstick for the
reason that the poem, when laid along the yardstick, is
never the "full poem" but an abstraction from the poem

---

* I do not, of course, intend to minimize the fact that some
of these battles have been highly profitable, or to imply that
the foregoing paragraphs could have been written except for the
illumination shed by the discussions of the last twenty-five years.

—such an argument will seem to such readers a piece of barren logic-chopping—a transparent dodge.

Considerations of strategy then, if nothing more, dictate some positive account of what a poem is and does. And some positive account can be given, though I cannot promise to do more than suggest what a poem is, nor will my terms turn out to be anything more than metaphors.*

The essential structure of a poem (as distinguished from the rational or logical structure of the "statement" which we abstract from it) resembles that of architecture or painting: it is a pattern of resolved stresses. Or, to move closer still to poetry by considering the temporal arts, the structure of a poem resembles that of a ballet or musical composition. It is a pattern of resolutions and balances and harmonizations, developed through a temporal scheme.†

* For those who cannot be content with metaphors (or with the particular metaphors which I can give) I recommend Rene Wellek's excellent "The Mode of Existence of a Literary Work of Art" (*The Southern Review*, Spring, 1942). I shall not try to reproduce here as a handy, thumb-nail definition his account of a poem as "a stratified system of norms," for the definition would be relatively meaningless without the further definitions which he assigns to the individual terms which he uses. I have made no special use of his terms in this chapter, but I believe that the generalizations about poetry outlined here can be thoroughly accommodated to the position which his essay sets forth.

† In recent numbers of *Accent*, two critics for whose work I have high regard have emphasized the dynamic character of poetry. Kenneth Burke argues that if we are to consider a poem as a poem, we must consider it as a "mode of action." R. P. Blackmur asks us to think of it as gesture, "the outward and dramatic play of inward and imagined meaning." I do not mean to commit either of these critics to my own interpretation of dramatic or symbolic action; and I have, on my own part, several rather important reservations with respect to Mr. Burke's position. But there are certainly large areas of agreement among our positions. The reader might also compare the account of poetic structure given in this chapter with the following passage from Susanne Langer's *Philosophy in a New Key:* ". . . though the *material* of poetry is

Or, to move still closer to poetry, the structure of a poem resembles that of a play. This last example, of course, risks introducing once more the distracting element, since drama, like poetry, makes use of words. Yet, on the whole, most of us are less inclined to force the concept of "statement" on drama than on a lyric poem; for the very nature of drama is that of something "acted out"—something which arrives at its conclusion through conflict—something which builds conflict into its very being. The dynamic nature of drama, in short, allows us to regard it as *an action* rather than as a formula for action or as a statement about action. For this reason, therefore, perhaps the most helpful analogy by which to suggest the structure of poetry is that of the drama, and for many readers at least, the least confusing way in which to approach a poem is to think of it as a drama.

The general point, of course, is not that either poetry or drama makes no use of ideas, or that either is "merely emotional"—whatever *that* is—or that there is not the closest and most important relationship between the intellectual materials which they absorb into their structure and other elements in the structure. The relationship between the intellectual and the non-intellectual elements in a poem is actually far more intimate than the conventional accounts would represent it to be: the relationship is not that of an idea "wrapped in emotion" or a "prose-sense decorated by sensuous imagery."

---

verbal, its import is not the literal assertion made in the words, but *the way the assertion is made,* and this involves the sound, the tempo, the aura of associations of the words, the long or short sequences of ideas, the wealth or poverty of transient imagery that contains them, the sudden arrest of fantasy by pure fact, or of familiar fact by sudden fantasy, the suspense of literal meaning by a sustained ambiguity resolved in a long-awaited key-word, and the unifying, all-embracing artifice of rhythm."

The dimension in which the poem moves is not one which excludes ideas, but one which does include attitudes. The dimension includes ideas, to be sure; we can always abstract an "idea" from a poem—even from the simplest poem—even from a lyric so simple and unintellectual as

> *Western wind, when wilt thou blow*
> *That the small rain down can rain?*
> *Christ, that my love were in my arms*
> *And I in my bed again!*

But the idea which we abstract—assuming that we can all agree on what that idea is—will always be *abstracted:* it will always be the projection of a plane along a line or the projection of a cone upon a plane.

If this last analogy proves to be more confusing than illuminating, let us return to the analogy with drama. We have argued that any proposition asserted in a poem is not to be taken in abstraction but is justified, in terms of the poem, if it is justified at all, not by virtue of its scientific or historical or philosophical truth, but is justified in terms of a principle analogous to that of dramatic propriety. Thus, the proposition that "Beauty is truth, truth beauty" is given its precise meaning and significance by its relation to the total context of the poem.

This principle is easy enough to see when the proposition is asserted overtly in the poem—that is, when it constitutes a specific detail of the poem. But the reader may well ask: is it not possible to frame a proposition, a statement, which will adequately represent the total meaning of the poem; that is, is it not possible to elaborate a summarizing proposition which will "say," briefly and in the form of a proposition, what the poem "says" as a poem, a proposition which will say it fully and will say it exactly, no more and no less? Could not the poet, if he had chosen, have framed such a proposition? Cannot we as readers and critics frame such a proposition?

The answer must be that the poet himself obviously did not—else he would not have had to write his poem. We as readers can attempt to frame such a proposition in our effort to understand the poem; it may well help toward an understanding. Certainly, the efforts to arrive at such propositions can do no harm *if we do not mistake them for the inner core of the poem*—if we do not mistake them for "what the poem *really* says." For, if we take one of them to represent the essential poem, we have to disregard the qualifications exerted by the total context as of no account, or else we have assumed that we can reproduce the effect of the total context in a condensed prose statement.*

But to deny that the coherence of a poem is reflected in a logical paraphrase of its "real meaning" is not, of course, to deny coherence to poetry; it is rather to assert that its coherence is to be sought elsewhere. The

---

* We may, it is true, be able to adumbrate what the poem says if we allow ourselves enough words, and if we make enough reservations and qualifications, thus attempting to come nearer to the meaning of the poem by successive approximations and refinements, gradually encompassing the meaning and pointing to the area in which it lies rather than realizing it. The earlier chapters of this book, if they are successful, are obviously illustrations of this process. But such adumbrations will lack, not only the tension—the dramatic force—of the poem; they will be at best crude approximations of the poem. Moreover—and this is the crucial point—they will be compelled to resort to the methods of the poem—analogy, metaphor, symbol, etc.—in order to secure even this near an approximation.

Urban's comment upon this problem is interesting: he says that if we expand the symbol, "we lose the 'sense' or value of the symbol *as symbol*. The solution . . . seems to me to lie in an adequate theory of interpretation of the symbol. It does not consist in substituting *literal* for symbol sentences, in other words substituting 'blunt' truth for symbolic truth, but rather in deepening and enriching the meaning of the symbol."

characteristic unity of a poem (even of those poems which may accidentally possess a logical unity as well as this poetic unity) lies in the unification of attitudes into a hierarchy subordinated to a total and governing attitude. In the unified poem, the poet has "come to terms" with his experience. The poem does not merely eventuate in a logical conclusion. The conclusion of the poem is the working out of the various tensions—set up by whatever means—by propositions, metaphors, symbols. The unity is achieved by a dramatic process, not a logical; it represents an equilibrium of forces, not a formula. It is "proved" as a dramatic conclusion is proved: by its ability to resolve the conflicts which have been accepted as the *données* of the drama.

Thus, it is easy to see why the relation of each item to the whole context is crucial, and why the effective and essential structure of the poem has to do with the complex of attitudes achieved. A scientific preposition can stand alone. If it is true, it is true. But the expression of an attitude, apart from the occasion which generates it and the situation which it encompasses, is meaningless. For example, the last two lines of the "Intimations" ode,

> *To me the meanest flower that blows can give*
> *Thoughts that do often lie too deep for tears,*

when taken in isolation—I do not mean quoted in isolation by one who is even vaguely acquainted with the context—makes a statement which is sentimental if taken in reference to the speaker, and one which is patent nonsense if taken with a general reference. The man in the street (of whom the average college freshman is a good enough replica) knows that the meanest flower that grows does not give *him* thoughts that lie too deep for tears; and, if he thinks about the matter at all, he is inclined to feel that the person who can make such an assertion is a very fuzzy sentimentalist.

We have already seen the ease with which the statement "Beauty is truth, truth beauty" becomes detached from its context, even in the hands of able critics; and we have seen the misconceptions that ensue when this detachment occurs. To take one more instance: the last stanza of Herrick's "Corinna," taken in isolation, would probably not impress the average reader as sentimental nonsense. Yet it would suffer quite as much by isolation from its context as would the lines from Keats's "Ode." For, as mere statement, it would become something flat and obvious—of course our lives are short! And the conclusion from the fact would turn into an obvious truism for the convinced pagan, and, for the convinced Christian, equally obvious, though damnable, nonsense.

Perhaps this is why the poet, to people interested in hard-and-fast generalizations, must always seem to be continually engaged in blurring out distinctions, effecting compromises, or, at the best, coming to his conclusions only after provoking and unnecessary delays. But this last position is merely another variant of the paraphrastic heresy: to assume it is to misconceive the end of poetry—to take its meanderings as negative, or to excuse them (with the comfortable assurance that the curved line is the line of beauty) because we can conceive the purpose of a poem to be only the production, in the end, of a proposition—of a statement.

But the meanderings of a good poem (they are meanderings only from the standpoint of the prose paraphrase of the poem) are not negative, and they do not have to be excused; and most of all, we need to see what their positive function is; for unless we can assign them a positive function, we shall find it difficult to explain why one divergence from "the prose line of the argument" is not as good as another. The truth is that the apparent irrelevancies which metrical pattern and metaphor introduce do become relevant when we realize that they function in a good poem to modify, qualify, and develop the total attitude which we are to take in coming to terms with the total situation.

If the last sentence seems to take a dangerous turn toward some special "use of poetry"—some therapeutic value for the sake of which poetry is to be cultivated— I can only say that I have in mind no special ills which poetry is to cure. Uses for poetry are always to be found, and doubtless will continue to be found. But my discussion of the structure of poetry is not being conditioned at this point by some new and special role which I expect poetry to assume in the future or some new function to which I would assign it. The structure described—a structure of "gestures" or attitudes—seems to me to describe the essential structure of both the *Odyssey* and *The Waste Land*. It seems to be the kind of structure which the ten poems considered in this book possess in common.

If the structure of poetry is a structure of the order described, that fact may explain (if not justify) the frequency with which I have had to have recourse, in the foregoing chapters, to terms like "irony" and "paradox." By using the term irony, one risks, of course, making the poem seem arch and self-conscious, since irony, for most readers of poetry, is associated with satire, *vers de société,* and other "intellectual" poetries. Yet, the necessity for some such term ought to be apparent; and irony is the most general term that we have for the kind of qualification which the various elements in a context receive from the context. This kind of qualification, as we have seen, is of tremendous importance in any poem. Moreover, irony is our most general term for indicating that recognition of incongruities—

which, again, pervades all poetry to a degree far beyond what our conventional criticism has been heretofore willing to allow.

Irony in this general sense, then, is to be found in Tennyson's "Tears, Idle Tears" as well as in Donne's "Canonization." We have, of course, been taught to expect to find irony in Pope's *Rape of the Lock,* but there is a profound irony in Keats's "Ode on a Grecian Urn"; and there is irony of a very powerful sort in Wordsworth's "Intimations" ode. For the thrusts and pressures exerted by the various symbols in this poem are not avoided by the poet: they are taken into account and played, one against the other. Indeed, the symbols—from a scientific point of view—are used perversely: it is the child who is the best philosopher; it is from a kind of darkness—from something that is "shadowy"—that the light proceeds; growth into manhood is viewed, not as an extrication from, but as an incarceration within, a prison.

There should be no mystery as to why this must be so. The terms of science are abstract symbols which do not change under the pressure of the context. They are pure (or aspire to be pure) denotations; they are defined in advance. They are not to be warped into new meanings. But where is the dictionary which contains the terms of a poem? It is a truism that the poet is continually forced to remake language. As Eliot has put it, his task is to "dislocate language into meaning." And, from the standpoint of a scientific vocabulary, this is precisely what he performs: for, rationally considered, the ideal language would contain one term for each meaning, and the relation between term and meaning would be constant. But the word, as the poet uses it, has to be conceived of, not as a discrete particle of meaning, but as a potential of meaning, a nexus or cluster of meanings.

What is true of the poet's language in detail is true of the larger wholes of poetry. And therefore, if we persist in approaching the poem as primarily a rational statement, we ought not to be surprised if the statements seems to be presented to us always in the ironic mode. When we consider the statement immersed in the poem, it presents itself to us, like the stick immersed in the pool of water, warped and bent. Indeed, whatever the statement, it will always show itself as deflected away from a positive, straightforward formulation.

It may seem perverse, however, to maintain, in the face of our revived interest in Donne, that the essential structure of poetry is not logical. For Donne has been appealed to of late as the great master of metaphor who imposes a clean logic on his images beside which the ordering of the images in Shakespeare's sonnets is fumbling and loose. It is perfectly true that Donne makes a great show of logic; but two matters need to be observed. In the first place, the elaborated and "logical" figure is not Donne's only figure or even his staple one. "Telescoped" figures like "Made one anothers hermitage" are to be found much more frequently than the celebrated comparison of the souls of the lovers to the legs of a pair of compasses. In the second place, where Donne uses "logic," he regularly uses it to justify illogical positions. He employs it to overthrow a conventional position or to "prove" an essentially illogical one.

Logic, as Donne uses it, is nearly always an ironic logic to state the claims of an idea or attitude which we have agreed, with our everyday logic, is false. This is not to say, certainly, that Donne is not justified in using his logic so, or that the best of his poems are not "proved" in the only senses in which poems can be proved.

But the proof is not a logical proof. "The Canonization" will scarcely prove to the hard-boiled naturalist that the lovers, by giving up the world, actually attain a better world. Nor will the argument advanced in the poem convince the dogmatic Christian that Donne's lovers are really saints.

In using logic, Donne as a poet is fighting the devil with fire. To adopt Robert Penn Warren's metaphor (which, though I lift it somewhat scandalously out of another context, will apply to this one): "The poet, somewhat less spectacularly [than the saint], proves his vision by submitting it to the fires of irony—to the drama of the structure—in the hope that the fires will refine it. In other words, the poet wishes to indicate that his vision has been earned, that it can survive reference to the complexities and contradictions of experience."

The same principle that inspires the presence of irony in so many of our great poems also accounts for the fact that so many of them seem to be built around paradoxes. Here again the conventional associations of the term may prejudice the reader just as the mention of Donne may prejudice him. For Donne, as one type of reader knows all too well, was of that group of poets who wished to impress their audience with their cleverness. All of us are familiar with the censure passed upon Donne and his followers by Dr. Johnson, and a great many of us still retain it as our own, softening only the rigor of it and the thoroughness of its application, but not giving it up as a principle.

Yet there are better reasons than that of rhetorical vain-glory that have induced poet after poet to choose ambiguity and paradox rather than plain, discursive simplicity. It is not enough for the poet to analyse his experience as the scientist does, breaking it up into parts, distinguishing part from part, classifying the various parts. His task is finally to unify experience. He must return to us the unity of the experience itself as man knows it in his own experience. The poem, if it be a true poem is a simulacrum of reality—in this sense, at least, it is an "imitation"—by *being* an experience rather than any mere statement about experience or any mere abstraction from experience.

Tennyson cannot be content with *saying* that in memory the poet seems both dead *and* alive; he must dramatize its life-in-death for us, and his dramatization involves, necessarily, ironic shock and wonder. The dramatization demands that the antithetical aspects of memory be coalesced into one entity which—if we take it on the level of statement—is a paradox, the assertion of the union of opposites. Keats's Urn must express a life which is above life and its vicissitudes, but it must also bear witness to the fact that its life is not life at all but is a kind of death. To put it in other terms, the Urn must, in its role as historian, assert that myth is truer than history. Donne's lovers must reject the world in order to possess the world.

Or, to take one further instance: Wordsworth's light must serve as the common symbol for aspects of man's vision which seem mutually incompatible—intuition and analytic reason. Wordsworth's poem, as a matter of fact, typifies beautifully the poet's characteristic problem itself. For even this poem, which testifies so heavily to the way in which the world is split up and parceled out under the growing light of reason, cannot rest in this fact as its own mode of perception, and still be a poem. Even after the worst has been said about man's multiple vision, the poet must somehow prove that the child is father to the man, that the dawn light is still somehow the same light as the evening light.

If the poet, then, must perforce dramatize the oneness of the experience, even though paying tribute to its diversity, then his use of paradox and ambiguity is seen as necessary. He is not simply trying to spice up, with a superficially exciting or mystifying rhetoric, the old stale stockpot (though doubtless this will be what the inferior poet does generally and what the real poet does in his lapses). He is rather giving us an insight which preserves the unity of experience and which, at its higher and more serious levels, triumphs over the apparently contradictory and conflicting elements of experience by unifying them into a new pattern.

Wordsworth's "Intimations" ode, then, is not only a poem, but, among other things, a parable about poetry. Keats's "Ode on a Grecian Urn" is quite obviously such a parable. And, indeed, most of the poems which we have discussed in this study may be taken as such parables.

In one sense, Pope's treatment of Belinda raises all the characteristic problems of poetry. For Pope, in dealing with his "goddess," must face the claims of naturalism and of common sense which would deny divinity to her. Unless he faces them, he is merely a sentimentalist. He must do an even harder thing: he must transcend the conventional and polite attributions of divinity which would be made to her as an acknowledged belle. Otherwise, he is merely trivial and obvious. He must "prove" her divinity against the common-sense denial (the brutal denial) and against the conventional assertion (the polite denial). The poetry must be wrested from the context: Belinda's lock, which is what the rude young man wants and which Belinda rather prudishly defends and which the naturalist asserts is only animal and which displays in its curled care the style of a particular era of history, must be given a place of permanence among the stars.

APPENDIX ONE
CRITICISM, HISTORY, AND
CRITICAL RELATIVISM

The preceding chapters obviously look forward to a new history of English poetry (even though, quite as obviously, the discussions of poetry which they contain do not attempt to write that history). Indeed, the discussions may very well seem to take history too little into account. Yet, though the discussions have been concerned with the poems as poems, the mind of the poet, it must be admitted at once, is not a *tabula rasa*. I certainly have not meant to imply that the poet does not inherit his ideas, his literary concepts, his rhythms, his literary forms—that he does not inherit, in the first place, his language itself.

What is possible for a Donne, therefore, may not be possible for a Pope, and materials which may lie to hand for a Pope, may not be available for a Keats. I make the point here, not because it is not already obvious to the reader, but because I want the reader to harbor no lingering doubt that it is completely obvious to me.

But I insist that to treat the poems discussed primarily as poems is a proper emphasis, and very much worth doing. For we have gone to school to the anthropologists and the cultural historians assiduously, and we have learned their lesson almost too well. We have learned it so well that the danger now, it seems to me, is not that we will forget the differences between poems of different historical periods, but that we may forget those qualities which they have in common. We are not likely to ignore those elements which make the great poems differ from each other. It is entirely possible, on the other hand, that the close kinship that they bear to one another may be obscured—those qualities that make them *poems* and which determine whether they are *good* poems or *bad* poems.

I am thoroughly aware that the terms *good* and *bad* are suspect, and that their introduction here may be considered even impertinent. *Good* and *bad,* we have been taught, are meaningless terms when used absolutely. They must refer to some standard of values, and values, we know, are hopelessly subjective. We resent the arrogance implied in judgments which seem to have any tinge of absoluteness about them, and, as a rule, no profession of personal humility on the part of the critic who renders them is sufficient to assuage us. We have come to believe less and less in any absolute criteria; and, even assuming that such criteria exist, we feel that no critic could know and apply them without a certain egotism: how is a critic, who is plainly the product of his own day and time, hopelessly entangled in the twentieth century, to judge the poems of his own day—much less, the poems of the past—*sub specie aeternitatis!*

But in giving up our criteria of good and bad, we have, as a consequence I believe, begun to give up our concept of poetry itself. Obviously, if we can make no judgments about a poem *as a poem,* the concept of poetry as distinct from other kinds of discourse which employ words becomes meaningless. Recently, I heard a professor of literature propose before a group of professors and critics of more than average distinction that the new history of American literature should assume, for its purposes, that literature was synonymous with "anything written in words," it being obvious that any narrower criterion would be hopelessly subjective.

It should be added that the company addressed registered varying degrees of shock; and yet the speaker was merely carrying to its logical conclusion tendencies which three-quarters of his audience exemplified in practice. We have no confidence in absolutes of any kind; we know too much about ourselves to rest happily in subjective judgments. We try, therefore, to be more objective, more "scientific"—and in practice we usually content ourselves with relating the work in question to the cultural matrix out of which it came.

The studies of particular poems which fill up the earlier chapters of this book take as their assumption that there is such a thing as poetry, difficult as it may be to define, and that there are general criteria against which the poems may be measured. If there is any absolutism implied, I prefer not to conceal it, but to bring it out into the open. The foregoing discussions of poetry may, indeed, be hopelessly subjective. But, for better or for worse, the judgments are rendered, not in terms of some former historical period and not merely in terms of our own: the judgments are very frankly treated as if they were universal judgments. But if I am perfectly willing to expose the assumptions on which my own judgments rest, I am equally desirous of exposing the assumptions which underlie the typical varieties of attack on such judgments.

I believe that the typical attacks fall into a pattern—a pattern which will help to explain the state into which literary criticism, and ultimately the Humanities in general, have fallen in our day. I want to point out, therefore, that the notes which follow are concerned with something more than the defense of a particular critical method. They have to do—and this must be my justification for their presence here—they have to do with the whole question of whether we can have literary criticism at all.

The attempt to locate the "poetry" in a special doctrine or a special subject matter or a special kind of imagery, as we have seen in earlier pages, speedily breaks down. It must break down, if literature exists as literature; for different poems state what are apparently contradictory doctrines and employ very different materials. Yet if we are to emphasize, not the special subject matter, but the way in which the poem is built, or—to change the metaphor—the form which it has taken as it *grew* in the poet's mind, we shall necessarily raise questions of formal structure and rhetorical organization: we shall be forced to talk about levels of meanings, symbolizations, clashes of connotations, paradoxes, ironies, etc.

Moreover, however inadequate these terms may be, even so, such terms do bring us closer, I feel, to the structure of the poem as an organism—the formal structure as it is related to the relatively complex effect which even a simple poem gives. And the formal pattern suggested by these terms seems to carry over from poem to poem. If it does, then we are allowed to approach a poem by Donne in the same general terms through which we approach a poem by Keats; or a poem of Wordsworth's, through the same terms which will apply to a poem by Yeats. I repeat: I do not mean to ignore important differences between poets. Yet what must be sought is an instrument which will allow for some critical precision, and yet one which may be used in the service, not of Romantic poetry or of metaphysical poetry, but of *poetry*.

It is just at this point that one encounters the first line of misapprehension or of considered disagreement. The ordinary critic is usually quite willing to allow the poetry of the moderns or of the seventeenth-century metaphysical poets to be as complex as anyone may care to regard it. He raises no objections, for both of these poetries, he feels, are eccentric and "special." But the poetry of the nineteenth century, he is sure, is not, and need not be, complex. And the treatment accorded poetry in the earlier chapters of this book, he is convinced, attempts to read an unwarranted complexity into nineteenth-century poems—to "overintellectualize" them.

But though this objection is a rather general one (since most of us derive our concept of poetry from the nineteenth-century poets), I think that it may be treated with more clarity in terms of a concrete instance; and Mr. Donald Stauffer has furnished us with a particularly usable one since it involves one of the chapters of this book as it first appeared in the volume *The Language of Poetry.* Furthermore, the fact that Mr. Stauffer writes as a friendly critic makes his statement against complexity in poetry all the more pertinent.

With reference to the account of Wordsworth's sonnet on Westminster Bridge (p. 5), Mr. Stauffer writes as follows: "[In Brooks's account] Wordsworth's flash of insight—that even the man-made city participates in the life of nature—becomes not a part of a powerful conviction slowly achieved, as Wordsworth himself describes it in *The Prelude,* but an analyzable paradox."

Mr. Stauffer's reprobation seems to involve two items: (1) the fact that the experience as given in the critical account of the poem cuts across the general experience of the poet's life—that is, the critical account of the poem does not square with the received biographical account; and (2) the fact that the paradox is "analyzable"—a fact which apparently implies to Mr. Stauffer a violation of the nature of the experience which the poem records. The second item, since it involves a problem that will appear again under various forms, may be postponed for the moment.

As for the first objection: it raises the whole question of the relation of criticism to biography. Is the experience of "On Westminster Bridge" simply a morning out of Wordsworth's life, a morning to be fitted neatly into his biography? Or, is the experience of "On Westminster Bridge" to be considered *as a poem*—the dramatization of an experience (real or imagined, or with elements of both) in which the poet may make what use he cares to of contrast, surprise—even shock? Mr. Stauffer's objection seems to be that the conviction that the man-made city was a part of nature was arrived at slowly in Wordsworth's own life, and therefore he feels that this conviction cannot come to the protagonist of the poem as a flash of intuition—cannot come to the protagonist with some sense of shock.

I am not so much concerned with whether it is Mr. Stauffer or I who am most nearly right about the sonnet, but I am greatly concerned with the nature of Mr. Stauffer's argument. For he seems to me to confound the protagonist of the poem with the poet and the experience of the poem as an aesthetic structure, with the author's personal experience.

My assumption that Mr. Stauffer is guilty of this confusion seems to me confirmed by Mr. Stauffer's general skittishness about any attempt to deal with rhetorical structure. "Mr. Brooks," he writes, "is determined to find all things original, spare, and strange in any set of verses before he will accord them the name of poetry." The terms are Mr. Stauffer's, not mine; but I think that I can afford to accept them for the sake of the argument. Is there not a sense, and an important sense, in which "original, spare, and strange" must apply to all poetry worthy of the name? Surely, there is a sense in which all true poetry must be original.

Mr. Stauffer would not allow that even the simplest of Wordsworth's poems that he admires can be trite. And "trite," I submit, is a fair enough antonym to "original." I agree, of course, that the original poem need not be an esoteric poem. It can certainly make use of words, themes, and subject matter which are ordinarily thought of in isolation as trite. But the poem itself? Can it be trite? And still poetry? Surely, in the good poem, that which in ordinary experience is thought of as commonplace is renewed, made fresh and compelling. Even Dr. Johnson, certainly no friend to the esoteric, demanded that the thoughts in poetry be "new" as well as "just."

In the same way, even "strange" characterizes the good poem—nowhere more than where the familiar matter of today is rendered fresh and unfamiliar. Mr. Stauffer's own Romantics will furnish abundant evidence on this point. What else is Wordsworth talking about when he says that his primary function in the *Lyrical Ballads* was to remove the "film of familiarity" from daily objects?

The third term, "spare," hardly comes off any better. I would prefer to substitute for it the term "functional." But I think that I can afford to accept the metaphor which "spare" implies and still make my point. Mr. Stauffer and I may quarrel about the proper degree of spareness—about what is healthily spare and what is not—but Mr. Stauffer can accept no more easily than I, the opposite of spareness. He too will have to reject the obese poem, the overstuffed poem. Wordiness, mere external decoration, unrelated sentiment—these, he must agree, are faults; and if they are faults, then we are driven to admit that some kind of relation must obtain between the individual word or incident and the poem as a whole. If Mr. Stauffer will accept the proposition that *every* word in a poem plays its part,

then we can have no radical disagreement over princi-
ples and can agree to disagree over particular interpre-
tations. On the other hand, I do not see how Mr.
Stauffer can reject the proposition that every word in
a good poem counts and still continue to use the term
"poem" in a meaningful sense.

The question of form, of rhetorical structure, simply
has to be faced somewhere. It is the primary problem
of the critic. Even if it is postponed, it cannot ultimately
be evaded. If there is such a thing as poetry, we are
compelled to deal with it. And this is my justification
for considering with some minuteness the passage in
which Mr. Stauffer summarizes his objections: "I am
being unfair to Mr. Brooks, as he, I think, is unfair to
poetry as a whole. But I do so because I feel his position
excludes from the reader's enjoyment great areas of
poetry. . . . He says truly that 'We must be prepared
to accept the paradox of the imagination itself.' Part
of the paradox of the imagination is that a poet may
write with simplicity and sentiment and still remain
a poet."

One naturally sympathizes with Mr. Stauffer's ob-
jection to what has seemed to him a too narrow dogma-
tism. Moreover, it is entirely possible that the essay on
which he has based his objection reflects just that—
though I could hope that the essay, placed as it is now
within the context of this book, will no longer appear
narrowly dogmatic. But a deeper issue is involved.
What does Mr. Stauffer's "simplicity" mean? What can
it be made to mean? If one means that a poet may be
able to write without giving a sense of pomposity—
that he can give a sense of casual and simple directness
—the point can surely be granted at once. If the state-
ment means that the poet can make his poem *one* by
reducing to order the confusions and disorders and
irrelevancies of ordinary experience in terms of one uni-

fying insight, again granted. The poet not only *may* do this; he must. But if Mr. Stauffer means that matters of structure are irrelevant—that the poet can render his truth "simply" and directly, then I am afraid that the generous motive of protecting the diversity of poetry has betrayed him into the common error that besets our criticism. To state it in its most pervasive form, it conceives of the "form" as the transparent pane of glass through which the stuff of poetry is reflected, directly and immediately. To state it in its crudest form, it conceives of form as a kind of box, neat or capacious, chastely engraved or gaudily decorated, into which the valuable and essentially poetic "content" of the poem is packed.

I am confident that it is this embarrassingly over-simple conception of the relation of form to content that underlies Mr. Herbert Muller's attack on my position, particularly as it is outlined in *Modern Poetry and the Tradition*. Mr. Muller, like Mr. Stauffer, is troubled by what he terms my "exclusiveness."

> More serious and central, however, is Mr. Brooks' exclusiveness. In practice, he consistently disparages Augustan, Romantic, and Victorian poetry. . . . But there is certainly reason for pause before taking up a critical position that logically requires one to regard as of an "inferior" order most of the literature the world has been content to think great; for the Bible is as full of didactic heresy as Dante or Milton, and there is as little wit in the old epic or saga as in the pure song or psalm.
>
> In effect, Mr. Brooks takes as narrow a view of the uses of the imagination as did the old moralists and schoolmen; and the clue here is his ultimate criterion of "ironic contemplation." Apart from his tendency to use it rather carelessly, equating the simple with the naïve and the passionate with the sentimental, no forthright expression of a faith or ideal can bear such contemplation—and so what?

It is true that in *Modern Poetry and the Tradition* I suggested the need for a radical revision of the history of English literature, and that I there criticized certain aspects of the eighteenth- and nineteenth-century poetry. I hope that the treatment accorded to particular eighteenth- and nineteenth-century poems in this book, will perhaps put that criticism in better perspective. I should certainly dislike to be thought to maintain that English poetry ceased with the death of Donne, to be resumed only in our own time.

But though I believe that we need to revise drastically our conventional estimate of the course of English poetry, I had not realized that I had succeeded in doing so with the thoroughness which Mr. Muller suggests. The new broom has swept embarrassingly clean if it has managed to put the Bible, Dante, and Milton, in a heap, out of doors. If an attack on the didactic heresy entails this, then I agree with Mr. Muller that it does exact far too great a price.

But are we really forced into so unpleasant a dilemma? Why is it that some "didactic" poems are great, and others not? Admitting that Dante had a didactic purpose, is it not relevant to our problem here that Dante was not content merely to set forth Catholic dogma—that he wished to dramatize it? Mr. Muller expostulates that "no forthright expression of a faith or an ideal can bear" an "ironical contemplation." But the great poetic expressions of a faith can, and do. To me, it is significant that Dante, in dramatizing his faith, was willing to portray more than one pope in hell. Surely there is more than mere propagandizing for a dogma and an institution in a view which can envisage Christ's vicar among the damned. Indeed, I should say that Dante was quite willing to expose his preachment to something very like an "ironical contemplation."

Is it not also relevant to our problem that Milton presents Lucifer with full dramatic sympathy—with so much, indeed, that some readers have felt that he injured the effectiveness of his *Paradise Lost* as Christian "propaganda" by inadvertently making out a case for Lucifer rather than for God? A weaker poet—and a more forthright propagandist—would have risked no such ambiguity. He would have set up Lucifer as a straw man to be overthrown rather than as a powerful being who challenges the place of hero.

Mr. Muller sums up his attack as follows: "[Brooks] considers only technique, mechanism, outward show. He overlooks the underlying attitudes, the world view, the quality of mind, the informing spirit—all that makes Donne's poetry much greater than Herbert's, and very different from Mr. Ransom's, and that enables a Shakespeare or a Goethe to be as simple, forthright, eloquent as he pleases." If the "form" of which I have spoken is but outer envelope, an embellished husk, then Mr. Muller is perfectly right in rejecting it for something more inward ("informing spirit"), or deeper ("underlying attitudes"). Obviously, it is not for me to say that I did not overlook "the underlying attitudes, the world view, the quality of mind. . . ." Perhaps I did, but I can assure Mr. Muller that it was not by intention. I attempted in the earlier book (as I have attempted here) to deal with attitudes, superficial and underlying, but to deal with them in terms of the organization of the given poem itself. (I believe that ultimately, if we are to deal with poems as poems, we shall have to show how the attitudes reveal themselves in the poems.) I have talked less about "world views" and "informing spirits" because I have been primarily interested in the specific view taken in the particular poem, and interested in how the attitude of the poem was made to inform the poem—and not primarily interested in historical or psychological generalizations about the poet's mind. But if Mr. Muller has missed these things—and if he has missed them, less acute readers must have missed them—I believe that it is because Mr. Muller refuses to take a discussion of tone, attitude, and ironic qualification as other than a treatment of superficial mechanisms. He persists in seeing "form" as something *external* and *radically frivolous*.

For, to say that Shakespeare could be as "simple" and "forthright" as he pleased suggests that the poetry resides in certain truthful or exalted poetic statements which need only to be stated simply and forthrightly. But this assumption, as Mr. Muller himself knows, is desperate: for on this assumption one can never explain why such poetic material, when stated in clear expository prose is not poetry, or why only those who are great poets managed to locate and exploit "poetic material."

Perhaps it is caution which has therefore caused Mr. Muller to add, to "simple" and "forthright," the adjective "eloquent"; but, by adding it, Mr. Muller has succeeded in begging his whole case. For what is it to be *eloquent?* Mr. Muller has not tried to define it. The definition, however, has to be attempted if literary criticism is to exist. Yet, if we attempt to define it, can we be sure that Mr. Muller will not reproach us for dealing only with external matters—only with "technique, mechanism," and "outward show"?

The dualism of form and content thus puts a stop to criticism by compelling us to locate the poetry in the truth of the statement made by the poem or contained in the poem (actually, a paraphrase of the poem, not the poem itself); or, to locate the poetry in the "form" conceived as a kind of container, a sort of beautified envelope. As a corollary, the role of imagery becomes divided between a logical function and a decorative: to use Dr. Johnson's terms, between "illustration" and "decoration."

Both Mr. Stauffer and Mr. Muller, it may be said, are engaged in defending Augustan and Romantic and Victorian poetry against what they regard as the overweening claims of a particular standard. Their protests take the form of a plea for tolerance in the application of a particular set of criteria or of an attack on the generality claimed for that particular set of criteria. They do not argue the impossibility of applying generally *any* one set of criteria.

Yet it is this last argument which provides the most logical and thoroughgoing defense of the integrity of the various "poetries" of the past. And it is this argument for which the conventional pattern of English studies of the past fifty years has prepared us. The position taken is this: that one simply may not apply to Romantic poetry any standards except those of Romantic poetry itself, or, to Augustan poetry, any save those sanctioned by the Augustans. Each period is thus carefully sealed off from possible intrusion from the outside. The appeal from absolute standards of any kind to a complete relativism in criticism is bold but self-consistent. It rationalizes the procedure of our great graduate schools; and it challenges the critical position assumed in this book, forthrightly and directly, by denying the basic assumptions upon which that position is based.

The claims of such a critical relativism have been argued most ably and plausibly by Mr. F. A. Pottle in his recent *Idiom of Poetry*. There is so much in the book with which one must agree, the line of inquiry is so intelligent, that it seems a little ungracious to press disagreements. And yet, it is precisely because the book represents the most acute and logically consistent statement of what is usually a muddled and self-contradictory view, that a positive and detailed answer is demanded.

"The basic fallacy in nearly all recorded criticism," Mr. Pottle remarks, "is that it assumes a fixed or absolute sensibility or basis of feeling: a natural, correct basis of feeling that all right men have had since the beginning of time, or that the critic has arrived at by special grace. The view I am propounding is that an absolute basis of feeling has no more existence than an absolute frame of space. All original criticism is subjective, being a report of the impact of the work upon the critic's sensibility; all criticism is relative; and the question as to a 'right' sensibility does not arise."

The postulates which underlie this position are set forth with admirable lucidity at the end of Chapter I:

"1) *Poetry always expresses the basis of feeling (or sensibility) of the age in which it was written.*

"2) *Critics of the past were as well qualified to apply a subjective test to poetry as we are.* . . .

"3) *Poetry is whatever has been called poetry by respectable judges at any time and in any place.* ('Respectable' may be thought to beg the question. I mean to include in the term those critics who had the esteem of their own age, as well as those whom we admire.)

"4) *The poetry of an age never goes wrong.* Culture may go wrong, civilization may go wrong, criticism may go wrong, but poetry, in the collective sense, cannot go wrong."

The fact of revolutions of taste, of course, has to be admitted. Augustan poetry does seem radically different from Romantic poetry; Romantic, from modern. Taste seems to change, and, according to Mr. Pottle, does change. But he rejects the assumption that taste necessarily improves under these revolutions. There is no "progress" in good taste. Further, he rejects the assumption that research and learning in themselves will recover for us all the poets of the past. He even rejects the assumption, dear to Wordsworth, that there exists a correct, "permanent" style which can be attained by the poet who transcends the limitations of his own age.

One is compelled to sympathize with the motives for making the rejections. Science does progress; it cumulates. But criticism is not a science in this sense—a judgment in which I heartily concur. We certainly have no right to have any confidence in our judgments over earlier judgments merely because ours come later in time.

The "possibility of absolute judgments in those who have equipped themselves with the necessary education" is less easily disposed of. The equipment provided by a knowledge of literary history is obviously of great importance. One must agree when Mr. Pottle remarks that "It would seem to me obvious that one cannot fully understand Shakespeare or Milton or Pope without becoming a good deal of an antiquary." Yet he goes on to take the position that "when I am honest with myself, I have to admit that erudition, though it gives understanding (a very precious thing), never by itself confers the rapture of intuitive poetic experience." Mr. Pottle is himself a distinguished literary historian, and the disavowal which he makes is therefore all the more generous. But one could wish that it had been made in other terms.

For should not one make a distinction between the kind of understanding with which literary history usually concerns itself and the special understanding of poetic structure with which it has rarely concerned itself but which is vital to real appreciation? And furthermore, is "rapture" precisely the term with which to describe real appreciation? Indeed, does not the antithesis between "erudition" and "rapture" tend to beg the whole question by suggesting that the critical problem is an essentially irrational one—by placing the rapture outside the pale of understanding? *

* I should not press so hard the antithesis suggested by the terms if I did not feel that the conception of poetry which it

Mr. Pottle's disposition of the third possibility, namely, that there is a correct, "permanent" style which transcends the limitations of any one age, deserves full quotation. "One may well question," he writes,

if the taste of all past ages proves upon examination to be so bad, how can one be sure that his own is not worse? . . . How does one derive his notion of this permanently correct way of writing? But I should reject this explanation on another ground: its lack of simplicity. It is like the machinery of the epicycles. For what recourse could be more desperate than that of accusing all the great authors of the past of bad taste? Is it not simpler and a great deal more satisfactory to abandon as meaningless the search for an absolutely good style, and to agree that good taste in literature is, like good taste in language, the expression of sensibility in accordance with the accepted usage of the time? To agree that our original critical judgments are, in the final analysis, subjective; and that the sensibility or basis of feeling to which we refer for a measurement is a variable whose characteristics can be recorded historically

implies was clearly suggested in other parts of *The Idiom of Poetry*. For example, Mr. Pottle seems to make the "poetry" of a poem reside in the "memorable images," images which, for an appropriately attuned mind, give "a state of heightened consciousness." The passage on page 70 is decisive: "In the ordinary or popular sense of the term, poetry is language in which expression of the qualities of experience is felt to predominate greatly over statement concerning its uses. But we must not forget what we have said about sensibility and shifts of sensibility. The qualities of experience are neither perceived nor expressed in the same way by different organizations of sensibility."

Mr. Pottle, it is true, speaks of "structure." But the only "structural" purpose which he recognizes is that performed by "the element of prose" which furnishes "a background on which the images are projected, or a frame in which they are shown, or a thread on which they are strung." That is, if I interpret correctly, "the element of prose" serves to arrange for display the little nodules of "poetry" which apparently have no more intimate relation with their framework or with each other. This, it seems to me, represents another variant of the old form-content dualism with the "form" susceptible, in this case, to rational analysis and the "content" susceptible only to irrational appreciation.

after they are past, but whose future changes are unpredictable?

But is the case really so desperate as this last paragraph implies? To assume absolute standards does not imply that one has to damn right and left without qualification. I hope that the earlier chapters of this book will indicate that even to adopt such relatively unpopular criteria as functional imagery, irony, and complexity of attitude will still allow one to find many poems in the past which are worthy of praise.

I am principally concerned here, however, with the argument that the doctrine of critical relativism provides a simpler theory. Is it really simpler? Will it not actually involve us in more complexities than would any doctrine of absolute criteria?

Suppose that we adopt the theory of critical relativism. We will then judge Wordsworth, not by the standards of the Age of Pope nor by those of the Age of Donne. Each period will be considered *sui generis;* we will have criticisms, not Criticism. But if this procedure is proper, why should we not go on to recognize what is also clearly true: that there are subperiods within the major periods—that each generation can claim its own standards of criticism? And what of the not too rare rebel against his period, a Gerard Manley Hopkins among the Victorians, or a John Milton among the poets of the Restoration? Do they not have the right to demand judgment in terms of a special modification of sensibility? In short, does not the logic of the principle push us on to acceptance of the proposition that each poet is to be judged in terms of his own individual sensibility?

I think that the *reductio ad absurdum* is fair: for the reduction seems to me inherent in the principle itself. And if one considers the difficulty to be merely theoretical, let me point out that the merit claimed for critical relativism is that of simplicity. Undoubtedly, we can rough out the limits of our major periods, and agree, doubtless, on practical limits for their subdivisions; but we shall have to provide epicycle within epicycle in order to avoid the consequences of our initial assumptions. If, indeed, we are to save poetry—that is, as an art which can be dealt with meaningfully—we shall have to make our system tremendously and artificially complex.

Even so, I doubt that in terms of such a system poetry can survive as an art. For critical relativism wins its simplicity and objectivity only at the sacrifice of the whole concept of literature as we have known it. For what is the sensibility of our age? Is there any one sensibility? Do we respond to T. S. Eliot, Dashiell Hammett, Mary Roberts Rinehart, or Tiffany Thayer? The objective answer must be that some of us respond to one and some to another.* One may grant that the absolutist critic assumes an admittedly heavy burden, the obvious diversity of taste in this age and in other ages; yet, does the critical relativist in any wise escape such a burden? We know that there are cultural lags, that one region of the world differs from another, and that one class of society differs from another, for that matter. Historical periods (in the sense in which they color and mold sensibility) run horizontally as well as vertically. And we shall have just as much right to claim exemptions and special treatment on the horizontal basis as on the vertical.

A specific example may help to make this point clear. Mr. Pottle points out that whereas Percival Stockdale in the eighteenth century testifies to the fact that he

---

* If we give any other than a statistical answer, I think that we shall have already introduced the criteria which allow us to transcend—or rather commit us to transcending—a mere relativism.

was moved to raptures by the poetry of Pope, A. E. Housman, in the twentieth, states that he was not so moved. As a way of accounting for such phenomena, Mr. Pottle offers the following metaphor: "A radio looks the same when its dial is set for one wave length as for another. Are we, in fact, very much like receiving sets, born into the world with our dials locked to one wave length, or at least with a narrow range which we can extend very little? I am sure that we are, and that consequently all our literary judgments are purely relative to our 'set.' "

But the metaphor is double edged. If it will account for the diversity of opinion between "respectable judges" of different periods, it will also account for divergencies between the most respectable and the least respectable in the same period. Mr. Pottle has been very fair on this point, for in choosing Percival Stockdale as an instance, he has refused to confine himself to respectable judges. Stockdale, as he says, was "a ridiculous man and wrote a rather ridiculous book." But cannot we extend the application further—or rather, if we are interested in testing the principles involved, are we not compelled to extend it further? Can we even stop short of the young lady who confesses to raptures over her confessions magazine? I agree that we have no right to call Stockdale a liar when he testifies to his pleasure, but we can hardly call the young lady a liar either. The fact of the response in neither case is in question. But on the premises of critical relativism, have we not deprived ourselves of the right to say that her taste is "desperately bad"? How can we prove that her "set" is not merely tuned to a certain wave length? And on what objective basis can one evaluate wave lengths? Is it not the very principle of critical relativism that comparison of wave lengths is invidious?

The differences between "respectable judges" of different periods may well give us pause, and should induce humility and caution in the modern critic. In the case of different judgments of the emotional effect of *particular words and images,* the difference may point to shifts in language which we must take into account. But I do not think that the fact of difference forces us into relativism, and I am convinced that, once we are committed to critical relativism, there can be no stopping short of a *complete* relativism in which critical judgments will disappear altogether.

My concern is not so much with Mr. Pottle as with some of the consequences of his critical position in an age which has turned so heavily as ours toward naturalism and relativism. Mr. Pottle is no relativist in ethics. He subscribes "without reservation to a Christian orthodoxy and its attendant moral code." Though "poetry, in the collective sense, cannot go wrong," it is possible for him to say that "civilization may go wrong." But a hard-bitten and more consistent relativism will question whether we can say, objectively and scientifically, that a civilization may go wrong. Certainly we have many cultural historians today who apply their relativism in a thoroughgoing fashion, and who would consider Mr. Pottle's ethical absolutism an anomaly, an unscientific survival in an otherwise consistent system. With Mr. Pottle's religious position, I own, I am highly sympathetic; but I believe that I can predict that most proponents of relativism will dismiss it as an inconsistent outcropping of absolutism, and will proceed to parcel out literature among the cultural historians and the sociologists, respectively.* It is a process already well advanced.

To the thoughtful reader, it will be apparent at this point, if it has not already been apparent, that

---

* See, for example, "What to do with the Humanities," by George A. Lundberg, *Harper's,* June, 1943.

Mr. Pottle is not the villain of this piece; and that something more important than a mere carping at his book is the issue. The issue is nothing less than the defense of the Humanities in the hard days that lie ahead.

The Humanities are in their present plight largely because their teachers have more and more ceased to raise normative questions, have refrained from evaluation. In their anxiety to avoid meaningless "emoting," in their desire to be objective and "scientific," the proponents of the Humanities have tended to give up any claim to making a peculiar and special contribution. Yet, if they are to be merely cultural historians, they must not be surprised if they are quietly relegated to a comparatively obscure corner of the history division. If one man's taste is really as good as another's, and they can pretend to offer nothing more than a neutral and objective commentary on tastes, they must expect to be treated as sociologists, though perhaps not as a very important kind of sociologist. I do not mean, of course, to take the foolish position that the bad position in which the Humanities find themselves is purely the fault of the teachers of the Humanities. The Humanities have suffered under a variety of attacks which stem perhaps from the very nature of our age and of our civilization. But they have not been better defended, it seems to me—at least, more effectively defended— because the teachers of the Humanities have tended to comply with the spirit of the age rather than to resist it. If the Humanities are to endure, they must be themselves—and that means, among other things, frankly accepting the burden of making normative judgments.

But to say *merely* this much—though I believe that it is of first importance to say at least this much—would involve a misuse of Mr. Pottle's book. *The Idiom of*

Poetry contains some highly relevant warnings as to the difficulties which confront the critic. The difficulties are real, and it would be foolish to attempt any cavalier dismissal.

Mr. Pottle is quite right in pointing out that ideas change, customs change—language changes. In order to understand Shakespeare, we simply have to understand what Shakespeare's words mean. And the implications of this latter point are immense; for they go far beyond the mere matter of restoring a few obsolete meanings. Tied in with language may be a way of apprehending reality, a philosophy, a whole world-view. And the last person who can afford to deny the importance of the shadings of language is the person like myself who attaches great importance to the connotations, the feeling tone, the nuances of the poet's words. The problem has to be faced, and it is not an easy one.

Yet, though faced with the changing nature of language itself, I do not think that we are forced into a critical relativism. (If we identify the "poetry" with certain doctrines or with certain emotional effects which automatically proceed from a certain historical conditioning, we *are* forced into relativism, of course.) I believe, however, that the problem set by the changes of language from period to period is not different, in principle at least, from the problem presented by a poem written, say, in French or German.

One must learn the language, or one must put himself at the mercy of the translator—with the knowledge that the finer aspects of poetry elude translation. But men have been faced with the diversity of languages for centuries without feeling that universal standards were meaningless. And their instincts undoubtedly have been right. It is no accident that the *Odyssey* and the *Divine Comedy* have held a high place for a long time—even though we are perhaps in better position to see how much the later reader loses because his grasp of Greek or Italian is not that of a native speaker, and even though the distortions of translations may provoke a smile as we see just what the poem could mean at one period or another.

The problem raised by the older English literature does not differ in principle, I repeat, from the problem raised by literature written in other languages. In degree, of course, it is less serious—though the very fact that the older writer is using "English" may make the modern reader less cautious than he should be.

The truth of the matter is that an increased interest in criticism will not render literary history superfluous. It will rather beget more literary history—a new literary history, for any revised concept of poetry implies a revised history of poetry. I think that it is possible to foresee what some of the revisions will be, and in *Modern Poetry and the Tradition* I was rash enough to make some predictions about them. If the discussions of eighteenth- and nineteenth-century poems in the present book correct some misapprehensions, that is all to the good. What is relevant to say here is that the same discussions confirm my view that a new history is desirable and necessary—that new "facts" emerge that have to be taken into account, that whole series of problems which have been scanted in the past show themselves to be important, that certain poets deserve a higher place than they have been accorded in the past, and some a lower.

Such a history will, of course, not be final: but it ought to be more nearly so than the histories that it supersedes. (That it will have to face the charge that it is merely *our own* interpretation of past events should be beneficial in so far as this begets a proper humility in the historians. If the charge can, in truth, be leveled against any possible history stemming from our times, then relativism will have forced us to give up, not only literature, but history as well. We shall have to content ourselves with literary chronicles, masses of uninterpreted facts, mere bibliographies.)

Moreover, the new history of literature should be more truly a history of *literature:* that is, it should be better able to deal with literary structures and modes more closely than have the literary histories of the past. How rich and valuable such history can be is well illustrated by Mr. Arthur Mizener's "Some Notes on the Nature of English Poetry," to which I have made reference in an earlier chapter. Yet, in citing his essay as an instance of the sort of literary history which becomes possible to us as a result of a more critical approach to literature, I do Mr. Mizener an injustice perhaps by appearing to endow his essay with a pretentiousness to which the essay itself makes no claim. The essay actually is a study in the variation of one metaphor, the sun metaphor, through some two centuries of English poetry. About the theory of metaphor implied, I myself have some reservations; but the study is brilliant. And it does demonstrate the new "facts" which a more careful reading of even familiar poems presents to the literary historian, and the importance of those facts in accounting for the practice of the poets themselves.

I have stated that the attack on the general critical position maintained in this book has come primarily from "Romantic" sources—from critics whose opposition is based on an anxiety to protect the diversity of the various periods from an appeal to some universal criterion, or from critics whose opposition founds itself on a desire to protect "simple," "spontaneous," "directly eloquent" poetry from what they feel is an overweening tendency to intellectualize it.

But an attack can be made from another quarter, and though the answers I would make to it have been suggested earlier, particularly with regard to the critical position of Mr. Yvor Winters, the matter calls for a little more detailed reply. The general position to be considered is what may be called a kind of "neoclassic" position. It makes much of formal considerations in something of the old neoclassic sense of "formal." It stresses meter and decorum; and, in the person of Mr. Winters at least, it frankly stresses the moral.

Mr. Winters, it is true, has insisted that in calling the act of the poet "an act of moral judgment," he means something more than "an act of classification"—means indeed "a full and definitive account of a human experience." Now any human act is, of course, a moral act; and any act of judgment, including that of aesthetic judgment, has a moral aspect. But surely Winters expands morality too much by making it include all value judgments. He obscures distinctions that are important and ought to be maintained. The classic difficulty involved in lumping aesthetic judgments in with moral judgments is, of course, that one thus ties aesthetic values to a moral system: poetry tends to become the handmaid of religion or philosophy, whether Christian, Marxist, or some other.

This difficulty Winters tries to avoid by allowing a good deal of play in the approximation of the moral judgment made by the poem to the moral system held by the reader. As he puts it, "if the final act of adjustment is a unique act of judgment, can we say that it is more or less right, provided it is demonstrably within the general limits prescribed by the theory of morality which has led to it? . . . We can say that it is more or less nearly right." This is a common-sense solution that may seem satisfactory enough. The difficulty with it is that it is so loose and "common-sense" that in the hands of a crochety and dogmatic critic, any poem is liable to damnation on the score of the moral judgments which it makes, or which it is held it ought to make and does not. *The Waste Land* is a good case in point: for Mr. Winters, the poem does not judge modern civilization; it yields to it, and thus merely exhibits the confusion of modern civilization. Mr. Winters would actually render his criticism more responsible if he would either bring forward his system of morals overtly and explicitly or else would distinguish between moral judgments and aesthetic judgments.

But the far more important limitation of Mr. Winters' theory, his bias in favor of "rational meaning" and his assertion of the primacy of the concept, have already been touched on in Chapter Eleven. By ascribing priority to the concept and making it the "motive to emotion," Winters does not merely violate the natural history of language: he distorts the actual way in which poems "work."

For example, Mr. Winters writes in his *Anatomy of Nonsense:*

> It is the concept of fire which generates the feelings communicated by the word, though the sound of the word may modify these feelings very subtly, as may other accidental qualities, especially if the word be used skillfully in a given context. The accidental qualities of a word, however, such as its literary history, for example, can only modify, cannot essentially change, for these will be governed ultimately by the concept; that is, *fire* will seldom be used to signify *plum-blossom,* and so will have few opportunities to gather connotations from the concept, *plum-blossom.* The relationship, in the poem, between rational statement and feeling, is thus seen to be that of motive to emotion.

The passage is quite important, for Winters is saying much more than merely this: that *however rich the manifold of meanings and submeanings contained in a word, still there is a practical limit somewhere to the range of meanings; fire will seldom be used to signify plum-blossom.* If Winters were merely saying this, one would be disposed to agree with him at once. But Winters is actually doing something more. He is (1) managing to introduce a dualism of denotation and connotation and (2) he is assigning priority to the denotation: the "accidental qualities of a word" will be "governed ultimately by the concept." The dualism introduced is essentially that between intellect and emotion; the priority assigned, that assigned to "rational statement."

Winters himself has seen that the relationship is not so simple as he would imply. As he says "the sound of the word may modify these feelings very subtly, as may other accidental qualities, especially *if the word be used skillfully in a given context* [emphasis mine]." Precisely! In the poems with which we have been concerned the words *are* used skillfully and the given context is of immense importance. Under such conditions, not only the "feelings communicated by the word" are modified, but as we have seen, the meaning of the complex of words (from which the "rational" meaning is abstracted) may be modified too.

The whole point is of importance and much more than a mere quibble is involved, for we have in the paragraph which we have been discussing the foundation for Winters' subsequent statement that "Any rational statement will govern the general possibilities of feeling derivable from it," and the foundation for his description of the critical process which he says consists

(1) of the statement of such historical or biographical knowledge as may be necessary in order to understand the mind and method of the writer; (2) of such analysis of his literary theories as we may need to understand and evaluate what he is doing; (3) of a rational critique of the paraphrasable content (roughly, the motive) of the poem; (4) of a rational critique of the feeling motivated—that is, of the details of style, as seen in language and technique; and (5) of the final

act of judgment, a unique act, the general nature of which can be indicated, but which cannot be communicated precisely, since it consists in receiving from the poet his own final and unique judgment of his matter and in judging that judgment.

The crucial matter concerns, of course, the "paraphrasable content." What is the relation of this content to the rest of the poem? Most of all, who makes this paraphrase and in what terms; that is, what does he take into account in making the paraphrase? How accurate, how exact, can the paraphrase be and with what approximation to accuracy will the critic be satisfied? One *can* paraphrase the statement made by *Macbeth* as "Murder will out." The statement is true in so far as it goes; but it leaves out nearly everything of importance that the play "says." There will be few who will rest in so simplified a paraphrase; but there will be many who will be content with a paraphrase which is only less abstract and sketchy.

Will not the serious critic actually have to go through stages (4) and (5) before he is sure that his paraphrase is sufficiently accurate, and, in that case, what is the value of step (3) except as a tentative and provisional one?

One must sympathize with Mr. Winters' attack on mere impressionism in criticism, which, as Mr. Winters points out, ultimately leads to relativism and the abandonment of universal standards. One applauds too his attack on the fuzzier kinds of romanticism. But the alternative which Mr. Winters offers has all the limitations of neoclassical critical theory. "A great critic," he writes, "is the rarest of all literary geniuses: perhaps the only critic in English who deserves the epithet is Samuel Johnson." The statement is pat and to the point. It defines at least the bias of Mr. Winters himself —toward an essential dualism between intellect and emotion, toward a preoccupation with "rational meaning," and toward an overt moral. Mr. Winters' criticism, like that of Johnson, has its admirable qualities; but like Johnson's, though it can be extremely useful as a tool for exploration, it is hardly a criticism to rest in.

To detect a tendency toward such a neoclassicism in the criticism of John Crowe Ransom may seem merely perverse. If his criticism is to be regarded as "neoclassicist" at all, it is certainly a very special variant. Yet there is some justification for comparing it with Winters'. Whereas Winters insists on a rather rigorous and rational structure in a poem, the variant of which I speak insists on a rather tight and systematic structure of the images in a poem. It tends to find its clearest examples of such admirable rigor in metaphysical poetry, and the finest metaphysical poems, among the masterpieces of Donne. I certainly have little predisposition to quarrel with this account: the imagery of a good poem must be "functional"—it cannot afford to be merely decorative. And, again, I yield to few in my admiration for the triumphs of Donne. (Indeed, any reservations at all on this point may seem to come with poor grace from a critic who is frequently charged with attempting to push out of the boat any poem which does not possess the special character of Donne's poetry.)

But some reservations are in order, I believe—if not with regard to the praise accorded Donne, at least with regard to the terms on which the praise is accorded. Mr. Ransom, in his essay "Shakespeare at Sonnets," finds Donne a better lyric poet than Shakespeare because Donne's images "work out" and Shakespeare's frequently do not. I heartily agree with him that the poet's metaphors must "work out." So much the worse for Shakespeare when and if his do not. But I am inclined to feel that Ransom demands that all images work out as Donne's more "logical" images work out; and that, in my opinion, is to elevate one admirable poetic strategy into the whole art. There are ways *and* ways to gain the "objectivity" and the "realism" which, for Ransom, are the glory of Donne, and which Shakespeare, in his opinion, so often fails to obtain. Ransom's general reprehension of Shakespeare involves his shifting from figure to figure, his mixtures of metaphor, his failure to present "a figure systematically."

What is of more importance, however, is Ransom's tendency to praise—unless I misread him—Donne's logical rigor, not for its function in the development of the tone, but as an end in itself. The point is crucial, for it has everything to do with the essential function of metaphor. Does a poem find its unity in a rational or logical unity? Or does it find its unity in a unity of tone? Or, to transpose the question: Does the poem find its "truth" in a scientific or philosophical truth? Or does it find its truth in a dramatic truth? Does the poem achieve coherence in a system of propositions logically related to each other? Or does it find its coherence in a complex of attitudes dramatically related to each other?

Donne's display of "logic" is frequently so brilliant that we may be tempted to say that it functions in the poems "logically." But an inspection of any one of his poems indicates what the "logic" is actually being used for. The logic of "The Canonization," for example, will hardly satisfy the friend to whom it is addressed and who has (in the implied dramatic situation) been trying to persuade the lover to give up his love. The poem in which the logic is contained may well convince the friend that the lover is committed and determined, that he is not callow, that he is making his choice with open eyes. It will hardly convince him *logically* that the lover is a saint or that he is a phoenix or that he is winning a better world by giving up this world.

The real structure of "The Canonization" transcends the logical framework of its images. Moreover, it involves mixed metaphor and rapidly shifted figures. It achieves a unity, to be sure; but the unity which it achieves is an imaginative unity. It is not a logical unity unless we beg the whole question by adding "logic of its own nature." That, to be sure, it has; but so have most of the poems of Shakespeare.

Mr. Ransom concludes his discussion of Shakespeare with an examination of the famous "Tomorrow and tomorrow" speech from *Macbeth*. It is curious to compare his specific criticisms with those implied by Davenant's rewriting of the passage. Both boggle at *syllable* as a fit object for the tomorrows to creep to, and at "dusty" as a fit adjective to apply to "death." "The connections between part and part in this speech," Mr. Ransom writes, "are psychological, and looser than logical, though psychological will always include logical, and indeed act as their matrix. And the point is that mere psychological connections are very good for dramatic but not for metaphysical effects. Dramatically, this speech may be both natural and powerful; so I am told. Metaphysically, it is nothing."

In this connection, one ought to add Ransom's comments on the following lines from *Antony and Cleopatra:*

> *Now I must*
> *To the young man send humble treaties, dodge*
> *And palter in the shifts of lowness. . . .*

"Antony," writes Mr. Ransom, "is a figurative man, and full of feelings. The sending of humble treaties is not enough to express them, therefore he elects to dodge, and also to palter, and he will be in shifts of—of what? Lowness will do. And this vigorous jumping from one thing to another registers Antony very well, and may claim its theoretical justification under dramatic method. But in the coherent poetry of Donne and the metaphysicals there is nothing like it; no more than there is anything there like the peculiar jumpiness and straining of a modern such as, let us say, Mr. Joseph Auslander."

Now what concerns me especially is the distinction drawn here between "dramatic" and "metaphysical" effects and the nature of the coherence to be found in the metaphysical poets. As Mr. Ransom has pointed out, the "psychological will always include logical [connections], and indeed act as their matrix." I question whether the parts of any poem ever attain any tighter connections than the "psychological" or that the coherence, even of the metaphysical poets, is not ultimately a coherence of attitude. To ask more than this, I believe, is to ask that poetry be something that it does not pretend to be: philosophy. The *Macbeth* speech as metaphysics—using the term with a philosophical reference—may be nothing; but so is any Donne lyric, nothing. (I am not leaving out of account the possibility that one might have a piece of good metaphysics which happened to be at the same time good poetry, and I am willing to agree with W. M. Urban* that there is a sense in which all poetry is "covert metaphysics"; but, as he points out, science and religion as well as poetry are also "covert metaphysics." In any case, I am convinced that we do not find in Donne a poetry which eschews the "vigorous jumping from one thing to another" which Mr. Ransom finds so characteristic of Shakespeare's dramatic poetry.)

Consider "The Canonization" once more. The "jumping from one thing to another" occurs, not merely as the speaker satirizes the things to which his friends may compare him—to a fly, to a taper, to an eagle. It characterizes all the rest of the poem. To take one instance, the lovers build a kind of pretty rooms in sonnets, but the rooms are really tombs, and the rooms can be built (and, as tombs, become sacred) because the lovers have made of each other a hermitage.

Or, suppose we consider the "Valediction: forbidding mourning" with its celebrated compass comparison. How are the figures related here? Mr. Ransom comments on the succession of figures in the "Tomorrow" speech, thus: "But speaking now of lights, out with this one, a mere candle! Lights also imply shadows, and suggest that life is a walking shadow. Then the lights lead to the torches of the theatre, and the walking shadow becomes a strutting player, who after an hour will be heard no more. Finally, since one thing leads to another, we may as well make life into the thing the player says, the story, whose sound and fury have no meaning."

But are the connections between figures in the "Valediction" any more logical? The speaker says to his loved one: Since our parting is a death, let us die quietly as the virtuous man can afford to do. But dying as a dissolution is a kind of melting; and melting suggests tears; tears, floods and storms. Then the speaker thinks of another reason for them to make no outcry: they are priests of love and to let the common people know will be a kind of profanation: the value of their love constrains silence. This suggests a parallel between the noisy movement of the little earth when it quakes and the silence of the movement of the much greater spheres. The reference to the spheres brings to mind "sublunary" and we have a contrast between sublunary lovers and "heavenly" lovers, the elements of whose love is so different. But a consideration of the elements of which a thing is composed suggests "refinement," and then the contrast is made between a love that is like refined gold and that which is like a base metal. In addition to the superior value which men attach to gold, gold is the most ductile of metals. Gold can be stretched a long way as the love of the two lovers is going to be stretched and it can be beaten to airy thinness. (The poet, however, does not utilize this aspect of the matter in developing the analogy.) The idea of something which can stretch over a long distance, and yet not break, and therefore remain the same thing, causes the speaker to think of a pair of compasses—another *one* thing which seems two things though it is really one: one part travels while the other remains in the same spot.

I should not deny that Donne's figures—the last figures in particular—have a fuller development than Shakespeare's, and that the expanded figures, because of that expansion, possess an internal consistency. Furthermore, I should not deny that they have a sort of logic; but the links between the figures are associational ultimately, just as much as are the links which connect the Shakespearean figures. Most important of all, the coherency of Donne's poem, *on the level of strict logic,* is ragged and spotty as any analogical argument must be, and all poetry is committed, for better or worse, to that kind of argument. The essence of poetry is metaphor, and metaphor is finally analogical rather than logical. The presence or absence of strict logic, therefore, has no *direct* relation to the kind of coherency to which good poetry aspires, and without which it cannot be "good."

Mr. Arthur Mizener defends Shakespeare's kind of poetry, and makes some very helpful distinctions between it and the kind of poetry which Donne writes. Shakespeare's poetry, according to Mizener, is characterized by a soft focus; a metaphysical poem is in perfect focus, perhaps more than perfect focus (like those paintings in which every detail is drawn with microscopic perfection). In a good metaphysical poem each figurative detail may be examined in isolation and the poem as a whole presents itself to us as a neatly integrated hierarchy of such details. Mr. Ransom suggests that the metaphysical poet shows a special kind of courage in committing his feelings in this way "to their determination within the elected figure"; probably no one will question this claim, or the implication that the special intensity of good metaphysical poetry derives from this self-imposed restriction. But the metaphysical poet shows also a special kind of perversity. He achieves a logical form at the expense of richness and verisimilitude; for the more ingeniously he elaborates his elected figure, the more apparent will it be that it is either distorting or excluding the nonlogical aspects of his awareness of the subject.

In so far as Mr. Mizener is about the valuable and necessary business of making distinctions between kinds of poetry by emphasizing (and, in a few places, overemphasizing) the special strategies available to different poets, one must applaud. The characteristic strategy of Donne is not that of Shakespeare just as it is not that of Marvell or Herrick. Yet, the usefulness of such distinctions involves really a matter of levels. If we push some of the distinctions too far, or if we fail to supply certain qualifications, we end up, not with kinds of *poetry,* but with *separate poetries,* and thus with critical relativism.

Mr. Mizener is not a critical relativist, and it is no part of my intention to suggest that he is. But in a study such as this which attempts to find common structural principles in the diverse poems treated, it is necessary to take into account the ultimate validity of the distinctions which he has set up; and all the more necessary in view of some of his later remarks on the difference between the poetry of Donne and Yeats.

Between Donne and Yeats there are important differences, to be sure. I myself have perhaps muddied the waters in an earlier book by writing so as to imply to the unwary reader that there are none—that Yeats in his later poetry has adopted and practiced the "syllogistic" strategies of Donne. If so, Mizener's remarks on Yeats constitute, among other things, a proper corrective. But, read apart from this context and divorced from this purpose, there is danger that Mizener's treatment of Yeats may seem guilty of the same limitations with which he charges Ransom in Ransom's account of Shakespeare: that is, Mizener, failing to find in Yeats the "systematization" of images such as he finds in Donne, convicts him of writing a "soft" poetry, a "romantic" poetry, which takes refuge from the problems set by a rigorous structural pattern in the use of a kind of "overlap dissolve." Yeats's poetry, indeed, in Mizener's opinion, great in many respects as it is, remains to the end a "romantic" poetry—"full of enthusiastic and crotchety extremes which are forever on the verge of destroying its coherence of statement or its unity of style. It knows neither decorum of idea . . . nor decorum of vocabulary." This is in many respects an admirable account of the style of Yeats's later poetry; and yet it is amusing to reflect that, to the man of the eighteenth or nineteenth century, this account would have seemed like an apt description of Donne's style which, for such readers, certainly seemed full of "enthusiastic and crotchety extremes" and which also appeared to regard "neither decorum of idea . . . nor decorum of vocabulary."

The point is not, of course, that Yeats and Donne are "just alike": the differences exist. But it is of very great importance to see on what levels they exist. Most of all, it is important that in discriminating between them we do not make the mistake of equating the "coherence of statement" and "unity of style" which a good poem must attain with "decorum of idea," and "decorum of vocabulary," whether we take our conception of the decorous from Donne or Pope or Keats.

"Decorum of idea" and "decorum of vocabulary"— but what determines the decorum? Decorum ultimately there must be; but I am not sure that we can afford to accept any decorum finally (in terms of which we shall judge the goodness of a poem) except that ultimate decorum of the realized poem itself. Moreover, I think that this must always be applied on the level of tone; that is, we must ask whether or not the devices in question—be they sequence of ideas, development of metaphors, selection of words—function to develop a coherent and powerful structure of attitudes. If they do this, then they accord with, and are justified by, the only "decorum" that finally matters.

APPENDIX TWO
THE PROBLEM OF BELIEF AND
THE PROBLEM OF COGNITION

The position developed in earlier pages obviously seeks to take the poem out of competition with scientific, historical, and philosophical propositions. The poem, it has been argued, does not properly eventuate in a proposition: we can only *abstract* statements from the poem, and in the process of abstraction we necessarily distort the poem itself.

But there are several possible misapprehensions which one ought to guard against. In the first place, the theory proposed does not divorce the poem from the realm of meanings and evaluations. A person for whom the word "idiot" carried the connotations of, say, "wood-nymph" would have great difficulty with Macbeth's speech in which he says "Life is a tale/ Told by an idiot" just as a person who regarded murder as generally delightful would have difficulty with the play as a whole. We have to ask the reader to become acquainted with the poet's language (using the term in its broadest sense). But it is important to note what the reader is *not* asked to do. He is not asked to give up his own meanings or beliefs or to adopt permanently those of the poet. It will be sufficient if he will understand the unit meanings with which the poet begins—that is, that he understands the meanings of the words which the poet uses—and if he will so far suppress his convictions or prejudices as to see how the unit meanings or partial meanings are built into a total context.

I take it that this is what I. A. Richards means (or ought to mean) in the passage in his *Practical Criticism* where he says: ". . . the question of belief or disbelief, in the intellectual sense, never arises when we are reading well. If unfortunately it does arise, either through the poet's fault or own own, we have for the moment ceased to be reading and have become astronomers, or theologians, or moralists, persons engaged in quite a different type of activity." The point is not that when we read a poem we put to sleep all our various interests as human beings—the reason evidently for Richards' demurring at Coleridge's metaphor of a "willing suspension of disbelief." The point would be that in "reading well" we are willing to allow our various interests as human beings to become subordinate to the total experience.

T. S. Eliot's testimony to his difficulty with Shelley's beliefs in reading Shelley's poetry can be rephrased in these terms. Certain statements, explicit or implied, because they are not properly assimilated to a total context, wrench themselves free from the context, and demand to be judged on ethical or religious grounds. The fault may, of course, lie either with the poet or the reader: the poet may fail by not dramatizing the statement; the reader may fail by ignoring the context and considering the statement out of context.

A second misapprehension may be mentioned again here though it has been discussed in some detail in earlier pages. Because the poet uses the language of a particular time (and with the language, the ideology and the valuations of a particular time), we may easily come to feel that only in so far as we agree with the ideology and valuations of that time can we accept his poem. But this again is to misconceive the functions of the various elements in a poem. We do need to understand the language of the poem including the ideas and the allusions. We may need to have impressed upon us, for example, if we are to understand *Antigone,* the nature and importance of the Greek burial rites. But our understanding of the play, though it may depend upon our knowing what is at stake for the characters, does not depend upon our accepting the importance of such burial rites for ourselves. In short, if we see that any item in a poem is to be judged only in terms of its relation to the total effect of the poem, we shall readily grant the importance for criticism of the work of the linguist and the literary historian, but we shall deny the heresy which reduces literature to cultural history and thus begets a critical relativism.

But if the individual parts of a poem may not be judged in isolation from the whole, and if the meaning of the whole can only be "abstracted" in a thinned-out paraphrase, how are we, then, to test the "goodness" or "soundness" or "significance" of the "total meaning" of the poem? An answer has already been suggested, but the matter can bear, and perhaps demands, further elaboration.

It is interesting to reconsider T. S. Eliot's proposed test in the light of the preceding paragraph. He is willing to accept in a poem any possible world view provided that he feels that it is a world view which is "coherent," "mature," and "founded on the facts of experience." But in choosing such terms he indicates that he is testing the philosophical "truth" of the poem, not by the philosophical statement which the poem makes as a naked proposition but rather by considering whether the proposition implied is one that might be conceivably made by a tough-minded observer who had thought and felt seriously about experience. Eliot very properly avoids the pitfall involved in measuring the "statement of the poem" directly against some proposed philosophical yardstick. (*Good* poetry is by this test automatically limited to that poetry which happens to embody the philosophical doctrines of the reader.) But would not Eliot make his case stronger still by frankly developing the principle of dramatic propriety suggested by his statement and by refraining from attempting to extract any proposition from the poem at all? Could he not keep his test within the terms of the characteristic organization of the poem with some such account of affairs as this: He will regard as acceptable any poem whose unifying attitude is one which really achieves unity ("coherence"), but which unifies, not by ignoring but by taking into account the complexities and apparent contradictions of the situation concerned ("mature" and "founded on the facts of experience")? The advantages of such an account would be these: first, he would be dealing with the attitudes developed in the poem rather than with abstract propositions which he would have to interpret *as implied by the attitudes;* second, he would not be forced to go outside the poem* to find some criterion external to it, but would be able

* We are, of course, always forced to go outside the poem for the unit meanings on which the poem is founded—see p. 236. No theory of poetry can make poetry autonomous in the sense that it denies that every poem is rooted in language and in the language of a particular time. We *start* outside the poem. But there is another sense in which it may be held that we are forced to go *outside the poem:* in determining the power of the tensions generated, the fact of the reconciliations achieved, etc., the reader will have to have recourse to his own experience, and on occasion different readers may disagree. What will appear sentimental to one reader may appear, to another, to be a legitimate reconciliation. Again, no theory of criticism can do away with the subjective element (though the consequences of this ineradicable subjectivity are easily exaggerated). Yet, it seems to me that there is a real gain in attempting to judge a poem in terms of its characteristic structure, a dramatic structure, rather than in attempting to abstract propositions from the poem and to measure these by canons of scientific or philosophic truth.

to find a criterion in the organization of the poem itself by assessing the relative complexity of the unifying attitude—the power of the tensions involved in it, the scope of the reconciliation which it is able to make, etc. To illustrate from the particular poet whom Eliot instances: under the proposed scheme one would condemn Shelley's "Indian Serenade" as *sentimental* rather than as *silly* in the propositions about love which it implies. (The translation of attitudes into propositions is unnecessary; moreover, it is dangerous since it invites confusion about the way in which poems make statements.)

Having in mind the scheme proposed, one could say that a poem does not *state* ideas but rather *tests* ideas. Or, to put the matter in other terms, a poem does not deal primarily with ideas and events but rather with the way in which a human being may come to terms with ideas and events. All poems, therefore, including the most objective poems, turn out on careful inspection to be poems really "about" man himself. A poem, then, to sum up, is to be judged, not by the truth or falsity as such, of the idea which it incorporates, but rather by its character as drama—by its coherence, sensitivity, depth, richness, and tough-mindedness.

In *Modern Poetry and the Tradition* I suggested that Richards' distinction between "poetry of exclusion" and "poetry of inclusion" might be developed into a kind of scale for determining the value of poetry. Low in the scale one would find a rather simple poetry in which the associations of the various elements that go to make up the poem are similar in tone and therefore can be unified under one rather simple attitude—poems of simple affection, positive, "external" satires, etc. Higher in the scale, one would find poems in which the variety and clash among the elements to be comprehended under a total attitude are sharper. In tragedy, where the clash is at its sharpest—where the tension between attraction and repulsion is most powerful—one would probably find the highest point in the scale. So much for the positive side; but there is a negative side too, where one would place those poems which failed to secure unity at all—or achieved only a specious reconciliation of attitudes—the sentimental poem.

It cannot be claimed for such a test that it eliminates the subjective element in judgment. It does not, of course, and no meaningful criterion of poetry can ultimately eliminate the subjective. But the test proposed is by no means an impressionistic test, either. Indeed, we shall probably be able to use this test of complexity of attitude to set up what is essentially the same hierarchy of poems which we tend to accept on the basis of other tests. But the advantages of this particular criterion are two-fold: (1) we shall be able to set up our hierarchy in terms of the organizations of the poems themselves—not by having to appeal to some outside scale of values; (2) we shall, if this mode of evaluation rests upon what is really a more accurate account of the structure of poetry, be able to correct and improve the presently accepted hierarchy of poems.

That such a criterion is the normal development of the critical methods displayed in earlier pages of this book is probably obvious. One perhaps does not need to point out that the importance assigned to the resolution of apparently antithetical attitudes accounts for the emphasis in earlier pages on (1) wit, as an awareness of the multiplicity of possible attitudes to be taken toward a given situation; on (2) paradox, as a device for contrasting the conventional views of a situation, or the limited and special view of it such as those taken in practical and scientific discourse, with a more inclusive view; and on (3) irony, as a device for definition of attitudes by qualification. Moreover, the insistence on the element of conflict between attitudes will also throw more light upon Coleridge's account of the imagination* as the synthesizing faculty of the mind, and will emphasize further the sense in which poetry is essentially dramatic.

But if one makes so high a claim for poetry as a mental activity, it is possible that the reader will feel inclined to reinstate once more the old question: Why may we not, then, generalize on the basis of the attitudes adopted in the great and more important poems and thus get a world view which will provide a set of basic values? Cannot we catalogue and categorize the wisdom included in the great poetry in this fashion, and thus make poetry yield a directive wisdom, after all? We may, of course, if we like. But it needs to be pointed out that we are moving out of the realm of literary criticism if we do this. The real point is that, though any wise philosophy will probably take the greatest poetry into account, still this is a problem for philosophy or religion, and not for art. It is sufficient if we can show that poetry, though it does not compete with science and philosophy, yet involves a coming to terms with situations, and thus involves wisdom, though poetry as such indulges in no ethical *generalizations*.

It should be pointed out, however, how the position taken here differs from that taken by Richards; for, if we are not to judge poems by their truth as statements, it may seem that we are denying that they are in any sense cognitive. Richards' claims for poetry as the activity that would "save us" involved the hope that by discipline gained from reading the great poems—

---

* It "reveals itself in the balance or reconcilement of opposite or discordant qualities: of sameness, with difference; of the general, with the concrete; the idea, with the image; the individual, with the representative; the sense of novelty and freshness, with old and familiar objects; a more than usual state of emotion, with more than usual order. . . ."

a discipline in coming to terms with the world in relation to ourselves—we would be able to come to terms with any situation by which we were confronted. Thus, Richards would have us appeal, not to a body of dogma, but rather to a discipline and habit within ourselves which would prompt the proper attitude toward any set of events. Now, it is true that the kind of development of insight and self-criticism to be found in great poetry resembles that to be found elsewhere. But Richards puts a burden on poetry as an activity which poetry does not need to assume and which it probably cannot assume. I think that there are grounds for concluding that Richards' most recent position assigns to poetry a more modest place. Actually, whether or not Richards has reinstated metaphysics, he has evidently in his present position reinstated philosophy.*

Urban, in his *Language and Reality*, has made a full-scale attack on the account of language given by nominalistic positivism—an account which would parcel out the functions of language between the "referential" (scientific) and the "emotive" (poetic). Language, he maintains, has also a "representational" (intuitive or symbolic) function, a function necessary along with the others if language is to convey meaning at all. Poetry is not merely emotive, therefore, but cognitive. It gives us truth, and characteristically gives its truth through its metaphors (though not through metaphor conceived of as mere illustration or decoration). "All poetic symbols," he writes, "are . . . metaphors and arise out of metaphor. But a symbol is more than a metaphor. *The metaphor becomes a symbol when by means of it we embody an ideal content not otherwise expressible* . . . we use metaphor to *illustrate* ideas or assertions which are expressible wholly in abstract or non-figurative terms. The metaphor is a symbol when it

* See p. 265 below.

alone expresses or embodies our ideal meaning." (The distinction between "metaphor as symbol"—I have employed the term "functional metaphor"—and metaphor conceived of as mere illustration is, as I have tried to point out, crucial.)

Grounding poetry on "functional metaphor" as he does, Urban is able to combat those theories which conceive of poetry as "communicating" a "content" external to the poem, and which thus split the poem between its "form" and its "content." "The general principle of the inseparability of intuition and expression," Urban insists, "holds with special force for the aesthetic intuition. Here it means that form and content, or content and medium, are inseparable."

A poem, then, for Urban, is strictly untranslatable: what it "says" can be rendered only by the poem itself; but Urban is emphatic in maintaining that it does say something—that the poetic symbol gives cognition. (His position is so close to that which I have argued in earlier pages that it is worth devoting some space to his solution of the problem involved.)

For a problem is involved, and as Urban confesses, a difficult one to solve:

> We have here one of the most difficult problems in connection with language and cognition, as indeed in the entire theory of knowledge. We are apparently faced with a dilemma. If we are to interpret the "sense" of the symbol we must expand it, and this must be in terms of literal sentences. If, on the other hand, we thus expand it we lose the "sense" or value of the symbol *as symbol*. The solution of this paradox seems to me to lie in an theory of interpretation of the symbol. It does not consist in substituting *literal* for symbol sentences, in other words substituting "blunt" truth for symbolic truth, but rather in deepening and enriching the meaning of the symbol.

To substitute "literal for symbol sentences" is to commit oneself to the heresy of paraphrase discussed earlier in this book. The expansion of the symbol had better be, not for the purpose of providing a nonsymbolic surrogate for the poem, but rather, as Urban puts it, for the purpose of "deepening and enriching the meaning of the symbol." The discussion of the poem is not to be substituted for the poem: it should return us to the poem.

But Urban's further statement that "only [by expansion of the symbol] . . . can its truth or falsity be determined" calls for further comment; for, in spite of his warning against attempting to substitute "blunt" truth for symbolic truth, it is possible to take Urban's position to be another variant of those theories which claim cognition for poetry only at the price of considering it ultimately as distorted and imperfect philosophy.

Indeed, Susanne Langer in her *Philosophy in a New Key* taxes Urban with just this error. I am inclined to agree with her (though I am not sure that her own general position on the function of literary meaning is not somewhat reminiscent of the earlier Richards, and open to some of the same objections). I too feel that Urban is guilty of some apparent self-contradictions in his discussion of the problem. But it is possible, in the context of his whole book, to make out a case for his solution of what he calls the paradox of the interpretation of the literary symbol.

For Urban, poetry, along with religion and science, is "covert metaphysics." But though all poetry is covert metaphysics, the poem need not, and ought not, to aspire to become explicit metaphysics.

Poetry says what it means but it does not say *all* that it means; in attempting to say this "all" it often ceases to be poetry. . . . This is evidently a problem which, from the artist's point of view, can be solved only *in ambulando;* it is only his genius and tact which can discover the *via media,* the way between the horns of the dilemma. But from the philosopher's point of view a more reasoned and intelligible answer may be given to this question. The transition to metaphysics is inevitable, but the poet, as poet, is not the one to make it. He does well . . . to keep to his own symbolic form. For precisely in that symbolic form an aspect of reality is given which cannot be adequately expressed otherwise. It is not true that whatever is expressed symbolically can be better expressed literally. For there *is* no literal expression, but only another kind of symbol. It is not true that we should seek the blunt truth, for the so-called blunt truth has a way of becoming an untruth.

Why make the expansion at all, then? In what sense is the "transition to metaphysics . . . inevitable"? If I understand Urban, the expansion is called for only if we wish to relate the "truths" given by poetry to the truths given in other realms of discourse—to those given by science, for instance. If this is the point in question, one may grant it as an entirely reasonable concession. No critic that I know of is anxious to maintain that *only* poetry gives ultimate truth. If I understand Urban properly, then, the relationship of poetry to metaphysics is not that of handmaiden to mistress. Metaphysics criticizes and interprets the symbolic truth of poetry (*and* of science *and* religion); but it does not give us the "blunt truth" or the "naked truth." Nor does metaphysics dispense with symbolism; it has, as Urban emphasizes, its own symbols.

It is the philosopher who is to make the "transition to metaphysics." The poet "does well . . . to keep to his own symbolic form." Thus, though he insists— in opposition to the nominalistic positivists—that poetry is revelatory, Urban refuses to set the poet the task of revealing some extrapoetic truth: poetry is not merely the vehicle of a content which it is to "express." The test of "good poetry" is evidently that of "authentication": "We constantly speak of 'good' symbols and, what is even more to the point here, of 'authentic' symbols. By such expressions we always mean that the symbol expresses adequately for our type of consciousness that which could not be fully expressed in 'literal' sentences."

I shall argue that this test seems to differ not a great deal from the test which I proposed on pp. 254-57 above. That test, like Urban's, is finally one of "adequacy." "If," Urban writes, "intuition and expression are identical, or at least inseparable, then the only way to determine being or reality is in those forms in which statements about it are possible. Even though we think of the truth relation as one between 'idea' and 'thing,' such a relation can be determined, that is verified and confirmed, only when it is expressed. Truth, then, is always a function of expression, and the relation between an expression and that which is expressed can only be one of adequacy."

But the resemblance between the positions can perhaps be made still clearer by considering a few of Urban's comments on the function of poetry and its relation to dramatic language. In contrast to scientific symbolism, the object "in other regions of symbolism, such as those of art and religion . . . is not at all to operate or predict, but to understand." This "understanding," as contrasted with scientific description for purposes of operation and prediction, is peculiarly associated with the dramatic way of rendering relationships. Urban writes:

My own view is that, properly understood, the thesis of the primacy of the dramatic form must be maintained. It is part of my general thesis that all meaning is ultimately linguistic and that although science, in the interests of purer notation and manipulation, may break through the husk of language, its nonlinguistic symbols must again be translated back into natural language if intelligibility is to be possible. Natural language is dramatic and all meaning expressed in language must ultimately be of this type.

Urban not only sees poetry as constantly "employing the dramatic way of rendering life." He says that "indirectly all art is revelatory of man . . . no adequate account of what happens in human life, the central home of action and drama, is possible if 'relations of the mental type' [as opposed to the operational type of science] —and the dramatic way of rendering them—are left out."

This, I believe, is the essential point in Allen Tate's assertion that poetry gives "complete knowledge"—an assertion that has vexed critics of positivist persuasion. But how poetry is complete is specified: it does not leave out what science must leave out: "Literature is the complete knowledge of man's experience. By knowledge I mean that unique and formed intelligence of the world, of which man alone is capable."

For Urban too, poetry deals with "man's experience" —with *persons,* for

The one differentia of a person that is significant is, that he alone of all the parts of nature has consciousness of values and of the "ought" or obligation inseparable from the awareness of values. . . . To have this character is to be a "soul," and poetry in contrast to science, always speaks about souls. For the poet, then, the individual is always the centre and bearer of values, and his function, as poet, is to reveal them.

Urban maintains, of course, that the realm of values —the "world, the structure of which is determined by value appreciation"—is real, arguing as he does for the validity of metaphysics and for an objective theory of values. I should agree with him, but this is not the point which I am anxious to press here. It is rather the contrary: that even so, as Urban himself indicates, the characteristic and proper tests for the significance of poetry are to be developed from a consideration of its structure as dramatic utterance; that the poem is *not* to be conceived of as a statement, "clear," "beautiful," or "eloquent," of some truth imposed upon the poem from without.

In this regard, Urban seems to me in substantial agreement with Richards' earlier statement "that it is never what a poem says that matters, but what it is," and certainly with his later statement that "The saner and greater mythologies are not fancies; they are the utterance of the whole soul of man, and as such, inexhaustible to meditation. . . . Without his mythologies man is only a cruel animal without a soul—for a soul is a central part of his governing mythology—he is a congeries of possibilities without order and without aim." *
At the time he made this latter statement (*Coleridge on Imagination,* 1936), Richards specifically denied the validity of metaphysics. Perhaps he still does, but his latest pronouncement would indicate that, even on this subject, he approaches general agreement with Urban. He writes, for example, in 1941: "It is not any metaphysical doctrine, *as a doctrine,*" which we need. It is rather a study of the "most resourceful words," the "indispensable words, those which give structure to thoughts and connect them in larger structures." These are the words which most occasion metaphysical misunderstandings. "Such an inquiry," Richards goes on to say, "if well *designed* . . . would amount to a study

* Compare Urban's statement that "myth is indispensable from the standpoint of expression and intelligibility. Myth is dramatic language and only dramatic language is ultimately intelligible. . . . it was precisely the recognition on the part of Plato that cosmologically significant propositions could not be expressed in mathematical-logical language, which led him to resort to the dramatic language of myth. It was not that this language is an imperfect prescientific form, to be abandoned for the mathematical-logical; it was rather a clear recognition of the essential limitations of the latter."

of metaphysics. . . . But it would be a metaphysics approached from a new angle." *

This conception of metaphysics obviously comes close to Urban's conception of metaphysics as "the language of languages," concerned with "maximum content," the function of which is to interpret and mediate among the other symbolisms; and Urban has acknowledged the rapprochement.

But my purpose is not to welcome Richards as a returned prodigal. Richards is not a renegade but a pioneer who started out from a different set of assumptions; nor is it even to insist with Urban upon the necessity of metaphysics. It is rather to point out the area of substantial agreement between two close students of language whose starting points have been as diverse as those of Richards and Urban. One seems to me as cautious as the other with regard to making poetry the handmaiden of some doctrine which it is to reflect or "communicate." And yet one seems as fervent as the other in insisting upon the intrinsic importance of poetry as something far more serious than any idle fancy, and far more central to man's nature than any subjective "projection." Both point the literary critic to a reading of the poem itself—to the fullest realization of the symbolic structure that *is* the poem. The task is not easy; it is important; it is basic to any valid literary criticism.

* For Richards' lecture from which I have quoted, and for Urban's note on it, see *Furioso*, Summer, 1941.

THE CANONIZATION

For Godsake hold your tongue, and let me love,
Or chide my palsie, or my gout,
My five gray haires, or ruin'd fortune flout,
With wealth your state, your minde with Arts im-
prove,
Take you a course, get you a place,
Observe his honour, or his grace,
Or the Kings reall, or his stamped face
Contemplate, what you will, approve,
So you will let me love.

Alas, alas, who's injur'd by my love?
What merchants ships have my sighs drown'd?
Who saies my teares have overflow'd his ground?
When did my colds a forward spring remove?
When did the heats which my veines fill
Adde one more to the plaguie Bill?
Soldiers finde warres, and Lawyers finde out still
Litigious men, which quarrels move,
Though she and I do love.

Call us what you will, wee are made such by love;
Call her one, mee another flye,
We'are Tapers too, and at our owne cost die,
And wee in us finde the'Eagle and the Dove.
The Phœnix ridle hath more wit

    By us, we two being one, are it.
So to one neutrall thing both sexes fit,
    Wee dye and rises the same, and prove
    Mysterious by this love.

Wee can dye by it, if not live by love,
    And if unfit for tombes and hearse
Our legend bee, it will be fit for verse;
    And if no peece of Chronicle wee prove,
        We'll build in sonnets pretty roomes;
        As well a well wrought urne becomes
The greatest ashes, as halfe-acre tombes,
    And by these hymnes, all shall approve
    Us Canoniz'd for Love:

And thus invoke us; You whom reverend love
    Made one anothers hermitage;
You, to whom love was peace, that now is rage;
    Who did the whole worlds soule contract, and drove
        Into the glasses of your eyes
        (So made such mirrors, and such spies,
That they did all to you epitomize,)
    Countries, Townes, Courts: Beg from above
    A patterne of your love!

L'ALLEGRO

Hence loathed Melancholy
    Of Cerberus, and blackest midnight born,
In Stygian Cave forlorn
    'Mongst horrid shapes, and shreiks, and sights un-
        holy,
Find out som uncouth cell,
    Where brooding darkness spreads his jealous wings,
And the night-Raven sings;
    There under Ebon shades, and low-brow'd Rocks,
As ragged as thy Locks,

In dark Cimmerian *desert ever dwell.*
But com thou Goddes fair and free,
In Heav'n ycleap'd Euphrosyne,
And by men, heart-easing Mirth,
Whom lovely Venus *at a birth*
With two sister Graces more
To Ivy-crowned Bacchus *bore;*
Or whether (as som Sager sing)
The frolick Wind that breathes the Spring,
Zephir *with* Aurora *playing,*
As he met her once a Maying,
There on Beds of Violets blew,
And fresh-blown Roses washt in dew,
Fill'd her with thee a daughter fair,
So bucksom, blith, and debonair.
Haste thee nymph, and bring with thee
Jest and youthful Jollity,
Quips and Cranks, and wanton Wiles,
Nods, and Becks, and Wreathed Smiles,
Such as hang on Hebe's *cheek,*
And love to live in dimple sleek;
Sport that wrincled Care derides,
And Laughter holding both his sides.
Com, and trip it as ye go
On the light fantastick toe,
And in thy right hand lead with thee,
The Mountain Nymph, sweet Liberty;
And if I give thee honour due,
Mirth, admit me of thy crue
To live with her, and live with thee,
In unreproved pleasures free;
To hear the Lark begin his flight,
And singing startle the dull night,
From his watch-towre in the skies,
Till the dappled dawn doth rise;
Then to com in spight of sorrow,

And at my window bid good morrow,
Through the Sweet-Briar, or the Vine,
Or the twisted Eglantine.
While the Cock with lively din,
Scatters the rear of darkness thin,
And to the stack, or the Barn dore,
Stoutly struts his Dames before,
Oft list'ning how the Hounds and horn
Chearly rouse the slumbring morn,
From the side of som Hoar Hill,
Through the high wood echoing shrill.
Som time walking not unseen
By Hedge-row Elms, on Hillocks green,
Right against the Eastern gate,
Wher the great Sun begins his state,
Rob'd in flames, and Amber light,
The clouds in thousand Liveries dight
While the Plowman neer at hand,
Whistles o'er the Furrow'd Land,
And the Milkmaid singeth blithe,
And the Mower whets his sithe,
And every Shepherd tells his tale
Under the Hawthorn in the dale.
Streit mine eye hath caught new pleasures
Whilst the Lantskip round it measures,
Russet Lawns, and Fallows Gray,
Where the nibling flocks do stray,
Mountains on whose barren brest
The labouring clouds do often rest:
Meadows trim with Daisies pide,
Shallow Brooks, and Rivers wide.
Towers, and Battlements it sees
Boosom'd high in tufted Trees,
Where perhaps som beauty lies,
The Cynosure of neighbouring eyes.
Hard by, a Cottage chimney smokes,

From betwixt two aged Okes,
Where Corydon *and* Thyrsis *met,*
Are at their savory dinner set
Of Hearbs, and other Country Messes,
Which the neat-handed Phillis *dresses;*
And then in haste her Bowre she leaves,
With Thestylis *to bind the Sheaves;*
Or if the earlier season lead
To the tann'd Haycock in the Mead,
Som times with secure delight
The up-land Hamlets will invite,
When the merry Bells ring round,
And the jocond rebecks sound.
To many a youth, and many a maid,
Dancing in the Chequer'd shade;
And young and old com forth to play
On a Sunshine Holyday,
Till the live-long day-light fail,
Then to the Spicy Nut-brown Ale,
With stories told of many a feat,
How Faery Mab *the junkets eat,*
She was pincht, and pull'd she sed,
And he by Friars Lanthorn led;
Tells how the drudging Goblin swet,
To ern his Cream-bowle duly set,
When in one night, ere glimps of morn,
His shadowy Flale hath thresh'd the Corn
That ten day-labourers could not end,
Then lies him down the Lubbar Fend.
And stretch'd out all the Chimney's length,
Basks at the fire his hairy strength;
And Crop-full out of dores he flings,
Ere the first Cock his Mattin rings.
Thus don the Tales, to bed they creep,
By whispering Windes soon lull'd asleep.
Towred Cities please us then,

And the busie humm of men,
Where throngs of Knights and Barons **bold,**
In weeds of Peace high triumphs hold,
With store of Ladies, whose bright eies
Rain influence, and judge the prise
Of Wit, or Arms, while both contend
To win her Grace, whom all commend.
There let Hymen *oft appear*
In Saffron robe, with Taper clear,
And pomp, and feast, and revelry,
With mask, and antique Pageantry,
Such sights as youthfull Poets dream
On Summer eeves by haunted stream.
Then to the well-trod stage anon,
If Jonsons learned Sock be on,
Or sweetest Shakespear fancies childe,
Warble his native Wood-notes wilde.
And ever against eating Cares,
Lap me in soft Lydian Aires,
Married to immortal verse
Such as the meeting soul may pierce
In notes, with many a winding bout
Of lincked sweetnes long drawn out,
With wanton heed, and giddy cunning,
The melting voice through mazes **running;**
Untwisting all the chains that ty
The hidden soul of harmony.
That Orpheus *self may heave his head*
From golden slumber on a bed
Of heapt Elysian *flowres, and hear*
Such streins as would have won the **ear**
Of Pluto, *to have quite set free*
His half regain'd Eurydice.
These delights, if thou canst give,
Mirth with thee, I mean to live.

IL PENSEROSO

Hence vain deluding joyes,
    The brood of folly without father bred,
How little you bested,
    Or fill the fixed mind with all your toyes;
Dwell in som idle brain,
    And fancies fond with gaudy shapes possess,
As thick and numberless
    As the gay motes that people the Sun Beams,
Or likest hovering dreams
    The fickle Pensioners of Morpheus *train.*
But hail thou Goddes, sage and holy,
Hail divinest Melancholy,
Whose Saintly visage is too bright
To hit the Sense of human sight;
And therfore to our weaker view,
Ore laid with black staid Wisdoms hue.
Black, but such as in esteem,
Prince Memnons *sister might beseem,*
Or that Starr'd Ethiope *Queen that strove*
To set her beauties praise above
The Sea Nymphs, and their powers offended
Yet thou are higher far descended,
Thee bright-hair'd Vesta *long of yore,*
To solitary Saturn *bore;*
His daughter she (in Saturns *raign,*
Such mixture was not held a stain)
Oft in glimmering Bowres, and glades
He met her, and in secret shades
Of woody Ida's *inmost grove,*
While yet there was no fear of Jove.
Com pensive Nun, devout and pure,
Sober, stedfast, and demure,
All in a robe of darkest grain,

Flowing with majestick train,
And sable stole of Cipres *Lawn,*
Over thy decent shoulders drawn.
Com, but keep thy wonted state,
With eev'n step, and musing gate,
And look commercing with the skies,
Thy rapt soul sitting in thine eyes:
There held in holy passion still,
Forget thy self to Marble, till
With a sad Leaden downward cast,
Thou fix them on the earth as fast.
And joyn with thee calm Peace, and Quiet,
Spare Fast, that oft with gods doth diet,
And hears the Muses in a ring,
Ay round about Joves *Altar sing.*
And adde to these retired Leasure,
That in trim Gardens takes his pleasure;
But first, and chieftest, with thee bring,
Him that yon soars on golden wing,
Guiding the fiery-wheeled throne,
The Cherub Contemplation,
And the mute Silence hist along,
'Less Philomel *will daign a Song,*
In her sweetest, saddest plight,
Smoothing the rugged brow of night,
While Cynthia *checks her Dragon yoke,*
Gently o're th'accustom'd Oke;
Sweet Bird that shunn'st the noise of folly,
Most musicall, most melancholy!
Thee Chauntress of the Woods among,
I woo to hear thy eeven-Song;
And missing thee, I walk unseen
On the dry smooth-shaven Green,
To behold the wandring Moon,
Riding neer her highest noon,
Like one that had bin led astray

Through the Heav'ns wide pathles way;
And oft, as if her head she bow'd,
Stooping through a fleecy cloud.
Oft on a Plat of rising ground,
I hear the far-off Curfeu *sound,*
Over som wide-water'd shoar,
Swinging slow with sullen roar;
Or if the Ayr will not permit,
Som still removed place will fit,
Where glowing Embers through the room
Teach light to counterfeit a gloom,
Far from all resort of mirth,
Save the Cricket on the hearth,
Or the Belmans drousie charm,
To bless the dores from nightly harm:
Or let my Lamp at midnight hour,
Be seen in som high lonely Towr,
Where I may oft out-watch the Bear,
With thrice great Hermes, *or unsphear*
The spirit of Plato to unfold
What Worlds, or what vast Regions hold
The immortal mind that hath forsook
Her mansion in this fleshly nook:
And of those Dæmons *that are found*
In fire, air, flood, or under ground,
Whose power hath a true consent
With Planet, or with Element.
Som time let Gorgeous Tragedy
In Scepter'd Pall com sweeping by,
Presenting Thebs, *or* Pelops *line,*
Or the tale of Troy *divine.*
Or what (though rare) of later age,
Ennobled hath the Buskind stage.
But, O sad Virgin, that thy power
Might raise Musæus *from his bower,*
Or bid the soul of Orpheus *sing*

Such notes as warbled to the string,
Drew Iron tears down Pluto's *cheek.*
And made Hell grant what Love did seek.
Or call up him that left half told
The story of Cambuscan *bold,*
Of Camball, *and of* Algarsife,
And who had Canace *to wife,*
That own'd the vertuous Ring and Glass,
And of the wondrous Hors of Brass,
On which the Tartar *King did ride;*
And if ought els, great Bards *beside,*
In sage and solemn tunes have sung,
Of Turneys and of Trophies hung;
Of Forests, and inchantments drear,
Where more is meant than meets the ear.
Thus night oft see me in thy pale career,
Till civil-suited Morn *appeer,*
Not trickt and frounc't as she was wont,
With the Attick *Boy to hunt,*
But Cherchef't in a comly Cloud,
While rocking Winds are Piping loud,
Or usher'd with a shower still,
When the gust hath blown his fill,
Ending on the russling Leaves,
With minute drops from off the Eaves.
And when the Sun begins to fling
His flaring beams, me Goddes bring
To arched walks of twilight groves,
And shadows brown that Sylvan *loves*
Of Pine, or monumental Oake,
Where the rude Ax with heaved stroke,
Was never heard the Nymphs to daunt,
Or fright them from their hallow'd haunt.
There in close covert by som Brook,
Where no profaner eye may look,
Hide me from Day's garish eie,

While the Bee with Honied thie,
That at her flowry work doth sing,
And the Waters murmuring
With such consort as they keep,
Entice the dewy-feather'd Sleep;
And let som strange mysterious dream,
Wave at his Wings in Airy stream,
Of lively portrature display'd,
Softly on my eye-lids laid.
And as I wake, sweet musick breath
Above, about, or underneath,
Sent by som spirit to mortals good,
Or th' unseen Genius of the Wood.
But let my due feet never fail,
To walk the studious Cloysters pale,
And love the high embowed Roof,
With antick Pillars massy proof,
And storied Windows richly dight,
Casting a dimm religious light.
There let the pealing Organ blow,
To the full voic'd Quire below,
In Service high, and Anthems cleer,
As may with sweetnes, through mine ear,
Dissolve me into extasies,
And bring all Heav'n before mine eyes.
And may at last my weary age
Find out the peacefull hermitage,
The Hairy Gown and Mossy Cell,
Where I may sit and rightly spell
Of every Star that Heav'n doth shew,
And every Herb that sips the dew;
Till old experience do attain
To something like Prophetic strain.
These pleasures Melancholy *give,*
And I with thee will choose to live.

CORINNA'S GOING A-MAYING

Get up, get up for shame, the Blooming Morne
Upon her wings presents the god unshorne.
    See how Aurora *throwes her faire*
    Fresh-quilted colours through the aire:
    Get up, sweet-Slug-a-bed, and see
    The Dew bespangling Herbe and Tree.
Each Flower has wept, and bow'd toward the East,
Above an houre since; yet you not drest,
    Nay! not so much as out of bed?
    When all the Birds have Mattens seyd,
    And sung their thankful Hymnes: 'tis sin,
    Nay, profanation to keep in,
When as a thousand Virgins on this day,
Spring, sooner than the Lark, to fetch in May.

Rise; and put on your Foliage, and be seene
To come forth, like the Spring-time, fresh and greene;
    And sweet as Flora. *Take no care*
    For Jewels for your Gowne, or Haire:
    Feare not; the leaves will strew
    Gemms in abundance upon you:
Besides, the childhood of the Day has kept,
Against you come, some Orient Pearls *unwept:*
    Come, and receive them while the light
    Hangs on the Dew-locks of the night:
    And Titan *on the Eastern hill*
    Retires himselfe, or else stands still
Till you come forth. Wash, dresse, be briefe in praying:
Few beads are best, when once we goe a-Maying.

Come, my Corinna, *come; and comming, marke*
How each field turns a street; each street a Parke
    Made green, and trimm'd with trees: see how
    Devotion gives each House a Bough,

Or Branch: Each Porch, each doore, ere this,
    An Arke a Tabernacle is
Made up of white-thorn neatly enterwove;
As if here were those cooler shades of love.
    Can suck delights be in the street,
    And open fields, and we not see't?
    Come, we'll abroad; and let's obay
    The Proclamation made for May:
And sin no more, as we have done, by staying;
But my Corinna, come, let's goe a-Maying.

There's not a budding Boy, or Girle, this day,
But is got up, and gone to bring in May.
    A deale of Youth, ere this, is come
    Back, and with White-thorn laden home,
    Some have dispatcht their Cakes and Creame,
    Before that we have left to dreame:
And some have wept, and woo'd, and plighted **Troth,**
And chose their Priest, ere we can cast off sloth:
    Many a green-gown has been given;
    Many a kisse, both odde and even:
    Many a glance too has been sent
    From out the eye, Loves Firmament:
Many a jest told of the Keyes betraying
This night, and Locks pickt, yet w'are not a-Maying.

Come, let us goe, while we are in our prime;
And take the harmlesse follie of the time.
    We shall grow old apace, and die
    Before we know our liberty.
    Our life is short; and our dayes run
    As fast away as do's the Sunne:
And as a vapour, or a drop of raine
Once lost, can ne'er be found againe:
    So when or you or I are made
    A fable, song, or fleeting shade;

All love, all liking, all delight
  Lies drown'd with us in endless night.
Then while time serves, and we are but decaying;
Come, my Corinna, *come, lets goe a-Maying.*

ELEGY WRITTEN IN A COUNTRY CHURCH-YARD

The Curfew tolls the knell of parting day,
The lowing herd wind slowly o'er the lea,
The plowman homeward plods his weary way,
And leaves the world to darkness and to me.

Now fades the glimmering landscape on the sight,
And all the air a solemn stillness holds,
Save where the beetle wheels his droning flight,
And drowsy tinklings lull the distant folds;

Save that from yonder ivy-mantled tow'r
The moping owl does to the moon complain
Of such, as wand'ring near her secret bow'r,
Molest her ancient solitary reign.

Beneath those rugged elms, that yew-tree's shade,
Where heaves the turf in many a mould'ring heap,
Each in his narrow cell for ever laid,
The rude Forefathers of the hamlet sleep.

The breezy call of incense-breathing Morn,
The swallow twitt'ring from the straw-built shed,
The cock's shrill clarion, or the echoing horn,
No more shall rouse them from their lowly bed.

For them no more the blazing hearth shall burn,
Or busy housewife ply her evening care:
No children run to list their sire's return,
Or climb his knees the envied kiss to share.

Oft did the harvest to their sickle yield,
Their furrow oft the stubborn glebe has broke;
How jocund did they drive their team afield!
How bow'd the woods beneath their sturdy stroke!

Let not Ambition mock their useful toil,
Their homely joys, and destiny obscure;
Nor Grandeur hear with a disdainful smile
The short and simple annals of the poor.

The boast of heraldry, the pomp of pow'r,
And all that beauty, all that wealth e'er gave,
Awaits alike th' inevitable hour.
The paths of glory lead but to the grave.

Nor you, ye Proud, impute to These the fault,
If Mem'ry o'er their Tomb no Trophies raise,
Where thro' the long-drawn isle and fretted vault
The pealing anthem swells the note of praise.

Can storied urn or animated bust
Back to its mansion call the fleeting breath?
Can Honour's voice provoke the silent dust,
Or Flatt'ry sooth the dull cold ear of death?

Perhaps in this neglected spot is laid
Some heart once pregnant with celestial fire;
Hands, that the rod of empire might have sway'd,
Or wak'd to extasy the living lyre.

But Knowledge to their eyes her ample page
Rich with the spoils of time did ne'er unroll;
Chill Penury repress'd their noble rage,
And froze the genial current of the soul.

Full many a gem of purest ray serene,
The dark unfathom'd caves of ocean bear:
Full many a flower is born to blush unseen,
And waste its sweetness on the desert air.

Some village-Hampden that with dauntless breast
The little Tyrant of his fields withstood;
Some mute inglorious Milton, here may rest,
Some Cromwell guiltless of his country's blood.

Th' applause of list'ning senates to command,
The threats of pain and ruin to despise,
To scatter plenty o'er a smiling land,
And read their history in a nation's eyes,

Their lot forbad: nor circumscribed alone
Their growing virtues, but their crimes confin'd;
Forbade to wade through slaughter to a throne,
And shut the gates of mercy on mankind,

The struggling pangs of conscious truth to hide,
To quench the blushes of ingenuous shame,
Or heap the shrine of Luxury and Pride
With incense kindled at the Muse's flame.

Far from the madding crowd's ignoble strife,
Their sober wishes never learn'd to stray;
Along the cool sequester'd vale of life
They kept the noiseless tenor of their way.

Yet ev'n these bones from insult to protect
Some frail memorial still erected nigh,
With uncouth rhimes and shapeless sculpture deck'd,
Implores the passing tribute of a sigh.

Their names, their years, spelt by th' unletter'd muse,
The place of fame and elegy supply:
And many a holy text around she strews,
That each the rustic moralist to die.

For who, to dumb Forgetfulness a prey,
This pleasing anxious being e'er resign'd,
Left the warm precincts of the chearful day,
Nor cast one longing ling'ring look behind?

On some fond breast the parting soul relies,
Some pious drops the closing eye requires;
E'en from the tomb the voice of Nature cries,
E'en in our Ashes live their wonted Fires.

For thee, who mindful of th' unhonour'd Dead
Dost in these lines their artless tale relate;
If chance, by lonely contemplation led,
Some kindred Spirit shall inquire thy fate,

Haply some hoary-headed Swain may say,
'Oft have we seen him at the peep of dawn
'Brushing with hasty steps the dews away
'To meet the sun upon the upland lawn.

'There at the foot of yonder nodding beech
'That wreathes its old fantastic roots so high,
'His listless length at noontide would he stretch,
'And pore upon the brook that babbles by.

'Hard by yon wood, now smiling as in scorn,
'Mutt'ring his wayward fancies he would rove,
'Now drooping, woeful wan, like one forlorn,
'Or craz'd with care, or cross'd in hopeless love.

'One morn I miss'd him on the custom'd hill,
'Along the heath and near his fav'rite tree;
'Another came; nor yet beside the rill,
'Nor up the lawn, nor at the wood was he;

'The next with dirges due in sad array
'Slow thro' the church-way path we saw him born.
'Approach and read (for thou canst read) the lay,
'Grav'd on the stone beneath yon aged thorn.'

The Epitaph

Here rests his head upon the lap of Earth
A Youth to Fortune and to Fame unknown.
Fair Science frown'd not on his humble birth,
And Melancholy mark'd him for her own.

Large was his bounty, and his soul sincere,
Heav'n did a recompense as largely send:
He gave his Mis'ry all he had, a tear,
He gain'd from Heav'n ('twas all he wish'd) a friend.

No farther seek his merits to disclose,
Or draw his frailties from their dread abode,
(There they alike in trembling hope repose,)
The bosom of his Father and his God.

ODE

Intimations of Immortality from Recollections
of Early Childhood

> The Child is father of the Man;
> And I could wish my days to be
> Bound each to each by natural piety.

I

There was a time when meadow, grove, and stream,
The earth, and every common sight,
> *To me did seem*
> *Apparelled in celestial light,*
The glory and the freshness of a dream.
It is not now as it hath been of yore;—
> *Turn wheresoe'er I may,*
> *By night or day,*
The things which I have seen I now can see no more.

II

> *The Rainbow comes and goes,*
> *And lovely is the Rose,*
> *The Moon doth with delight*
Look round her when the heavens are bare,
> *Waters on a starry night*
> *Are beautiful and fair;*
> *The sunshine is a glorious birth;*
> *But yet I know, where'er I go,*
That there hath passed away a glory from the earth.

III

Now, while the birds thus sing a joyous song,
 And while the young lambs bound
  As to the tabor's sound,
To me alone there came a thought of grief:
A timely utterance gave that thought relief,
  And I again am strong:
The cataracts blow their trumpets from the steep;
No more shall grief of mine the season wrong;
I hear the Echoes through the mountains throng,
The winds come to me from the fields of sleep,
  And all the earth is gay;
   Land and sea
  Give themselves up to jollity,
   And with the heart of May
  Doth every Beast keep holiday;—
   Thou Child of Joy,
Shout round me, let me hear thy shouts, thou happy
   Shepherd-boy!

IV

Ye blessèd Creatures, I have heard the call
  Ye to each other make; I see
The heavens laugh with you in your jubilee;
  My heart is at your festival,
  My head hath its coronal,
The fulness of your bliss, I feel—I feel it all.
   Oh evil day! if I were sullen
   While Earth herself is adorning,
    This sweet May-morning,
   And the Children are culling
    On every side,
   In a thousand valleys far and wide,
   Fresh flowers; while the sun shines warm,
And the Babe leaps up on his Mother's arm:—

I hear, I hear, with joy I hear!
—But there's a Tree, of many, one,
A single Field which I have looked upon,
Both of them speak of something that is gone;
The Pansy at my feet
Doth the same tale repeat:
Whither is fled the visionary gleam?
Where is it now, the glory and the dream?

V

Our birth is but a sleep and a forgetting:
The Soul that rises with us, our life's Star,
Hath had elsewhere its setting,
And cometh from afar:
Not in entire forgetfulness,
And not in utter nakedness,
But trailing clouds of glory do we come
From God, who is our home:
Heaven lies about us in our infancy!
Shades of the prison-house begin to close
Upon the growing Boy,
But He beholds the light, and whence it flows
He sees it in his joy;
The Youth, who daliy farther from the east
Must travel, still is Natures Priest,
And by the vision splendid
Is on his way attended;
At length the Man perceives it die away,
And fade into the light of common day.

VI

Earth fills her lap with pleasures of her own;
Yearnings she hath in her own natural kind,
And, even with something of a Mother's mind,
And no unworthy aim,
The homely Nurse doth all she can

To make her Foster-child, her Inmate Man,
　　　Forget the glories he hath known,
And that imperial palace whence he came.

VII

Behold the Child among his new-born blisses,
A six years' Darling of a pigmy size!
See, where 'mid work of his own hand he lies,
Fretted by sallies of his mother's kisses,
With light upon him from his father's eyes!
See, at his feet, some little plan or chart,
Some fragment from his dream of human life,
Shaped by himself with newly-learned art;
　　　A wedding or a festival,
　　　A mourning or a funeral;
　　　　And this hath now his heart,
　　　　And unto this he frames his song:
　　　　Then will he fit his tongue
To dialogues of business, love, or strife;
　　　But it will not be long
　　　Ere this be thrown aside,
　　　And with new joy and pride
The little Actor cons another part;
Filling from time to time his "humorous stage"
With all the Persons, down to palsied Age,
That Life brings with her in her equipage;
　　　As if his whole vocation
　　　Were endless imitation.

VIII

Thou, whose exterior semblance doth belie
　　　Thy Soul's immensity;
Thou best Philosopher, who yet dost keep
Thy heritage, thou Eye among the blind,
That, deaf and silent, read'st the eternal deep,
Haunted for ever by the eternal mind,—

Mighty Prophet! Seer blest!
   On whom these truths do rest,
Which we are toiling all our lives to find,
In darkness lost, the darkness of the grave;
Thou, over whom thy Immortality
Broods like the Day, a Master o'er a Slave,
A Presence which is not to be put by;
Thou little Child, yet glorious in the night
Of heaven-born freedom on thy being's height,
Why with such earnest pains dost thou provoke
The years to bring the inevitable yoke,
Thus blindly with thy blessedness at strife?
Full soon thy Soul shall have her earthly freight,
And custom lie upon thee with a weight,
Heavy as frost, and deep almost as life!

I X

   O joy! that in our embers
   Is something that doth live,
   That nature yet remembers
   What was so fugitive!
The thought of our past years in me doth breed
Perpetual benediction: not indeed
For that which is most worthy to be blest;
Delight and liberty, the simple creed
Of Childhood, whether busy or at rest,
With new-fledged hope still fluttering in his breast:—
   Not for these I raise
   The song of thanks and praise;
  But for those obstinate questionings
  Of sense and outward things,
  Fallings from us, vanishings;
  Blank misgivings of a Creature
Moving about in worlds not realised,
High instincts before which our mortal Nature
Did tremble like a guilty Thing surprised:

But for those first affections,
Those shadowy recollections,
Which, be they what they may,
Are yet the fountain light of all our day,
Are yet a master light of all our seeing;
Uphold us, cherish, and have power to make
Our noisy years seem moments in the being
Of the eternal Silence: truths that wake,
To perish never;
Which neither listlessness, nor mad endeavour,
Nor Man nor Boy,
Nor all that is at enmity with joy,
Can utterly abolish or destroy!
Hence in a season of calm weather,
Though inland far we be,
Our Souls have sight of that immortal sea
Which brought us hither,
Can in a moment travel thither,
And see the Children sport upon the shore,
And hear the mighty waters rolling evermore.

X

Then sing, ye Birds, sing, sing a joyous song!
And let the young Lambs bound
As to the tabor's sound!
We in thought will join your throng,
Ye that pipe and ye that play,
Ye that through your hearts to-day
Feel the gladness of the May!
What though the radiance which was once so bright
Be now for ever taken from my sight,
Though nothing can bring back the hour
Of splendour in the grass, of glory in the flower;
We will grieve not, rather find
Strength in what remains behind;
In the primal sympathy

Which having been must ever be;
  In the soothing thoughts that spring
  Out of human suffering;
    In the faith that looks through death,
In years that bring the philosophic mind.

XI

And O, ye Fountains, Meadows, Hills, and Groves,
Forebode not any severing of our loves!
Yet in my heart of hearts I feel your might;
I only have relinquished one delight
To live beneath your more habitual sway.
I love the Brooks which down their channels fret,
Even more than when I tripped lightly as they;
The innocent brightness of a new-born Day
      Is lovely yet;
The Clouds that gather round the setting sun
Do take a sober colouring from an eye
That hath kept watch o'er man's mortality;
Another race hath been, and other palms are won.
Thanks to the human heart by which we live,
Thanks to its tenderness, its joys, and fears,
To me the meanest flower that blows can give
Thoughts that do often lie too deep for tears.

ODE ON A GRECIAN URN

Thou still unravish'd bride of quietness,
    Thou foster-child of silence and slow time,
Sylvan historian, who canst thus express
    A flowery tale more sweetly than our rhyme:
What leaf-fring'd legend haunts about thy shape
      Of deities or mortals, or of both,
        In Tempe or the dales of Arcady?
What men or gods are these? What maidens loth?

What mad pursuit? What struggle to escape?
    What pipes and timbrels? What wild ecstasy?

Heard melodies are sweet, but those unheard
    Are sweeter; therefore, ye soft pipes, play on;
Not to the sensual ear, but, more endear'd,
    Pipe to the spirit ditties of no tone:
Fair youth, beneath the trees, thou canst not leave
    Thy song, nor ever can those trees be bare;
        Bold Lover, never, never canst thou kiss,
Though winning near the goal—yet, do not grieve;
    She cannot fade, though thou hast not thy bliss,
        For ever wilt thou love, and she be fair!

Ah, happy happy boughs! that cannot shed
    Your leaves, nor ever bid the Spring adieu;
And, happy melodist, unwearied,
    For ever piping songs for ever new;
More happy love! more happy, happy love!
    For ever warm and still to be enjoy'd,
        For ever panting, and for ever young;
All breathing human passion far above,
    That leaves a heart high-sorrowful and cloy'd,
        A burning forehead and a parching tongue.

Who are these coming to the sacrifice?
    To what green altar, O mysterious priest,
Lead'st thou that heifer lowing at the skies,
    And all her silken flanks with garlands drest?
What little town by river or sea shore,
    Or mountain-built with peaceful citadel,
        Is emptied of this folk, this pious morn?
And, little town, thy streets for evermore
    Will silent be; and not a soul to tell
        Why thou art desolate, can e'er return.

O Attic shape! Fair attitude! with brede
    Of marble men and maidens overwrought,

With forest branches and the trodden weed;
    Thou, silent form, dost tease us out of thought
As doth eternity: Cold Pastoral!
    When old age shall this generation waste,
       Thou shalt remain, in midst of other woe
Than ours, a friend to man, to whom thou say'st,
    Beauty is truth, truth beauty,—that is all,
       Ye know on earth, and all ye need to know.

TEARS, IDLE TEARS

Tears, idle tears, I know not what they mean,
Tears from the depth of some divine despair
Rise in the heart, and gather to the eyes,
In looking on the happy Autumn-fields,
And thinking of the days that are no more.

Fresh as the first beam glittering on a sail,
That brings our friends up from the underworld,
Sad as the last which reddens over one
That sinks with all we love below the verge;
So sad, so fresh, the days that are no more.

Ah, sad and strange as in dark summer dawns
The earliest pipe of half-awaken'd birds
To dying ears, when unto dying eyes
The casement slowly grows a glimmering square;
So sad, so strange, the days that are no more.

Dear as remember'd kisses after death,
And sweet as those by hopeless fancy feign'd
On lips that are for others; deep as love,
Deep as first love, and wild with all regret;
O Death in Life, the days that are no more.

AMONG SCHOOL CHILDREN*

I

I walk through the long schoolroom questioning;
A kind old nun in a white hood replies;
The children learn to cipher and to sing,
To study reading-books and history,
To cut and sew, be neat in everything
In the best modern way—the children's eyes
In momentary wonder stare upon
A sixty-year-old smiling public man.

II

I dream of a Ledaean body, bent
Above a sinking fire, a tale that she
Told of a harsh reproof, or trivial event
That changed some childish day to tragedy—
Told, and it seemed that our two natures blent
Into a sphere from youthful sympathy,
Or else, to alter Plato's parable,
Into the yolk and white of the one shell.

III

And thinking of that fit of grief or rage
I look upon one child or t'other there
And wonder if she stood so at that age—
For even daughters of the swan can share
Something of every paddler's heritage—
And had that colour upon cheek or hair
And thereupon my heart is driven wild:
She stands before me as a living child.

* From William Butler Yeats's *The Tower*. By permission of The Macmillan Company, publishers.

I V

Her present image floats into the mind—
Did Quattrocento finger fashion it
Hollow of cheek as though it drank the wind
And took a mess of shadows for its meat?
And I though never of Ledaean kind
Had pretty plumage once—enough of that,
Better to smile on all that smile, and show
There is a comfortable kind of old scarecrow.

V

What youthful mother, a shape upon her lap
Honey of generation had betrayed,
And that must sleep, shriek, struggle to escape
As recollection or the drug decide,
Would think her son, did she but see that shape
With sixty or more winters on its head,
A compensation for the pang of his birth,
Or the uncertainty of his setting forth?

V I

Plato thought nature but a spume that plays
Upon a ghostly paradigm of things;
Soldier Aristotle played the taws
Upon the bottom of a king of kings;
World-famous golden-thighed Pythagoras
Fingered upon a fiddle-stick or strings
What a star sang and careless Muses heard:
Old clothes upon old sticks to scare a bird.

V I I

Both nuns and mothers worship images,
But those the candles light are not as those
That animate a mother's reveries,
But keep a marble or a bronze repose.

And yet they too break hearts—O Presences
That passion, piety or affection knows,
And that all heavenly glory symbolise—
O self-born mockers of man's enterprise;

VIII

Labour is blossoming or dancing where
The body is not bruised to pleasure soul,
Nor beauty born out of its own despair,
Nor blear-eyed wisdom out of midnight oil.
O chestnut tree, great rooted blossomer,
Are you the leaf, the blossom or the bole?
O body swayed to music, O brightening glance,
How can we know the dancer from the dance?

INDEX